Outsiders in the Greek Cities in the Fourth Century BC

During the fourth century BC the number of Greeks who did not live as citizens in the city-states of southern mainland Greece increased considerably: mercenaries, pirates, itinerant artisans and traders, their origins differed widely. It has been argued that this increase was caused by the destruction of many Greek cities in the wars of the fourth century, accompanied by the large programme of settlement begun by Alexander in the East and Timoleon in the West. Although this was an important factor, argues Dr McKechnie, more crucial was an ideological deterioration of loyalties to the city: the polis was no longer absolutely normative in the fourth century and Hellenistic periods.

With so many outsiders with specialist skills, Alexander and his successors were able to recruit the armies and colonists needed to conquer and maintain empires many times larger than any single polis had ever controlled.

T0384949

Outsiders in the Greek Cities in the Fourth Century BC

Paul McKechnie

Routledge
Taylor & Francis Group

First published in 1989
by Routledge

This edition first published in 2014 by Routledge
2 Park Square, Milton Park, Abingdon, Oxon, OX14 4RN
and by Routledge
711 Third Avenue, New York, NY 10017

Routledge is an imprint of the Taylor & Francis Group, an informa business

Publisher's Note
The publisher has gone to great lengths to ensure the quality of this reprint but
points out that some imperfections in the original copies may be apparent.

Disclaimer
The publisher has made every effort to trace copyright holders and welcomes
correspondence from those they have been unable to contact.

A Library of Congress record exists under LC control number: 88022972

ISBN 13: 978-0-415-74057-9 (hbk)
ISBN 13: 978-1-315-81558-9 (ebk)
ISBN 13: 978-0-415-74059-3 (pbk)

Outsiders in the Greek Cities in the Fourth Century BC

Paul McKechnie

ROUTLEDGE
London and New York

First published 1989 by Routledge
11 New Fetter Lane, London EC4P 4EE
29 West 35th Street, New York, NY 10001

© 1989 Paul R. McKechnie

Typeset by Witwell Ltd, Southport
and printed in Great Britain by
T. J. Press (Padstow) Ltd, Padstow, Cornwall

British Library Cataloguing in Publication Data

McKechnie, Paul
   Outsiders in the Greek cities in the
   fourth century B.C.
   1. Ancient Greece. Cities. Social life,
   B.C. 400–B.C. 300
   I. Title
   938'.06

   ISBN 0 415 00340 7

Library of Congress Cataloging in Publication Data

McKechnie, Paul
   Outsiders in the Greek cities in the fourth century
B.C./Paul McKechnie.
     p.   cm.
   Bibliography: p.
   Includes index.
   1. Greece-Social conditions-To 146 B.C. 2. Cities and
towns, Ancient-Greece-History. I. Title.
   HN650.5.A8M43 1989
   306'.0938–dc19

Contents

Preface

This book is an attempt at examining an important side of the social history of Greece in the later half of the classical period. It is intended to be of use to anyone studying this period beyond an elementary level – so that quotations from Greek are given in English, and some more recondite parts of my D.Phil. thesis (of which the book is a straightforward revision) have been shortened or even omitted. I have generally latinised the English spelling of Greek personal names, and used what I take to be the most familiar forms of place names.

Money towards doing the research on which this book is based came from the Department of Education and Science (through a Major State Studentship) and also the Electors to the Prendergast Studentship (Cambridge University) and the judges of the Ancient History Prize Competition (Oxford University). Besides these I must thank Routledge, not only for publishing the book but also for encouraging revision work by the award of the Croom Helm Ancient History Prize (1986).

Connoisseurs of the work of Professor David Lewis will, I hope, find at least some faint reflection of his teaching in this book. His was the chief guiding hand in my work on the thesis – in so far as I was not too stubborn to be guided. Mr George Cawkwell and Dr Simon Hornblower also gave comment and guidance, as did Professor George Forrest and Dr Michel Austin, who examined me for the D.Phil. On the other hand, the book's defects are – or reflect – my own defects.

The typing work at various times of Mrs June Russell, Mrs Dorothy Palmquist and Mrs Jane Chirambo has been a help and a great encouragement. And I must express my love and thanks to Jenny McKechnie, who a dozen times has heard me say, 'I've finished it!' – without being likely to believe it until the printed book arrives.

P. McK.
Kamuzu Academy, Malawi

Abbreviations

Abbreviations of periodical titles are given either in *Année Philologique* form or an expanded version of it. The following abbreviations for standard works are used.

APF	J. K. Davies, *Athenian Propertied Families* (Oxford, 1971).
CAH	*Cambridge Ancient History* VI (Cambridge, 1927); VII (second edition), Part I (Cambridge, 1984).
FGrHist	F. Jacoby, *Die Fragmente der Griechischen Historiker* I (Berlin, 1923–9; Leiden, 1940–).
HCT	A. W. Gomme, A. Andrewes and K. J. Dover, *A Historical Commentary on Thucydides* I–V (Oxford, 1945–81).
IG	*Inscriptiones Graecae* (Berlin, 1873).
Kock	T. Kock, *Comicorum Atticorum Fragmenta* I–III (Leipzig, 1880–8).
Koerte	A. Koerte, *Menandri quae supersunt; reliquiae apud veteres scriptores servatae edidit A. Koerte* (Leipzig, 1959).
Lewis and Short	C. T. Lewis and C. Short, *A Latin Dictionary* (Oxford, 1879).
LSJ	H. G. Liddell and R. Scott, *A Greek–English Lexicon* (ninth edition, Oxford, 1968).
ML	R. Meiggs and D. M. Lewis, *A Selection of Greek Historical Inscriptions to the End of the Fifth Century B.C.* (Oxford, 1969).
Nauck *TGF²*	A. Nauck, *Tragicorum Graecorum Fragmenta* (second edition, Leipzig, 1889).
OGIS	W. Dittenberger, *Orientis Graeci Inscriptiones Selectae* I–II (Leipzig, 1903 and 1905).
OLD	P. G. W. Glare, *Oxford Latin Dictionary* (Oxford, 1982).

1

Introduction

Greeks and their cities

City-state life, to most Greeks of the fourth century BC, was the normative pattern of human existence.[1] Most of the city-states of Greece, Asia and Italy and Sicily had been established for several generations. The younger cities – in the west and on the Black Sea – had mostly been founded as colonies, each with settlers from one, or sometimes more than one, of the older cities. This process of colonisation had happened gradually, much of it in the eighth and seventh centuries. Colonies typically were independent states from the start.

The colonising movement reinforced the discrete nature of the communities which sent out colonies. Attempts to expand by engrossing the land of a neighbouring Greek community were comparatively rare. The Spartans succeeded in defeating the Messenians and exploiting their land for 300 years, but in nearly all other cases attempts at forcible occupation of this kind proved impracticable. This state of affairs led to subdivision of communities by colonisation being the preferred strategy for coping with the situation which arose when there were too many people in a city for the city's land to support.

City-states varied widely in size. The extent of their independence differed: some colonies accepted the mother city's choice of annual magistrates, for instance, and some small cities, while independent, are not likely to have been able to pursue foreign policies distinct from the foreign policy of a large neighbouring city. But the number of city-states was large. E. Ruschenbusch documents the existence of over 630 states in classical Greece.[2] The sources he draws on refer to quite a wide scatter of dates over more than two centuries, and it may be that not all the cities he names were in existence and independent at once. On the other hand, many of the smaller states Ruschenbusch notes are mentioned only once in the literary or epigraphical record:

there may have been a large number of small states whose names have not come down in the texts.

The Greek world by the beginning of the fourth century was established as a very successful society. Colonies outside Greece managed to live with their non-Greek neighbours, generally able to defend themselves when necessary. Peoples in contact with the Greeks were influenced by their material culture. The Payava tomb in the British Museum, from the Lycian coast at Xanthus, is an example of this sort of influence. In Caria the Mausoleum was the outstanding example of a Hellenising tendency which was changing society radically in the fourth century.[3] Greek soldiers were in increasing demand by non-Greek as well as Greek employers,[4] because their style of equipment and training proved the most effective in action until the Macedonian phalanx and cavalry became fully developed under Philip II and Alexander the Great.

At least since the time of Aeschylus and Herodotus there had been theoretical speculation by Greeks about neighbouring peoples and the differences and contacts between them and the Greeks. Many city-state Greeks knew that in Persia or Egypt, and in parts of Greece such as Thessaly, there were larger states with a system of centralised bureaucracy. Some Asian Greek communities had obligations to send tribute or soldiers to the Persian kings' satraps. But the Persians' attempt to extend their control into Greece in the early fifth century had failed. Herodotus' *History* was available from the middle of the century as a permanent reminder to the reading public of this Greek victory.

So when Greek philosophers began to write about the organisation of human societies they were writing for a readership which had a confident attitude towards the Greek way of life.

The pragmatic pay-offs of city-state life were evident to those in the Greek cities who had education and leisure at their disposal. These were the people who, Aristotle said, could have 'the virtue of a citizen'.[5] And Aristotle, and Plato before him, examined the requirements of human life and aimed to show rigorously that these requirements imply the city-state as the context for their satisfaction. Plato argues from material needs;[6] Aristotle's argument is more theoretical.[7] Each philosopher was not only shaping, but also reflecting, the ideas prevalent in Greece: nobody could think of the city-state as dispensable.

And indeed, when Plato and Aristotle were writing, the Greek city, as a type of political entity, had several centuries of life still ahead of it. But while Aristotle was writing the *Politics*[8] his former pupil Alexander the Great was conquering the Persian empire and changing everything. Hegemony had been held by others before him, for briefer or longer periods. But in a short time Alexander succeeded in taking over Persia and Egypt. His Macedonian successors had more power and wealth than any Greek rulers before him. They divided between themselves the Greek world as well as the East, and took a degree of control over city governments which the League of Corinth had not given to Philip II. Nearly all Greek cities ceased, at this point, to be independent states.

So at the moment of the Greeks' most sophisticated analysis of its nature and value the city-state suffered a loss of political freedom which proved irreversible. It is not surprising if this appears to be a cruel irony. The self-assurance and broad outlook which form the background to the *Republic* and the *Politics* gradually gave way to the rather cramped town-councillor mentality evident in Plutarch's *Praecepta Rei Publicae Gerendae*. One should not forget that Plutarch wrote nearly 500 years later, but the feeling of the real politics being elsewhere pervades his advice. The late fourth century was the crucial moment when local power, the power of city governments, ceased to be the sovereign power in most of the Greek world.

The reasons for the transfer of power to larger political entities – the Hellenistic kingdoms – were complex. But this book will suggest that one of the important factors in the Hellenistic kingdoms' success in gaining and maintaining power was the way in which by the fourth century a large number of people were not living as settled inhabitants of city-state communities. These people, though not themselves in most cases powerful individuals, formed an important element in the complex of power relations which led to the subversion of local autonomy: it will be argued that they provided the linking elements in a society where mobility and cosmopolitanism were increasingly important factors; and that the Hellenistic kings found that Greek armies and servants without strong city loyalties could easily be directed for the purpose of establishing imperial governments over territorial areas in Greece as well as Asia and Egypt. These governments were effective and long-lasting, although their monarchical and international nature was contrary to the dominant political ideology of the Greek cities they ruled.

An outside world

It is wise to remember that the description and analysis of Greek life as the life of an aggregation of city-states is in essence and origin the Greeks' own. It comes from the ancient texts. There is a bias in the material of literary and epigraphic texts towards what the city-dwellers, and particularly the city elites, were going to make it their business or pleasure to read. This is why there is a danger that it may seem irrelevant or eccentric to focus on people who were outsiders from the city point of view. These people are referred to in the texts – sometimes in passing, sometimes with curiosity, occasionally with disapproval. They were the exiles, who used to have a city to live in but (at a given time) had one no longer; the mercenaries, who might stay in a place as long as a war, or an employer's money, lasted; the raiders who could live a short time on the loot of one place; the physicians, builders, sculptors, courtesans, cooks, philosophers, traders, actors and others whose movements would depend on local demand and professional success.

These people had widely different routes to their highly varied ways of life. The point of this book is not to argue that their importance in the fourth century was the product of a single factor working on Greek society. The reason for studying them together is to suggest that in the fourth century Greece was becoming a more international (meaning interlocal) society – partly because of the cumulative effect on communities of having increasingly complex dealings with people from outside. A related purpose of the book is to argue that outsiders, many of them unhappy, displaced and powerless people, could be (and were) used effectively by Hellenistic rulers as a means to augmenting the power of their governments.

The chapters that follow describe the ways of life of outsiders in some detail. There are arguments to show that in the fourth century there were more such outsiders than there had been before. The Greeks examined in the book, and described as outsiders, are Greeks who had no settled home in a city. This criterion has been applied with as much rigour as the sources allow: either they should have been living outside any city (physically, as a mercenary on campaign would do – at any rate for a part of a given year)[9] or they should be people who might live in a city for periods of time (days, months, even years) but would expect, during their stay in a given place, that at some time they would move to another place.[10] Greeks of the latter kind are less obviously *outside* the city than those who habitually slept outside city walls,[11] and there might be a temptation to consider the difference between them and other metics unimportant; but the approach used in this study is much encouraged by the work of D. Whitehead on metics. Whitehead, who stresses the idea of being a 'home-changer' and argues for the use of the English word *immigrant* as a good translation of *metoikos*,[12] speaks of non-citizen scholars and itinerant craftsmen becoming 'true "home-changers"' when they abandoned their '*esprit de retour*'.[13]

The feature common to all the Greeks defined here as outsiders was that (whatever the differences in their skills, their earning power and the length of their stay within the city walls) they derived their income from an occupation which required or permitted mobility. In all the areas of wage labour or business examined in this inquiry, there is evidence showing growth during the fourth century in the numbers of people making an income from these mobile occupations. In some areas there was growth beyond recognition between 400 and 300 (for example, in the area of mercenary service),[14] in others more modest growth (for example, the area of long-distance trading),[15] and in some occupations growth was accompanied by very significant advances in techniques[16] or in forms of recruitment.[17] The combined growth in many areas amounted to the rise of a world outside the city as a new and influential aspect of the whole Greek world.

Subversion

An important feature of the change from the Classical to the Hellenistic pattern of power relations in government was that the ideologies of particularist city government were affected surprisingly little by the existence of kings who could command the cities' allegiance and obedience. Democratic feeling and practice persisted for hundreds of years, if in qualified forms.[18] And upper-class political ambition in Greece centred on success and influence in one's own community.[19] The nobility maintained its importance at a local level (and safeguarded its property) by reliance on the Macedonian kings, but these Macedonian kings succeeded in including a very large non-Macedonian Greek element in their governments and infrastructures.

So the establishment and operation of Hellenistic governments were effective in making marginal in practice an ideology which continued to be dominant in the tradition of upper-class education and literature.[20] A great social change is involved, but does not take a form quite analogous to R. MacMullen's idea of 'un-Roman Activities' in the late Roman period:[21] MacMullen's picture is of 'un-Roman Activities' becoming more pervasive until 'there was little "Roman" left in the Roman empire – the "un-Roman" elements . . . now controlled the world in which they lived'.[22] The Greek outsiders' activities in the fourth century did not have the effect of destroying a society – nor even of making it un-Greek, since they were Greeks themselves – but they did create conditions which allowed an important change in social organisation.

There are points of similarity between this study and MacMullen's *Enemies of the Roman Order*, though. Both consider the effects which people as disparate as philosophers and brigands had on society,[23] and both assess governmental reactions to the problems caused by outsiders.[24] MacMullen argues that 'the drift of directing

5

power outward and downward from the Roman aristocracy is well known; its corollary is the simultaneous movement of anti-Establishment impulses in the same direction'.[25] Here, by contrast, anti-Establishment impulses are not really the heart of the matter. What is at issue is the growth of an element – or a complex of elements – in Greek society which stood outside the cities' control; the extent to which the people who formed that element in society were less subject than other Greeks to the conservative impulses of city-state thought;[26] and the ways in which that element was effective – or was exploited – in producing the social and political change which made up the beginning of the Hellenistic Age.

Modern explanations

The fifth century in Greece was a period of great achievements. Greek democracy was one of the greatest of them. Most of all in its Athenian manifestation, it is widely studied today and valued as an important part of the heritage of human society. There could be debate about what was Athenian democracy's finest hour, but somewhere in the fourth century things ceased to be what they had been. Athens ceased to be powerful or democratic; Sparta, the great rival, ceased to be powerful. There was a decline: not technological and arguably not economic. It might even be said that political sophistication grew, with federalism and the idea of common peace, not to mention Alexander's apparent internationalism. But there was a decline, or at least a change, in areas with a human importance.

This is why explanation of the fourth century is an important crux in the study of Greek history. A good many views have been put forward, particularly to answer the questions why Greece came to be ruled by Macedonian kings, and whether the city-state as an institution was in decline in some sense in the fourth century. Space does not allow a summary of all the views which have been put forward. But perhaps it will not seem too much to select three themes present in modern attempts at explanation of the phenomena, and to suggest how the findings of this study affect the implications of these explanatory themes. The themes chosen are intended to represent contrasting lines of thought in explanation of the turn events took in Greece in the fourth century. They are: first, the theme of the necessity for Greek unity; second, the theme of the overwhelming power of the Macedonian monarchs; and third, the theme that Macedonian rule and the decline of democracy were consequences of the success of the ruling class in Greece in class struggle with the lower classes.

Authors who have mentioned the necessity for Greek unity have in general evinced a measure of regret at its imposition by the might of the Macedonian kings. E. Barker, arguing that the fourth-century political thought of Greece was of unity (he draws attention to hegemonies and federations), states that the effect of this political thought was limited by the persistence of ideas giving a high importance to the autonomous city.[27] The necessity of unity is stated with a sigh ('the free city-state is not built for long endurance in the world of politics ... and who ... can feel otherwise about the great State than that it was a "cruel necessity"?').[28] A few pages later Barker points to the need for colonial expansion and settlement to make provision for 'men who ... were falling into a life of roaming vagrancy'[29] as a justification for the 'new monarch' of the fourth century BC.[30]

Other authors make statements about the difficulties of the world of city-states and the advantages of the Macedonian kings with less display of disappointment. In his book *The Warring States of Greece* A. R. Burn says,[31] 'the fourth century BC ... in political history ... reveals the moral bankruptcy of the city-state world'. W. W. Tarn, arguing for another form of this approach, characterises Alexander as superseding the Athenians as the standard-bearer of intellectual progress:[32]

> if we feel – and justly feel – that during Alexander's lifetime Greece has lost importance, that depends, not on military defeat or on Alexander's conquests in Asia, but simply on the fact that Athens had, for the moment, lost to Alexander her primacy in the world of ideas; it was Alexander who was now opening up new spheres of thought.

A fully developed argument for the imperative towards Greek unity in the fourth century needs both the Burn/Tarn and Barker perspectives. The need and the opportunity for expansion of the Greek world were the same thing. Trends in the development of the Greek world had led to the availability of colonists to settle cities, mercenaries to fight wars, an expanding community of traders to undertake distribution and exchange in areas newly settled by Greeks, and (fewer in number but of as great importance) the specialist builders, artists, philosophers, doctors, cooks and *hetaerae* who were needed to make the difference between a community of settlers and a Greek city.[33]

The weighting of the elements in the argument for the need for Greek unity affects the degree of regret available for the demise of independence and democracy. Barker's sympathy for autonomy is expressed in a framework more clearly determinist than that of Burn's or Tarn's Panhellenist comments: Burn suggests a decline of the city-state because of moral corruption, and Tarn makes a case for humanity progressing through an individual's genius. Thus a 'need' for unity has been perceived by different authors in terms of inevitability, or of moral neediness, or of the impulse towards the intellectual advancement of mankind.

The tendency of this book is against accepting that a 'need' for unity in any of these terms existed. The intention is to describe a situation which could be exploited – and not quite with the intention of establishing 'Greek unity': the kings' chief aim was to establish their own power. The Macedonian states found that the human resources for the establishment of a new kind of Greek government (for filling courts, camps and capital cities)[34] were at their disposal even though talented Greeks in the city-state tradition still lived in their homes and concentrated on the life of their own communities.

This is a positive argument: that Hellenistic kingdoms could not have been founded much earlier than they were because the Greek elements in their power and culture were crucial and were not in general recruited from among the settled Greeks of the powerful city-states. If it is accepted, the suggestions of moral or intellectual decline in the cities become unnecessary.[35] The argument contains no provision to the effect that 'Greek Unity' or 'the Great State' had become inevitable as well as practicable by 338; this is another point in its favour.

The second theme, that of the overwhelming power of the Macedonian monarchs, is not usually presented by modern authors as the whole explanation for the eclipse of the power of the Greek cities. But it appears in many places, often as a more or less unstated assumption. T. T. B. Ryder, commenting on the appearance of Isocrates' *Philippus* in the period after the peace of Philocrates, says,[36] 'it is doubtful whether Philip would ever have stopped short of being the dominant partner in any alliance, and probable that he always intended to establish some sort of control in Greece'. It would not be possible to say this if Philip's power were not regarded as so overwhelming that it would have been unreasonable for him to doubt his ability to subdue Greece. Similarly J. K. Davies's chapter on 'The Opportunists' explains Philip's success in relation to the resemblances and differences between him and the other monarchs and quasi-monarchs influenced by Dionysius I,[37] and answers affirmatively the question 'whether we can explain Philip's transformation from regional dynast to master of Greece purely in terms of his having been able to add a second role, as mercenary commander, to that of traditional king'.[38] He succeeded, and Jason of Pherae and the rest succeeded much less well, because of the differential in the military and economic power controlled by Philip and by each of the others.[39]

This is attractive as an explanation of why Greece fell under Philip's power, but it does not begin to explain the Hellenistic state. Without the development of a form of state allowing for government of the world of city-states, the Macedonians' hegemony over Greece would have gone the same way as the hegemonies of the Athenians, the Spartans and the Thebans. A good deal of the change involved in arriving at the Hellenistic state came about as a result of the needs of Alexander's Asian expedition, and many of the initiatives involved were taken by individuals;[40] but if it had not been the case that Hellenistic government could achieve things which Classical government had found difficult, such as control of piracy or the problem of exiles,[41] then its potential rivals would have had more chance of flourishing. And this new form of government was emphatically not only an application to a wider sphere of the traditional Macedonian forms.[42] Those were forms very like ones which most of Greece had abandoned in the Archaic Age. Hellenistic government, which cemented the victories of Philip, Alexander and Antipater over the city-state Greeks, was a form of Macedonian kingship deeply influenced by the problems and opportunities present in fourth-century Greece on account of Greeks without cities.

Explanations are, or suggest, meanings for the events they explain. The Greek Unity theme, and the Macedonian Power theme, both imply that the chief enigma needing explanation in the complexes of events leading to the establishment of Hellenistic governments is the enigma of the restriction of the autonomy of city-states. G. E. M. de Ste Croix disputes this view, asserting that the effect of Hellenistic government against democracy was more important than the general circumscription of the powers of Greek governments. He says:[43]

> modern historians have shown little concern with this aspect of the destruction of democracy; and when they have noticed the disappearance at all, their interest in it has been submerged by attention to the supersession of 'city-state' or 'republican' forms of government (which of course may be either democratic or oligarchic) by the monarchy of the Hellenistic Kingdoms or the Roman Principate.

This is a radical rejection of the meanings implicit in the first two themes discussed here and (not incidentally) of the motives of the scholars whose work has been on the lines of these explanatory themes.[44] De Ste Croix, it is worth noting, starts his analysis from the other end – his aim is to discuss the destruction of democracy by reference to moments involving critical transformations, and not to explain or evaluate any comparatively short historical period. He uses this perspective to allow him to concentrate on issues in the lives of ordinary people, and in *The Class Struggle in the Ancient Greek World* he develops not only the theme of the value of Greek democracy to succeeding ages, but also the theme of the protection and the degree of power it gave to poor people in Greece – even taking into account that women, slaves and non-citizens were excluded from participating in the government of democratic states.

Democracy, as de Ste Croix argues,[45] afforded free poor Greek people some protection against exploitation by the rich. The argument that the partial nature of this protection and the restricted range of its beneficiaries should not blind the modern student to its importance is put forward very strongly by de Ste Croix. Fourth-century changes, though, made a difference from a pragmatic point of view. A general case could be made for suggesting that with the weakening of Athens after 404 democracy was a less effective form of protection against economic exploitation – Athens could do less for democratic parties in other states than in the fifth century. But this argument is vulnerable to the objection that it does no more than describe a further limitation on a system which was already limited in its effects: a change in degree rather than in kind.

The particular case of outsiders, though, is clearly relevant. The increasing size, and economic and strategic importance, of the community of Greeks living outside the cities created during the fourth century a mass of economically active people who had nothing to gain from the continuance of the system of making political decisions by a majority vote of citizens. Greek democratic states were in effect large private clubs with closed membership (oligarchic states were smaller private clubs with exclusive membership). Once there was a significant number of free people outside the system of democratic or oligarchic government, and some of them were educated, articulate men who could have been influential had they been allowed to become involved in government, objections could arise to the position which closed associations of citizens held as governing bodies in the Greek world.[46]

Many of the more successful outsiders lived in Greek cities with metic or equivalent status, and their position is important for analysis of what happened to democracy in the fourth century. And de Ste Croix has an idealised view of metic status as affording protection against economic exploitation, which ought to be treated with reservation;[47] so that it must seem doubtful whether it is right to minimise the importance of the point that democracy protected a privileged minority (those who were not slaves, women, children, free non-citizens or non-Greeks) in democratic cities. Democracy was restricted to cities: no ancient Greek political unit more comprehensive than a city-state was governed by a constitution which de Ste Croix would be likely to recognise as democratic.[48] So the establishment in the fourth century of governments over and above the 'city-state' or 'republican' governments must be regarded both as interesting in itself and as no less valuable an object of constitutional analysis and speculation than the decline over several hundred years of democratic forms in (what was from 338) local government in Greek areas.

A. Lintott sums up the politics of Greek cities in the fourth century when he says:[49]

> it is almost too easy to draw a moral or deduce a necessity from the history of the Greek cities in the fourth century: their perpetual external and civil wars left them at the mercy of a new power, the ruthless and single-minded Philip of Macedon. Yet it is not immediately clear how far political behaviour in the cities had declined from what it had been in the fifth century, their supposed zenith, nor is it easy to pick out significant changes in their social and economic conditions.

The three themes considered in this section are in effect attempts to get at the causes of the change in Greek society in the fourth century, which involved the Greek states' becoming subject to Macedonian kings: the Greek Unity theme treats the change as a (sad) illustration of the power and importance of large states in an ancient civilisation; the Power of Macedon theme yields inescapable analysis of why Philip, Alexander and Antipater beat the Greeks; and the Decline of Democracy theme treats Philip as the lucky find of the ruling classes in Greek states. It is the intention of this book to suggest that an identifiable community existed outside the cities whose influence on the course of change was great enough to require a reconsideration of modern explanations of fourth-century history.

Notes

1 G. E. M. de Ste Croix, *The Class Struggle in the Ancient Greek World* (London, 1981), p. 9, though mentioning the city–countryside division in the Archaic and Classical periods, talks of the common culture of groups living in both areas. As p. 10 adds, Greek culture was city culture in a still more marked way in areas where Greek settlement began in the Hellenistic period.

2 E. Ruschenbusch, 'Die Zahl der griechischen Staaten und Arealgrösse und Bürgerzahl der "Normalpolis"', *ZPE* 59 (1985), pp. 253–63.

3 S. Hornblower, *Mausolus* (Oxford, 1982), pp. 223–74 and 332–53.

4 See chapter 4 below.

5 Aristotle, *Politics* 1278a10.

6 Plato, *Republic* 369a1–370e4.

7 Aristotle, *Pol.* 1252a–b.
8 Aristotle, *Pol.* 1311b2, refers to the assassination of Philip II, placing the book after 336. 1276a25–30 refers to when Babylon was captured, but is not explicit about what occasion is meant.
9 On mercenaries cf. below, chapter 4. Virtually all Greek traders must have lived in cities in winter, whether as metics or as citizens (but here cf. below, pp. 178–9) but in summer they formed a very important part of the world outside the city: clearly they could not sensibly be excluded from this inquiry.
10 Cf. below, the beginning of chapter 6.
11 Citizens and other settled country-dwellers also slept outside the walls. But the point should not be obscured by this.
12 D. Whitehead, *The Ideology of the Athenian Metic* (Cambridge, 1977), p. 7.
13 Whitehead, *Ideology*, p. 18; the point is also made that any foreigner staying even a fairly short period in Athens (cf. *Ideology*, p. 9) became a *metoikos*. The case of potters in the late fifth century is apposite here. Many of them moved out of Athens (B. R. MacDonald, 'The emigration of potters from Athens in the late fifth century BC and its effect on the Attic pottery industry', *AJA* 85 (1981), pp. 159–68; cf. below, chapter 6, n.18) and MacDonald argues that 'the disaster in Sicily in 413, may have prompted some craftsmen to abandon Athens, especially metics who had previously considered permanent residency' (p. 166; MacDonald quotes Hyperides, 3(*Athenogenes*). 29 and 33, referring to the law forbidding metics to leave Athens in wartime and making them subject to arrest if they did so and later returned to Athens). This illustrates how adverse circumstances could lead some apparently settled metics to behave as Greeks outside the city rather than as Whitehead's 'true "home-changers"'.
14 Cf. below, pp. 91–2.
15 Cf. below, chapter 7.
16 Any number of technical advances could be mentioned. J. K. Davies, *Democracy and Classical Greece* (Glasgow, 1978), pp. 166–7, gives an overview of the fourth century as 'a spectacularly creative period in Greek culture' (p. 166). One of very few texts which make explicit the recognition by a contemporary that innovation and advance in scientific and technical areas were fairly widespread is Theophrastus, *HP* IX.16.8–9: having described how Thrasyas of Mantinea used to gather ingredients for drugs from a wide range of places, and how Thrasyas' pupil Alexias was as skilled as his master in drug-making and experienced in other aspects of medicine, Theophrastus says (section 9), 'so these practices [*sc.* travel for scientific purposes] seem to be in evidence much more now than formerly.' Cf. below, p. 147.
17 Cf. below, pp. 157–60.
18 Comparisons between Classical, Hellenistic and Roman periods given at de Ste Croix, *Class Struggle*, pp. 300–15.
19 A. H. M. Jones, *The Greek city from Alexander to Justinian* (Oxford, 1940), pp. 166–9, discusses how rich people exercised influence in

Greek cities in the Hellenistic period – and how the democratic systems set up by Alexander came to be run by the rich.

20 This tradition in effect made the Classical period 'Classical' during antiquity: Plutarch's Greek Lives, for instance, are mostly lives of men living in the fifth and fourth centuries. Polybius, who wrote in the second century BC and had a wide perspective on history, wrote a biography of Philopoemen ('the last of the ancient Greeks': a representative of the tradition of local autonomy) before his exile in Italy turned him to dealing with the rise of Rome.

21 See R. MacMullen, *Enemies of the Roman Order* (Cambridge, Mass., 1967), p. vi.

22 MacMullen, *Enemies*, p. ix.

23 Cf. below, chapters 5 and 6. Cf. also MacMullen, *Enemies*, pp. 46–94, 192–241.

24 See in particular MacMullen, *Enemies*, p. 216, where, commenting on the difficulties caused to Roman government by circumcellions, Bagaudae, Arabs and others, MacMullen says, 'by declaring them enemies or outlaws, the government put into formal words the simpler wish that they would all go away, behave themselves, or die. No chance of that. The need for legislation only acknowledged how vigorous they had become, and their vigor continued unabated, ultimately transforming the world from which the insiders – the acquiescent or directing members of the dominant civilization – tried to exclude them.'

25 MacMullen, *Enemies*, p. 242.

26 It would be unwise to underestimate the continuing association between aristocratic values and civic values: see, e.g., W. Donlan, *The Aristocratic Ideal in Ancient Greece* (Lawrence, 1980), pp. 155–8.

27 E. Barker, 'Greek political thought and theory', in *CAH* VI (Cambridge, 1927), pp. 505–35, at p. 509.

28 Barker, 'Greek political thought', p. 510.

29 Barker, 'Greek political thought', p. 509.

30 Barker, 'Greek political thought', pp. 512–13.

31 A. R. Burn, *The Warring States of Greece* (London, 1968), p. 112.

32 W. W. Tarn, 'Greece: 335 to 321 BC', *CAH* VI (Cambridge, 1927), pp. 438–60, at p. 443.

33 Cf. below, chapter 6.

34 Cf. below on skilled workers, courtiers and mercenaries.

35 There is no real reason to think there was such a decline. Cf. A. Lintott, *Violence, Civil Strife and Revolution in the Classical City* (London and Canberra, 1982), pp. 252–62. E. Ruschenbusch, *Untersuchungen zu Staat und Politik in Griechenland vom 7.–4. Jh. v. Chr.* (Bamberg, 1978), pp. 60–1, gives a tabular presentation of ancient references to show the relative prevalence of civil strife in the fifth and fourth centuries: if increasing incidence of civil strife could be seen as an index of moral decline, Ruschenbusch's findings would not support a theory of moral decline in the fourth century.

36 T. T. B. Ryder, *Koine Eirene* (Oxford, 1965), pp. 99–100.

37 Davies, *Democracy*, pp. 228–53.

38 Davies, *Democracy*, p. 249. The qualification concerns the importance of legitimacy (p. 250): 'In terms of power,' Davies says (p. 249), 'the answer is probably yes.'

39 This is in effect the conclusion of Davies's chapter (cf. n. 38) in which the question why Philip was the most successful is put at the beginning (*Democracy*, p. 228).

40 Which is in effect simply to acknowledge that conquering the Persian empire made a difference to the conquerors, as would be expected.

41 Cf. pp. 122–6 and 24–8.

42 G. L. Cawkwell, *Philip of Macedon* (London, 1978), p. 19, says, 'Philip transformed the ancient world, confronting the city-states of Greece with the national state of Macedon ...' And at the end of the book (p. 183) he speculates whether Philip, had he lived, might not have consolidated gains round the Mediterranean instead of advancing to conquer the Persian empire ('if he had so preferred, Macedonia might have become the homeland of a mighty power'). This apparent suggestion that a distinctively Macedonian empire (rather than a number of Hellenistic kingdoms) could have come into being in the 330s and 320s is implausible in view of the rapid pace of change in Macedonian society during Philip's reign.

43 De Ste Croix, *Class Struggle*, p. 315.

44 There are several parallel references in de Ste Croix, *Class Struggle*, for example p. 71 ('the anti-democratic instincts of the majority of scholars'), and cf. the comments on the Athenian policy of 'naval imperialism' at p. 293.

45 De Ste Croix, *Class Struggle*, p. 315, notes as a result of the Athenian policy the 'disappearance of the limited measure of political protection afforded to the lower classes against exploitation by the propertied'.

46 'Cynic monarchism', for example, can be considered a theoretical expression of the frustration with which some philosophers regarded the democratic transactions of the cities in which they sojourned (see S. Hornblower, *The Greek World, 479–323*, London, 1983, p. 155). Skilled workers who had come from a well-off background and who had mobile practices of their various crafts lived without citizen rights, and so could clearly not be expected to take a Periclean attitude to democracy.

47 De Ste Croix, *Class Struggle*, p. 289: 'And surely metics could not be exploited intensively: if they were, they would simply move elsewhere.' This is a naive expectation, in view of de Ste Croix's theoretical framework: one would not usually expect a Marxist to put forward a proposition so closely analogous to 'surely employees cannot be exploited intensively: if they were, they would simply get new jobs'. The fact is more probably that some metics could improve their lot by moving, but others could not.

48 S. Hornblower, *Greek World*, p. 236, argues that because it embodies a representative principle 'Greek federalism was often more democratic than the often urban-dominated primary assemblies of the city-states.' But federalism does not figure in the comments on democracy in de

Ste Croix, *Class Struggle*. Athens in the fifth century, and Thebes in the fourth, ruled areas beyond their own walls, but these empires had no say in the government of the cities which held them.

49 Lintott, *Violence*, p. 252, and cf. above, n. 35.

2

Outsiders and exiles:
establishment perceptions

The stay-at-home ideology

It is a commonplace of fourth-century rhetoric that people who travel, or who live away from home, are disreputable characters.

Philon, for example, who went to Oropus as a metic during the rule of the thirty at Athens, is represented in Lysias as disloyal to his Athenian compatriots:[1] 'he wanted to be a metic among them rather than to be a citizen among you'. Similarly, Aphobus' headlong getaway to Megara after his conviction in the matter of Demosthenes' estate is brought up against him by his former ward.[2] The same point comes in the other way round in Isaeus: he avers in a speech written for Hagnon and Hagnotheus (relatives of a mercenary who died at Acre[3]) that his clients 'have never gone abroad anywhere except where you [*sc.* the Athenians] commanded: and they have not been useless to the city while they have been here'.[4]

Orators had to appeal to juries composed of Athenian citizens, the majority of whom lived their whole lives in Athens and Attica or in Athenian military or naval service abroad. So the orators' testimony reflects the feeling of those with fixed homes that people who did not share in settled Greek life were reasonable objects of suspicion.

But (even given this unavoidable degree of bias in the sources, which is only partly compensated for by the few available strands of evidence for the feelings and ideologies of some of the Greeks who lived without city ties)[5] the sources for the history of Greece in the fourth century, and in particular the political works of Isocrates, offer a number of glimpses of the world outside the cities, and of a 'floating population' in Hellas.[6] It is a diverse world, and there is a risk connected with an inquiry of the sort undertaken here that the constraints imposed by the nature of the primary sources may make it almost impossible for the student to develop an accurate picture of what the people in the world outside the cities were like. Isocrates speaks of wanderers (*planomenoi*) and contrasts them with city-dwellers[7] (*politeuomenoi*; other authors referring to wanderers use the distinction implied here but do not make it explicit).[8] His aim in doing so is to warn or frighten his audience about the nature of political conditions in Greece. The wanderers form an element in the armoury of images which he used over more than forty years to communicate his Panhellenist message, and outsiders who were earning a living and not posing a threat to property were not (could not be) used in developing that image.

But even destitute wanderers encompassed a spectrum of different kinds of people. And *plane*, a word which means either simple 'travel', as in Herodotus,[9] or 'error', as in the philosophers,[10] could be a temporary or a permanent life of moving from city to city. Certainly some wanderers would spend periods living in cities as metics, and a period of residence in a city might be followed by further travel.

It is clear that the people Isocrates wrote about and worried about were mainly mercenary soldiers, or exiles, or both. While modern authors have studied both mercenary service and exile,[11] less attention has been given to the wandering life adopted by some mercenaries and characteristic of exiles.[12] People who followed this sort of existence, while they were open to the type of rhetorical attack aimed at Philon and Aphobus (there was always prejudice which could be exploited against them), attracted some speculation and discussion of their lot in literature. The aim of this chapter is to examine the literary texts, bearing in mind that they tend to represent the aristocratic city-dwelling point of view, and from them to assess how the social phenomenon of outsiders developed and how it was understood by the settled people of the cities. The case for thinking that there were more wanderers than before will be set out, along with the theorists' reactions and speculations.

Isocrates' *Aegineticus*

A sophist to his fingertips, Isocrates, whose references to wanderers were calculated to strike fear into the settled property-owners of Greece, could produce a sympathetic portrayal of the life of people who had lost their home. His *Aegineticus* – the only extant forensic speech of the Classical period written for delivery outside Athens – gives the history of a family's separation from its home.

A man called Thrasyllus had inherited from Polemaenetus the soothsayer his soothsaying books and some property (*Aegineticus* 5; further references will be by number only). He began to practise soothsaying,[13] became a wanderer and lived in many cities (6). There were a number of women in his life, including the mother of the narrator's opponent (6). Thrasyllus' wandering career was profitable enough for him to return to Siphnos as the richest of its citizens, and to marry into the best family on the island (7). Not at all the sort of person Isocrates was warning his audiences about: indeed, once his money was made, he aimed to stabilise the result of his social climbing by a marriage connection with the aristocracy.

What he apparently did not do (wisely, it turned out) was turn his money into land. After his death his sons, Sopolis and Thrasylochus, inherited the property: they had a mother and sister living (9, 11). The property must have consisted wholly or mainly of movables, since most of it was at some time left with the narrator's friends in Paros, and recovered at the risk of his life when Pasinus (otherwise unknown) took Paros with the help of Siphnian exiles, who massacred six of the narrator's male relatives (18–19). Later the narrator and Thrasylochus, with their respective mothers and sisters (Sopolis was already absent), were exiled from Siphnos (20, 22). The whole fortune inherited from Thrasyllus they managed to take with them (20), but the narrator's property, presumably not made up of movables, was lost (23). After the escape they arrived in Melos (21), where they had friends (22), but at Thrasylochus' suggestion moved on to Troezen.

From Troezen or Melos – it is not clear which, but almost certainly the former, not least because it seems a much more likely source of mercenaries – the Siphnian exiles made an attempt to capture Siphnos (38). It failed (39). Sopolis went to Lycia, and died there (40); some time after his brother's death Thrasylochus, who with the narrator had by then moved to Aegina, fell ill – fatally ill, as it proved (24, 11). His mother and sister stayed in Troezen (25), where the narrator's mother and sister had already died of disease (22). Before his death Thrasylochus adopted the narrator by the terms of a will and bequeathed him his sister and his property; at the time of the lawsuit they are still living as metics in Aegina (12).

Now the narrative shows that the two families were in some ways quite exceptional. They were not only oligarchs, but the leading oligarchic families of Siphnos (7, 36). Sopolis was chosen to lead the attempted *revanche* (38). Perhaps more exceptionally still, the property left to his children by Thrasyllus could be saved – not once but twice – and taken with the exiles as they travelled. The narrator's property, by contrast, was lost – as was that of all landowning exiles. The fact of having ready money probably helped gain Sopolis the command of the exiles. But in other respects the record of their wanderings may be less untypical: of the six who left Siphnos, three died of disease,[14] and Sopolis too died, though the cause of death is unspecified (failure to recover from his wound?) (39–40). They left

Melos to join a community of Siphnians in Troezen (31), so putting the wish to remain in the circle of the Siphnian oligarchs above the tie of friendship and the reputed unhealthiness of Troezen (22). Seibert points out that Conon arrived in Melos in 393 and used it as a base, and states that while in Melos the Siphnians believed themselves in danger of persecution by victorious democrats, connected presumably with the prospect of Conon's arrival. (He cites the evidence about Conon to support this account of the Siphnians' fears.)[15] But there are difficulties with this view. Did anyone at Melos know that Conon was coming? Surely it would be unlikely. And Seibert's assumption that all the new exiles went to Melos together is not supported by the *Aegineticus* or any other ancient source.[16] Similarly, where Isocrates says that Thrasylochus and the narrator went to Aegina (24), Seibert says that 'many later continued their flight to Aegina'.[17] On the contrary, it seems almost certain that when Thrasylochus went to Troezen from Melos he joined the other Siphnians, and when he went to Aegina from Troezen he left them behind.

Granted the limits on the usefulness of a single family's story, the *Aegineticus* is still an exceptional document. Points of detail emerge. For instance, the Siphnians were able to travel – the ordinary Siphnians as well as the leading families; this emerges from the fact that the Siphnians from Troezen attended the funeral in Aegina (31). Note too that both Thrasylochus and Sopolis, and presumably some others, chose to settle elsewhere than with the community in Troezen. In the case of settlers with money, at least, perhaps it is no surprise that they were welcomed as metics,[18] but it is worth knowing that a community of exiles concentrated in one place would act as a centre from which individuals would go and settle in small numbers as metics elsewhere. Thus exile, wandering and temporary settlement were likely to be followed sooner or later by absorption into a new community as metics.[19] Finally, and significantly, even rich people became poor when they lost their citizenship. As Seibert notes, poverty (caused by exile) led to loss of social position:[20] advantages of birth ceased to be worth much and the value of guest friendship depended on the conscience of one's foreign friends.

Theorists' perceptions

It has been remarked above[21] that a distinction is sometimes drawn between destitution and the voluntary and lucrative non-city life of paid professional people, but that in some literary texts the distinction is obscured and the more prosperous, more voluntary outsiders become invisible. When the distinction goes, it is taken away for rhetorical reasons, as with Isocrates, but also on occasion for reasons of apparently less partisan analysis – as by Aristotle, whose comments will be discussed in this section. At times Isocrates goes a step beyond merely ignoring the existence of another outlook on wanderers' lives, and argues against taking an optimistic view of non-city life. Some philosophers, he says, 'dare to write that the life of beggars and exiles is more enviable than that of other men'. But he makes it very clear that he does not share this opinion.[22] Probably Isocrates was referring to some written material which is not now extant, but there were arguments open to philosophers in his generation in favour of non-citizenship or exile. One avenue might have been to show that sophists could prosper from professional travel. Gorgias of Leontini and Prodicus of Ceos, according to Socrates in Plato's *Hippias Major*,[23] both earned more from wisdom than other craftsmen from their crafts. And travel in general was known to have something to offer: a clever philosopher could have argued for a similarity between the travels of exiles and those of aristocratic tourists as mentioned in Herodotus.[24]

But whatever sophistic manoeuvre Isocrates was countering at the beginning of the *Helen*, the pessimistic view of exile and wandering was dominant. And an account such as that in the *Aegineticus* is worth considering for the information it gives about how people felt on becoming outsiders. Clearly the characters in the story experienced difficulty in adjusting to life outside the city: in fact, Thrasylochus and the narrator of the *Aegineticus* found exile a thoroughly disagreeable experience. Every day in Aegina they spent 'lamenting each other's troubles and our exile and our loneliness': no day was without tears, or so says their speech-writer.[25] He says the same about the Plataeans in exile, and after their city's destruction he wrote, 'we were all equally lacking in all necessities and we became wanderers and beggars'.[26] The rhetorical exaggeration of how often the Siphnians and Plataeans wept over the loss of their place in Greek society (their being reduced from city-dwellers to wanderers) will not prevent the modern reader from realising what a serious view they had to take of their worsened circumstances. A Greek whose city rejected him, or whose city ceased to exist, lacked the central one of the several terms in which he could define himself to the outside world. In the 'political animal' passage from the beginning of the *Politics* Aristotle reflects and expounds the view that a man without a city is a man lacking an important part of his humanity:[27]

> ... It is clear that the city-state exists *by nature*, and that man is by nature a city-state animal, and that someone who is cityless by nature (and not by chance) is either a rogue or a superhuman

being. Like the 'kinless, lawless, heartless . . .' person complained of by Homer. And that sort of man is by nature also a desirer of war, since he is an 'unconnected piece' like in draughts.

Now although Thrasyllus would probably not have been described by Aristotle as cityless (since, even when he chose to live as a traveller, he remained a citizen at Siphnos, where he later settled down again and brought up a family),[28] and Thrasyllus' children were without a city by chance, Aristotle's reservations only go to show the depth of his worry about anyone who really did choose to put himself outside the community. Such a choice would amount, in Aristotle's view, to a militant act of self-definition over against the normal (Hellenic) human pattern of life. Aristotle fears that such people will desire and encourage war. His quotation from Homer comes from a passage where Nestor is discouraging Diomedes from causing civil strife:[29] 'Kinless, heartless, lawless is the man who longs for murderous civil strife.' And the use of a passage reproaching the stirrer-up of civil strife (and having no obvious reference to being *without* a city) shows that in Aristotle's view the propensity to stir up strife is the chief characteristic of the cityless, not an occasional or accidental attribute. His theoretical justification follows: that the city-state is prior to the individual, and that the individual, when isolated, is not self-sufficient; he speaks[30] of 'the person who cannot share, or who is self-sufficient so that he needs no part in a city, so that he is either an animal or a god'. Here both sides of the alternative put forward in the earlier excerpt are strengthened ('either a rogue or a superhuman being' / 'either an animal or a god'). This dilemma is not intended to dispose Aristotle's readers to fall at the feet of outsiders and worship – the effect is to reinforce and rationalise existing suspicion.

Though a philosopher could express in such unequivocal terms as these his distrust of those who lived their lives outside the cities, his eloquence fades by comparison with the pleas found in the closing passages of some defence speeches on charges for which exile could be a penalty. Where the philosopher speaks for the settled, the 'political' population against the wanderers who trouble it, the speech-writer puts words into the mouth of a citizen facing the prospect of becoming (though not, to use Aristotle's phrase, *by nature*) such a wanderer. Antiphon's imaginary defendant in *Tetralogy* I, for instance, describes his fate if convicted:[31] 'if I am convicted and executed now, I shall leave this dreadful business hanging over my children; and if I am convicted and exiled, I shall be a beggar in foreign lands, a cityless old man'. A number of other speakers make the same point.[32] Exile was of course the most complete form of separation from the city-state, and exile by judicial decision (as opposed to exile of a party as a result of a *coup d'état*) left no prospect of fighting one's way back.[33] It also involved the confiscation of the condemned's property. The comment about being a beggar was no exaggeration.

People who found that they could no longer live in a city community as citizens or metics with a secure place in the city's life faced a beggarly, dangerous and humiliating future. Beggarly, if they had no income and no guest-friends to go to; dangerous, from sickness or violence; humiliating because being stateless implied alienation (in the strict Latin-derived sense: becoming-foreign) from Greek people and from the typical Greek way of life. If, as Aristotle states, many such people were desirous of war, then it was by no means irrational that they should be so: to the political exiles, like the Siphnians in the *Aegineticus*, the overthrow of the home government would mean their chance to return; to others, war meant employment and hence a means of support.[34]

Increasing numbers of outsiders

A large build-up of individual cases brought on the situation Isocrates wrote about in his political speeches. Only a strange combination of circumstances left the insight at the individual level which the *Aegineticus* affords, and for the most part the fates of particular communities form the most detailed data the sources can provide. In the next chapter the development of events at the communal level is dealt with – and the effects of the destruction or foundation of cities on people and social conditions are considered. But here the aim is to relate the overall outline of events in the fourth century to the increase in numbers of men available for mercenary service.

This increase was sharp and took effect between the end of the fifth century and the peace of Philocrates.[35] Up to the last years of the fifth century the Peloponnesian war was the dominant factor in Greek life. Only a few years after it ended, the wanderers and mercenaries (closely associated in Isocrates' comments) had become a noticeable feature of Greek life. Two events in the immediate aftermath of the war were particularly important not only in themselves but in effect as models for later episodes. The first was the tyranny of the Thirty at Athens, and the second, the expedition of the Ten Thousand with Cyrus. The point which here ought to be brought to the fore is, in Parke's words,[36] that 'Cyrus, by raising the Ten Thousand, closed one period in the history of Greek mercenaries as he opened another'. His army became the first wandering army, and its career marked the beginning of the period in which mercenary soldiery were an important, instead of a peripheral, factor in Greek wars and Greek society.

The Peloponnesian war ended with the return of exiles to Athens.[37] But the victory of the Spartans brought only a brief respite after the unprecedented spate of exilings which had occurred throughout Hellas during the war.[38] Before long the Thirty decided to limit citizen rights at Athens to 3,000 men,[39] and, as Lysias comments in his speech *Against Eratosthenes*, those who escaped death were in danger in many places, wandered to many cities and were banned everywhere, went short of necessities, and left their children in foreign, some in hostile, lands – before they came to Peiraeus.[40] The pattern of mass exiling by a controlling faction followed by an attempted (in the Athenian case, successful) return of the exiles is a completely typical feature of the fourth century in Greece till Alexander. This is not to say that the pattern was *new* at this time,[41] only that as mercenary soldiery and mercenary service were peripheral features of Greek life until Cyrus, and then became important, so until the Thirty Tyrants the practice of exiling political opponents wholesale (hundreds or thousands at a time) was exceptional, but after their example the instances of it multiplied.[42]

If the troubles of Athens set a pattern for revolutionary politics in the post-war period, then they have also left behind a unique record of how the Athenian citizen community coped with the task of living together after its reunification: notwithstanding the amnesty, the recriminations concerning the rule of the Thirty continued at least throughout the 390s, as Lysias' speeches show. The reason must be that, amnesty or no amnesty, the upheavals of 404/403 were not easily forgotten by the Athenians. There is no other case where it is possible to see in any detail how life continued after the restoration of exiles to a city.[43]

For the Athenian democrats, the exile–wandering–return sequence was a direct result of defeat in the Peloponnesian war. In contrast, the fact that Cyrus wished to raise an army, and had the money and good name needed to succeed in doing so, was not: nevertheless, the continuation of the Cyreians' existence, as a wandering army, can be explained at least in part by the observation that the Arcadian and Achaean hoplites who formed a majority of the army could have expected, had they gone home, to be required to serve the Spartans in an allied contingent, instead of serving paying customers. The Spartan campaigns in Asia arose out of the aftermath of the Peloponnesian war, and these campaigns made disbandment in effect an unattractive option for many of the Cyreians. The continued existence of Cyrus' army contributed to shaping the future of the mercenary armies of Greece.

Throughout the 390s there were more wars, of which the general effect was to hinder any attempt to return to the political and social pattern of the days before 431. The repeated tactical successes of Iphicrates' mercenary army in Corinth illustrate why it became preferable from an employer's point of view to be able to hire mercenaries who would not wish to go home in winter.[44] Through these years, and through the failure of the peace of Antalcidas to stem the almost relentless tide of wars, Isocrates was in middle life, writing and teaching. In the *Panegyricus*, composed about 380, he is already making the plea for a Panhellenic expedition against Persia which he continued to make, with differing degrees of shrillness, for more than forty years afterwards. He speaks against the wars of the Greeks:[45] 'we take such risks about small matters when we could get plenty safely; we are destroying our own country, and neglecting to harvest Asia'. Later he mentions how the wars and civil struggles cause homelessness and drive many men to serve as mercenaries:[46]

> we find more trouble for ourselves than necessary, starting wars and civil struggles for ourselves – so that some people die lawlessly in their own land, some wander on foreign soil with their children and wives, and many, forced by lack of daily necessities to serve as mercenaries, ... meet their death.

Now, though N. H. Baynes, in his essay 'Isocrates',[47] points out most convincingly that 'safety' – ability to enjoy property in security – is the cardinal aim of Isocrates' pronouncements on both domestic and foreign policy,[48] he is hardly justified in the opinion that 'Isocrates remains a puzzle – just a bundle of contradictions'.[49] On the contrary, Isocrates' claim to have spent his whole life warring with the barbarians (with words, of course, he means) carries a good deal of conviction.[50] He had in mind several possible champions of the Hellenic cause at different times: Athens, Dionysius I of Syracuse, Jason of Pherae, Philip;[51] and the detailed proposals he put forward were, as Baynes says, very inconsistent with each other;[52] but there is a single notion behind the whole thing – that of marching east to seize the Persians' wealth. This is the heart of Isocrates' message (an almost distressingly simple one), and the puzzles of the *Nicocles* and the *Archidamus* are unimportant by comparison. Isocrates saw a number of symptoms in the Greece of his day,[53] and thought there was one remedy which would cure them all.

The language of his speeches gives some clue as to how serious he thought the disease was that he hoped to see cured.[54] It is possible, however, to go a little way towards stating the size of the problem of wanderers in terms less subjective than those in which Isocrates dealt. At some time not far from 366, for example, Isocrates wrote in his

Archidamus that there were more exiles (at the moment of writing) from one city than there had been previously from the whole Peloponnese.[55] This is not informative about how many there were in absolute terms, but two important inferences can be drawn from it in relation to the number of exiles in Hellas in the mid-fourth century: first, that one event could change the general position a good deal (in this case, the mass exiling in one city); and second, that impressions or comparative results are easier to come by than statistics or absolute figures. Seibert, in a very brief section entitled 'Statistisches Zahlenmaterial', has collected the testimonies referring to numbers of exiles – and ten bodies of exiles from the period under consideration in this inquiry are numbered in the ancient sources.[56] The largest single body of exiles attested in the period is of 3,000: the Messenians who in 401 joined the exiles from Cyrene and were killed wholesale in an attempted return of exiles to that city;[57] the smallest, from Mantinea in 385/384, is of 60.[58] They are scattered figures, and Seibert is right to avoid attempts at statistical inference from them. But however erratic the numbers of exiles were, and although the sources do not invite statistical treatment, there are some important events, which had happened many years before the decree was issued in 324 whereby exiles were restored,[59] and which created exiles who were still homeless at the time of the decree. Their continued existence as exiles is an aspect of the continuity between the age of Isocrates and the time of the decree.

First, the problem of Arcadia, and particularly of Tegea, seems not to have been solved between 370 and 324. It would be more than plausible to guess that Tegea was the 'one city' Isocrates referred to in the *Archidamus*: 800 fled from it, and over 1,400 from the whole of Arcadia, in the civil struggle at the foundation of the single confederacy of Arcadia,[60] and the inscription setting terms for the return of exiles to Tegea in accordance with the decree of Alexander can, in the absence of any evidence to suggest the contrary, be recognised as referring to these same exiles, or their children.[61]

Second, as the same chapter of Diodorus in which the story of the decree is told shows, the Samians exiled by Timotheus in 365 were still in exile in 324.[62]

Third, the years between 358 and 347 had seen the destruction of six cities in central and north Greece: the inhabitants of Potidaea and Sestos had been sold into slavery,[63] but the Methoneans and very possibly the Narycaeans and Zereians had simply been scattered.[64] The citizens of the largest of the six cities, Olynthus, were also sold as booty,[65] but in 316 Cassander gathered them up again and settled them in his new city, Cassandreia.[66] Fourth, again in the same chapter of Diodorus as the decree, the Oeniadae had been expelled from their city by the Aetolians at some time before 324.[67]

Xenophon records that the Tegean exiles were 800 in number.[68] He almost certainly means 800 *men*, since he records later on that 'the youngest of the Tegean exiles, about 400' were part of a Spartan garrison.[69] Counting women and children in proportion to adult men, they may have numbered about 2,500 or 3,000. The Samians will probably have been more than this,[70] the Methoneans, Narycaeans, Zereians and Oeniadae each fewer, yet certainly enough to number between them thousands rather than hundreds. There were more than 10,000 Olynthians in 347.[71] However, even though a brief glance at the middle years of the fourth century shows up a large and continuing problem of exile (Alexander could truly say to *those* exiles, 'we were not responsible for your becoming exiled'),[72] E. Badian's contention that mercenaries declared traitors to the League of Corinth during Alexander's campaign against Darius became exiles in great numbers,[73] and that mercenaries disbanded by the satraps in 324 ended up at Taenarum after wandering in Asia and living by foraging,[74] is certainly right. So in spite of Alexander's attempt to settle mercenaries (his own) in new cities – which, as Parke notes,[75] 'reminds one of Isocrates' advice to Alexander's father that he should solve the problem of the Greek unemployed by conquering Asia Minor and settling colonies between Cilicia and Sinope' (Isocrates, *Philippus* 120–2) – the result of the eastern conquests was the exact opposite of what Isocrates had hoped. The problem, which had persisted throughout the century, took a turn for the worse during the reign of Alexander the Great.

The connection between the exilings of the mid-century and the decree of 324 makes it necessary to undertake the study of exiles in these years with the decree in mind – as Seibert does.[76] But Badian suggests that the decree was a response to 'an unprecedented and apparently insoluble social problem' created by Alexander himself.[77] Arguing that only the exiles within easy reach of Olympia attended to hear the decree, he concludes that 'we shall not go far wrong, if we postulate a figure of the same order [*sc.* as the 20,000 in D.S. 18.8.5] for those exiles who did not attend the Games'.[78] Regrettably, he glosses over Diodorus' explicit statement,[79] 'all the exiles had gathered together for the festival – there were more than 20,000 of them', which deserves at least the dignity of an open denial;[80] and it ought to be taken into account that there may perhaps have been 20,000 exiles altogether, of whom not all were at Olympia: in principle, Diodorus is as likely to have misinterpreted his source one way as the other. Badian goes on to say (same page), 'it is beyond belief that such numbers could be produced by the normal play of *stasis* in the cities'. Such numbers as Badian's conjectural 40,000, that is; but in view of the great mass of exiles 'left over' from the middle of the century who still needed settlement in 324 BC, 20,000 is a perfectly credible number.

It is certain that the facts of wandering and exile affected the thought of Isocrates.[81] Another fourth-century theorist found it necessary to treat questions raised by this pervasive problem: writing possibly at some point in the 360s, Aeneas Tacticus, after outlining precautions to be taken by a city if there are exiles,[82] advises some very careful measures with regard to outsiders in the city: they are to have their arms confiscated; no one is to take them in without permission – not even innkeepers; they are to be locked into their inns at night; and periodically the scruffy ones are to be expelled.[83] On the other hand, visitors to the city from near by, with educational or other good reasons for their presence, ought merely to be registered.[84] The great mistrust expressed here, and attested in Polyaenus II.30.1, is of poor strangers with no reason for being in a particular city rather than the next: mistrust, in effect, of wanderers.

Aeneas' treatise reflects the mundane concern for day-to-day security felt by the Greeks in their cities. So his testimony is more to the point here than that of Demosthenes, who, as noted below,[85] argued in the 350s that in spite of the 'prevailing poverty' no Greek would serve the Great King against Greeks: here the 'prevailing poverty' is treated as a small consideration beside any Greek's presumed pro-Hellenic feelings. Aeneas' work is also more to the point (in terms of its nearness to the world of events) than the outstanding political texts of the fourth century, Plato's *Republic* and *Laws* and Aristotle's *Politics*. Though these books have as their theme, or part of it, the constitution of an ideal city-state in the context of the Greek world, it was not the concern of their authors to comment on the existential details of city life, as Aeneas' theme required him to. Thus when, in the *Republic*, Plato comes to discuss how to maintain the number of households at 5,040, he is obliged to provide that if a son is disowned by his father (and the process of disowning is made difficult) and not adopted into a household within ten years, he is to be sent to a colony. With the number of households strictly limited,[86] Plato says, 'it is necessary to expel fatherless men to another country', but the plan to use a colony as a sort of 'governor' to regulate the pressure of population is not very convincing: its theoretical merit, indeed, is that it avoids giving a place in Plato's theoretical apparatus to the possibility of life outside the city-state. And Aristotle, though he derides Plato's plan to have 5,000 leisured citizens,[87] affirms that there is a best size for a city (beyond which it will not be manageable)[88] and yet outlines no practical non-violent way of keeping a city at that size. A case could be made for the conjecture that his and Plato's decisions to keep silent about the possibility of life outside the city-state[89] were affected by a consciousness of the problem of outsiders: better perhaps, though, only to note how the political theorists accepted and reinforced the idea of the city-state as the centre of life. Greeks without cities were at best marginal to their interests.

Service and money

What anybody without a city-state needed was an income. For citizens, though there were people who worked in urban trades, the predominant source of income was agriculture, either through their own labour or through control of slave or other dependent labour. But outsiders were very unlikely to work in agriculture. Once someone had lost citizenship, which for the majority of citizens was a facet in their position as freeholders or tenants of agricultural land, his (or her) most likely source of income was to earn wages or fees for services. Living on one's own movable wealth, or being supported by friends, were doubtless preferred courses of action but few can have had enough money, or rich and kind enough friends, for their life styles to affect the general situation much.

It has been pointed out many times how deeply untypical a way of life wage-earning was in ancient Greece.[90] The growth in the community of outsiders in Greece involved a large expansion in occupations producing a cash income and is thus connected both with the expansion in the use of mercenary armies and with the increased liveliness of the professional sector. In the lifetime of Hippocrates (perhaps 450 to 370) acceptance of the principle that the medical craft could be taught for fees, instead of only to relatives, led not only to increased prosperity and influence for the doctors but also to growth in the profession. To some degree the demand for professional services was created by their availability, just as the demand for mercenary armies was stimulated (at least) by their availability. The danger to the city-states was not the one which Isocrates envisaged: the armies of wanderers were not going to get organised and take over (except perhaps in isolated cases, as when Pasinus took Paros);[91] and the Panhellenist dream of maintaining the *status quo* by the settlement in Asia of the wanderers – a large-scale version of the 'governor' colonisation Plato wanted – was not going to be realised.

The permanent presence in Greece of people whose service was available for money made a difference to politics and life throughout the fourth century, and the Hellenistic rulers proved to be masters at exploiting the services available to them – to the detriment of the cities. That some provided high-level or prestigious services while others only marched and fought was not such an important fact as Isocrates apparently thought it, and the growth in numbers doing each of these things was of equal importance. Political conditions from the time of Sparta's victory in the Peloponnesian war, and conditions in individual communities in Aegean Greece, Sicily and Magna Graecia, all contributed to this growth.

Notes

1 Lysias XXXI (*Philon*). 9.
2 Demosthenes XXIX (*Aphobus* III). 3.
3 Isaeus IV (*Nicostratus*). 7.
4 Isaeus IV (*Nicostratus*). 27.
5 Cf. below, pp. 157–60 and 188–91.
6 Alexander Fuks's phrase (see 'Isocrates and the social-economic situation in Greece', *Ancient Society* 3, 1972, p. 26, and, for a list of key passages in Isocrates (many of which are referred to in this chapter), n. 33).
7 Especially at *Ep.* IX (*Archidamus*). 9, where he refers to 'larger and stronger armies being collected together out of the wanderers than out of the city-dwellers'. Cf. *Philippus* 96 and 120. 'Planomenoi,' Fuks states ('Isocrates', p. 27), 'is their usual designation in Isokrates,' and though some of the passage he cites in support are rather marginal to the issue, he is certainly right.
8 E.g. at Diodorus XVIII.53.6: Eumenes in 319 'was spending time in Cappadocia gathering up his former friends and those of the men that had campaigned with him before who were wandering about the country'. Here 'wanderers' does not designate a distinct social grouping over against city-dwellers. The context does not make it possible that it should. Without the fairly few explicit Isocratean references, therefore, wanderers could not fairly be used as a category word.
9 Herodotus I. 30, II. 103 and 116.
10 E.g. Plato, *Phaedo* 81a6; Aristotle, *De Anima* 402a21.
11 Notably H. W. Parke, *Greek Mercenary Soldiers* (Oxford, 1933); G. T. Griffith, *The Mercenaries of the Hellenistic World* (Cambridge, 1935); J. Seibert, *Die politischen Flüchtlinge und Verbannten in der griechischen Geschichte* (Darmstadt, 1979).
12 Cf. Isocrates, *Evagoras* 28.
13 Soothsayers in general are discussed in more detail below, pp. 156–7.
14 But note that Thrasylochus was consumptive (11) and already ill at the time of the revolution in Siphnos (20).
15 Seibert, *Flüchtlinge*, p. 105 and n. 850. Note 850 quotes Xenophon, *Hellenica* IV.8.7.
16 Seibert, *Flüchtlinge*, p. 105: 'Im Gegenzug mussten die bisher regierenden Kreise, die Reichen und Besitzenden, de Insel verlassen. Sie fanden zunächst auf der Insel Melos Aufnahme.' ('The circles which had

been in power up to that point – the rich, the property owners – had to leave the island. They found refuge next on the island of Siphnos.')
Aegineticus 31 mentions Siphnians going from Troezen to Thrasylochus' funeral in Aegina, and 38 touches on their expedition, but elsewhere no Siphnians are mentioned except the two families concerned in the case. If the Siphnians had been travelling as a body from Melos to Troezen, surely it would seem odd for Thrasylochus to have had to beg the speaker to come with him?

17 Seibert, *Flüchtlinge*, p. 105.
18 Xenophon, *Poroi* 2.1–3.5, especially 2.7. Cf. Whitehead, *Ideology*, p. 7.
19 The Samians exiled from Samos by the Athenians in 365 seem, from the dossier of inscriptions thanking their benefactors, to have stayed in a wide range of communities: see below, pp. 47–8.
20 Seibert, *Flüchtlinge*, p. 377.
21 Above, pp. 2–4.
22 Isocrates, *Helen* 8.
23 282b–e.
24 To Herodotus' own travels add Solon's (Herodotus I.30.2; cf. above, n. 9) and the casual comment at Herodotus III.139.1 on the many Greeks arriving in Egypt when Cambyses undertook his campaign against it: 'some came to trade, as you would expect, and some as soldiers, but some come to see the country. And one of these was Syloson . . .'
25 Isocrates, *Aegineticus* 27. Electra in Euripides' *Electra* weeps every day: D. M. Lewis suggests to me that the image used in the speech may be derived from tragedy.
26 Isocrates, *Plataicus* 46: a different word (*aletai*) is used here for 'wanderers', but this appears to be because a noun rather than a participle is required in the sentence structure.
27 Aristotle, *Politics* 1253a1–6.
28 Isocrates, *Aegineticus* 7–9.
29 Homer, *Iliad* IX.63.
30 Aristotle, *Politics* 1253a28–9.
31 Antiphon II (*Tetralogy* I) 2.9.
32 E.g. [Lysias], XX (*for Polystratus*). 35, and especially (though not from a criminal case) Isocrates, *Plataicus* 55: 'for someone to have nowhere to go, and for him to become cityless and suffer troubles every day and see himself unable to look after his family – I need not say how much worse that is than other disasters!'
33 Timasion the Dardanian came fairly near being able to try this: Xenophon, *Anabasis* VIII.2.2 and V.6.23. His first attempt foundered by reason of lack of money for pay (*Anabasis* V.6.36) and his second came at a time when the army was in any case dissolving (VII.2.3–6) and was kept together by offers of employment (VII.2.8–11).
34 Cf. below, chapter 4.
35 This point is argued below, pp. 85–8.
36 Parke, *Greek Mercenary Soldiers*, p. 23.
37 D. S. XIV.6.1–3; Xenophon, *Hellenica* II.2.20.

38 See Seibert, *Flüchtlinge*, pp. 54–92.
39 Xenophon, *Hellenica* II.3.18.
40 Lysias XII (*Against Eratosthenes*). 97.
41 Leaving aside on this occasion the events of the Peloponnesian war, one need only turn to the Epidamnus affair for an example of a factional group looking for restoration (Thucydides I.26.3).
42 See Seibert, *Flüchtlinge*, pp. 92–147.
43 Though the story of Phlius (Xenophon, *Hellenica* V.2.8–10 and V.3.10–12) is interesting.
44 The authoritative account of the mercenary army in Corinth is W. K. Pritchett, *The Greek State at War* II (Berkeley and Los Angeles, 1974), pp. 117–25.
45 Isocrates, *Panegyricus* 133.
46 Isocrates, *Panegyricus* 167–8.
47 N. H. Baynes, *Byzantine Studies and Other Essays* (London, 1960), pp. 144–67.
48 Baynes, *Byzantine Studies*, pp. 153–60.
49 Baynes, *Byzantine Studies*, p. 160.
50 Isocrates, *Philippus* 130.
51 Athens: Isocrates, *Panegyricus, passim*; Dionysius I: Isocrates, *Ep*. I (*Dionysius*), *passim*; Jason of Pherae: Isocrates, *Philippus* 119–20; Philip; Isocrates, *Philippus, passim*. Earlier Aristagoras had tried out a similar idea in two places: see Herodotus V.49.1–50.3 and 97.1–2. *Epistulae Socraticorum* 28 (Orelli 30) (Speusippus to Philip), most readily accessible in L. Köhler, 'Die Briefe des Sokrates und der Sokratiker', *Philologus*, Suppl. 20, Heft 2 (1928), text at pp. 44–50, translation into German at pp. 85–9, commentary at pp. 116–23, is a letter sent to Philip in winter 343/342 after Isocrates, *Philippus*. On its authenticity see E. Bickermann and J. Sykutris, 'Speusipps Brief an König Philipp', *Berichte über die Verhandlungen der Sächsischen Akademie der Wissenschaften zu Leipzig* 80 (1928, No. 3), pp. 1–86, at pp. 29–33. It makes some shrewd points. At section 16 the text runs, '(Isocrates) has sent you the speech – the one which he wrote first to Aegesilaus, and changed it a bit then sold it to Dionysius the tyrant of Sicily. Third, after making some subtractions and additions, he wooed Alexander of Thessaly with it. Now at last he has shamelessly shot it off at you ...'
52 Baynes, *Byzantine Studies*, pp. 155–8.
53 Fuks's idea of the value of Isocrates' speeches as evidence ('Isokrates is first-rate evidence for the social-economic situation in Greece ...', 'Isocrates', p. 17) is perhaps rather optimistic, but his method of presenting a sort of synopsis of salient passages from the political writings to build up a picture of 'the elements of the situation as perceived by Isocrates' (p. 19) illustrates how largely the matter of poverty and wandering figured in Isocrates' political perception.
54 Fuks, 'Isocrates', p. 18: 'the *signalling* of the situation in Greece by Isokrates is terrifying' (examples are quoted), and p. 30: 'the impression gained from Isokrates is that to him the dimensions of the floating

population are very large indeed'. In contrast *Epistulae Socraticorum* 28 (Orelli 30) (Speusippus to Philip). 5–7 (cf. above, n. 51) does not mention the problem of wanderers when it puts forward elements of myth and early history relating to the Thracian Chalcidice with a view to supplying Philip with arguments suggesting that he might justifiably flatten every settlement in the place if he wished. The question of where the inhabitants would go is not raised.

55 Isocrates, *Archidamus* 68.
56 Seibert, *Flüchtlinge*, pp. 405–6. Ten, not including (*a*) the Phliasian exiles of 380/379 (characterised as 'a few men' by the other Phliasians), who raised and trained a force of 1,000 from defectors from the city *during* the siege of Phlius (Xenophon, *Hellenica* V.3.16–17), or (*b*) the Syracusan exiles of 317/316.
57 D. S. XIV.34.3 and 5.
58 Xenophon, *Hellenica* V.2.6.
59 D. S. XVIII.8.4–5.
60 Eight hundred from Tegea: Xenophon, *Hellenica* VI.5.10; 1,400 from all Arcadia: D.S. XV.59.2. Cf. W. E. Thompson, 'Arcadian factionalism in the 360's', *Hist.* 32 (1983), pp. 149–60.
61 *Syll.*³ 306 (new edition at A. J. Heisserer, *Alexander the Great and the Greeks* (Norman, 1980), pp. 206–8; cf. Seibert, *Flüchtlinge*, pp. 160–2).
62 D.S. XVIII.8.7; cf. Seibert, *Flüchtlinge*, p. 165.
63 Potidaea: D.S. XVI.8.5. Sestos: D.S. XVI.34.3.
64 Methone: city razed by Philip; inhabitants allowed to leave with one cloak each, D.S. XVI.34.4–5, cf. XVI.31.1. Naryx: city taken and razed by Phayllus; fate of inhabitants not mentioned, D.S. XVI.38.5. Zereia: fortress razed by Philip. Zereia was one of the Chalcidic townships. Fate of inhabitants not mentioned, D.S. XVI.52.9.
65 D.S. XVI.53.3.
66 D.S. XIX.52.2.
67 D.S. XVIII.8.6; also Plutarch, *Alexander* 49.5.
68 Xenophon, *Hellenica* VI.5.10; see also Seibert, *Flüchtlinge*, p. 405.
69 Xenophon, *Hellenica* VI.5.24.
70 Cf. the decrees of the restored Samian state, below, chapter 3, n. 150.
71 Demosthenes XIX (*Embassy*).226, cf. K. J. Beloch, *Die Bevölkerung der griechisch-römischen Welt* (Leipzig, 1886), p. 205.
72 D.S. XVIII.8.4.
73 See E. Badian, 'Harpalus', *JHS* 81 (1961), p. 29 and n. 90 (cf. p. 25, quoting Arrian, *Anabasis* 1.16.6): 'any known cases of this crime [*sc.* treason] must have been punished by the death penalty in absence (i.e., in practice, exile)'. There seems to be a logical flaw here: (i) anyone under sentence of death was surely under a curse and so not allowed to return home; (ii) a city cannot restore someone whom it has never made an exile – and the decree does not require sentences of death to be quashed. So the soldiers' being *de facto* exiles does not at all suggest that the decree was a response to the problem caused initially by them. Parke, *Greek Mercenary Soldiers*, p. 196 (not referred to by Badian), argues that the decree affected only the (few) mercenaries who had

taken to soldiering *because of* banishment: which makes better sense.
74 D.S. XVII. 111.1.
75 Parke, *Greek Mercenary Soldiers*, p. 195.
76 Seibert, *Flüchtlinge*, p. 30.
77 Badian, 'Harpalus', p. 30.
78 Badian, 'Harpalus', p. 28. G. Grote, on the other hand, speculates plausibly that the 20,000 'had mustered here from intimations that such a step was intended' (*History of Greece* XII, London, 1856, p. 131); cf. also Timoleon's request for settlers. Plutarch, *Timoleon* 22.3–5, and D.S. XVI.82.5.
79 D.S. XVIII.8.5.
80 Seibert, *Flüchtlinge*, p. 158, also fails to mention this point.
81 Cf. above, n. 54.
82 Aeneas Tacticus 10.5–7.
83 Aeneas Tacticus 10.9–10.
84 Aeneas Tacticus 10.10: cf. below, p. 152.
85 Below, p. 93 n. 121.
86 Plato, *Laws* 928e–929d. The quotation is from 928e.
87 Aristotle, *Politics* 126a17–18: 'one can make any suppositions one likes – only nothing impossible'.
88 Aristotle, *Politics* 1326a34–7.
89 Aristotle admits that there will be a great number of slaves, metics and foreigners in the city (*Politics*, 132a18–20), and Plato devises terms for the residence of metics (*Laws* 850a–d) under which the metic must leave after twenty years – but where he is to go is not mentioned.
90 And de Ste Croix, *Class Struggle*, pp. 179–204, gives a good survey. At p. 182 he notes, 'The first appearance in antiquity of hired labour on a large scale was in the military field, in the shape of mercenary service.' It was precisely in Greece in the fourth century that mercenary service began to be available, and to be taken up, on a large scale (see below, especially pp. 85–8). So it is clear that wage labour had its first large development at the period when many people were being forced to live outside the cities (inside which it was normal for a free citizen not to gain his income in the form of wages).
91 Isocrates, *Aegineticus* 18–19.

3

Cities founded or destroyed in the fourth century

Effects of local crises

Since the Dark Age, in settling Greece, the Black Sea coasts and
Sicily and Italy, the Greeks had developed to a point where the
number of self-governing communities forming their world was
possibly in excess of 1,000. In mainland and Aegean Greece alone, E.
Ruschenbusch calculates, there were about 750 states, over half of
them with fewer than 400 adult male citizens.[1] He makes no
calculation for Italy and Sicily. These communities were generally
settled and inhabited in a stable way, though smaller ones were
sometimes taken over by larger neighbours;[2] and if a community
ceased to exist, the direct or indirect cause was usually war.

Where a city was captured and overthrown by enemies, the men
would often be killed and the women and children sold as slaves.
When this happened, the question of wandering outsiders, or of
refounding the captured city, did not arise. But sometimes the
inhabitants were allowed to leave as part of a surrender on terms;
and sometimes, as events in Sicily in the fourth century illustrate,
strategic reasons less immediate than actual siege could lead to
evacuation. The complex of cities throughout the Greek world could
absorb victims of such destructions to some extent. Cities did not
usually have a systematic policy of excluding non-citizens. For those
unable to find a way of supporting themselves as aliens there were
mercenary units and bands of raiders by means of which some sort of
livelihood could be won.[3] Some wanderers died of starvation or
disease.

In this chapter the prevalence and the results of such destructions
of cities are considered. Despite the radical local particularism of
government in most of Greece, the Greek world functioned to some
degree as a unit where its response to exiles and wanderers was
concerned: Sicilian exiles were brought back to Sicily in Timoleon's
time from Cos and other Aegean islands,[4] and the 'barbarisation' of

Sicily gave Lysias a theme for his speech at the Olympic Games.[5] So the situation in Sicily and Italy, though their politics were remote from the main currents of the struggle between states in Greece and Macedonia, was an important part of the developing social situation in the Greek world, in which during the fourth century outsiders were of increasing importance. Events in the western part of the Greek world will be considered first.

Sicily under Dionysius I

The difficulties which the democratic government of Syracuse had in responding to Carthaginian aggression, a few years after victory over the Athenians, enabled Dionysius I to set himself up as tyrant.[6] The policy of evacuating the smaller Greek cities of Sicily to concentrate strength in Syracuse, which had led to the discontent that brought in the tyranny, was continued once Dionysius had power.[7] The policy was in effect permanent, and its results were very noticeable at the time of Plato's visit to Sicily. The city of Syracuse itself had grown under Dionysius I,[8] suffering depopulation only during the interrupted reign of Dionysius II,[9] but the policy of keeping the rest of Sicily weak had been successful. The Platonic letters allude to the fact repeatedly – and treat the ruin of the cities outside Syracuse as symptomatic of the trouble brought by tyrannical government in general: *Ep.* III.315c8–d7 notes that not a few people are saying that Plato had prevented Dionysius II from carrying out his proposal 'to refound the cities in Sicily and take the burden off Syracuse, and change his government from a tyranny to a kingship ...' but was now encouraging Dion to do the same (and so subverting Dionysius). The author naturally denies the charge,[10] but the interesting point is the way in which the refoundation of the Greek cities is presented as a key element in the turn away from tyranny.

Similarly in *Ep.* VIII there is a passage driving at the point that the Greek cities of Sicily need to be refounded. It is a retrospective explanation of how Syracuse came under the rule of one family,[11] a family 'which your fathers put in power when they were in a desperate situation, at a time when there was a grave danger that the Greek part of Sicily would become ruined, wholly barbarised by the Carthaginians'. This identifies 406/405 as the moment when Greek Sicily was in danger of ruin, and notes (agreeing with D.S. XIII.91–6) that that very danger brought about Dionysius' tyranny. The origin of the state of affairs at the time of writing (in the 350s) is explicitly given as the period of invasion before 400. Dionysius' policies had done nothing to halt the abandonment of smaller cities and concentration of Greeks into Syracuse: rather the reverse.

His policies were not a new idea in Sicilian government – not even the invention of his immediate predecessors in the democratic regime. The earlier fifth-century history of the island had seen similar events. At the time when mainland Greece was defeating Xerxes' invasion Gelon had come back from his victory over the Carthaginians and carried out temple-building at Syracuse;[12] his good work for the cities of Sicily is mentioned in a panegyrical passage in Diodorus.[13] He brought the Camarinaeans, more than half the Geloans, and the rich people from Sicilian Megara and Sicilian Euboea, into Syracuse as citizens.[14] But his brother Hieron, who reigned as tyrant after him, moved the Naxians and Catanians out of their cities (to Leontini),[15] replacing them with settlers from Syracuse and the Peloponnese.[16] At much the same time Theron, the tyrant of Acragas, who controlled Himera, saw Himera in need of more inhabitants and enrolled many Dorians and others.[17] Movement from city to city was clearly in some degree typical of Siceliot life, whereas it was unusual in the older parts of Greece. Alcibiades comments to the Athenians at Thucydides VI.17.2, 'the cities are populated by intermingled hordes of people, and they have easy migrations and acceptances of citizens'. Movement of this sort need not, however, have involved abandonment of land if, as D. M. Lewis has suggested to me, the normal pattern in Sicily involved fewer Greek landowners working the land themselves than in other areas.

At the very beginning of Dionysius' reign the Carthaginian advance led to the abandonment of the Greek cities of the south coast. When Acragas was evacuated by the democratic generals, and the Carthaginians demolished it, there was panic among the Greek population, as Diodorus notes:[18] 'when the disaster at Acragas was announced, such fear gripped the island that, while some of the Siceliots moved to Syracuse, others took away to Italy their children, their wives and their other property'. Acragas, a large city in any case, had apparently been full to bursting with refugees from places taken or threatened by the Carthaginians.[19]

The people saved from Acragas went to Leontini with Syracusan support,[20] and were presumably the 'exiles and sacrilegious persons from everywhere' whom Dionysius got behind him for his decisive thrust for power:[21] a neat example of how writers treat all outsiders as rogues,[22] though in this case they had been made refugees through no fault of their own. Before evacuating Gela and Camarina[23] Dionysius made some attempt to defend them. But the evacuations were compulsory[24] and made him some enemies – the Geloans and Camarinaeans went to Leontini,[25] a city which had supported the Athenian invasion and which was an enemy of Syracuse to the last.[26]

Once Dionysius was established at Syracuse, it became more than ever the centre about which not only Greek Sicily but also Greek Italy revolved. In Italy the Lucanians, and slightly later the Bruttians, posed a threat analogous to that of the Carthaginians in Sicily. The situation is summed up in Strabo:[27] 'the Greeks held the sea coast of the straits on both sides, and for a long time Greeks and barbarians were fighting each other. But the tyrants of Sicily ... did harm to all the peoples in the area – but specially to the Greeks.'

So in 393 the Italiots formed an alliance for mutual defence against Dionysius and the Lucanians.[28] Even before this date Rhegium had taken a line of clear opposition to Dionysius: the attempt to found and maintain a city at Mylae in 394 was the end product of a Rhegine policy of collecting up refugees from Naxos and Catane;[29] there were presumably people who had escaped (by being ransomed or running away) from the slavery into which Dionysius had sold them in 403 when their cities fell.[30] Dionysius' friends the Messenians succeeded in seizing Mylae, and the Naxians living there dispersed and settled among the Sicels and the Greek cities,[31] so the Rhegine attempt to use displaced people against Dionysius came to nothing. But the episode shows how it was possible to exploit outsiders for a political purpose – even when there was no ready-made group of exiles (such as Dionysius had found at Leontini) and it was necessary to gather them up.

The alliance formed by the Greek cities of Italy in 393 seems to have been identical with the 'Italiot League' referred to by Polybius, who outlines how the Italiots followed an Achaean organisational model in forming their association, some time after they had first accepted Achaean help towards bringing about a truce at the time of the burning down of the Pythagorean *synedria*.[32] J. A. O. Larsen dates the formation of the league as early as the last quarter of the fifth century, but he seems to allow too little time for the interval indicated by Polybius, and fails to mention D.S. XIV.91.1, where Diodorus places the alliance's formation in 393.[33] In 393 the danger from Dionysius was certainly apparent: he had just retreated (making a truce for one year) from his first attack on Rhegium.[34] The extent to which the Lucanians were a threat by that date, though, is less easy to determine. G. Pugliese Carratelli suggests that the Panhellenic foundation of Thurii in the fifth century may show a realisation of the need for Hellenes to hang together against the barbarians, though (significantly) the paper in which this suggestion is made has a good deal to say about non-hostile relations between the Italiots and their non-Greek neighbours after 400.[35] But by 390 the Lucanians held the formerly Greek city of Laus and, possibly at the suggestion of Dionysius,[36] were launching an attack on the land of Thurii.[37] The battle that followed at Laus was won by the Lucanians, but the peace which was concluded afterwards with the help of Dionysius' brother and admiral Leptines, who lost his command because of it,[38] seems to have lasted for a matter of decades.

Pressure on the Italian Greeks from Dionysius' side was more or less constant after the threat of a Carthaginian take-over in Sicily had receded. He followed his first campaign, which had provoked the formation of the Italiot League, with further campaigns in 390, 389 and 388/387. The year 390 ended with the Italiots' peace with the Lucanians,[39] and 389 with a temporary settlement imposed on the Italiots by Dionysius after his victory at the Eleporus river. The cities were granted peace and allowed autonomy, and on Rhegium's surrender Dionysius took 300 talents, all the Rhegines' ships (70), and 100 hostages; the population of Caulonia was moved to Syracuse.[40] In 388 Dionysius took Hipponium, sending the inhabitants to Syracuse and giving the territory to the Locrians, and then indulged his feelings against Rhegium by beginning a new siege, which ended eleven months later.[41] After the surrender 6,000 Rhegines were sent to Syracuse, and those who could not pay a mina as ransom were sold into slavery.[42]

There are some comments in ancient sources about Dionysius' presumed motives for continuing the Italian wars. Justin says,[43] 'Dionysius thought peace was a bad thing for his regime, and thought it dangerous to have such a large army doing nothing, so he deployed his forces across into Italy.' Diodorus tells the story of the Rhegines offering him the public hangman's daughter as his bride.[44] But his actions in moving the populations of whole cities into Syracuse suggest that a main motive may have been to augment his power by keeping his capital city strong enough to resist any likely non-Greek enemy, while weakening the rest of the area of Greek settlement so that no combination of states could eclipse him. Diodorus more or less skips the campaigns of the last twenty years of Dionysius I's life (387–367),[45] but other sources show that he attacked Croton after the fall of Rhegium.[46] This city is described by Diodorus as (in 389)[47] 'the most populous city and the one which had the most Syracusan exiles'. And it is clear that in the course of the fourth century Croton ceased to be the most populous city in Greek Italy, its mantle falling on Taras.[48] Since the moment of its conquest by Dionysius was the moment when it began to decline, it is possible that Dionysius may have taken at least a proportion of its population back to Sicily with him.[49]

Dionysius' transplants of Greeks to Syracuse are in one way like the Successors' policies, two generations later, of building up big cities in the areas they controlled, and in another way quite different. Syracuse, like Cassandreia or Antigoneia, was intended to protect the ruler who made it his base. But its formation was a defensive investment of human resources. It represented a more or less deliberate retreat from areas which had been successfully colonised by Greeks up to 350 years earlier. Dionysius created and exploited homelessness to give himself the means of building his unassailable fortress at Syracuse – and unassailable it was, until it passed into Dionysius II's less able hands.

But not all the people made outsiders by Dionysius I became insiders at Syracuse. During the Carthaginian invasion some went east and found that Carthaginian rule was not so terrible as Greek propaganda made out:[50] these received their property back.[51] Messene, by contrast, was refounded by Dionysius after its destruction by the Carthaginians in 396.[52] Some of the Messenians had been killed in the fighting, others had fled to the nearest cities, but most of the people took to the mountains and were scattered to the fortresses in the countryside.[53] Their period without a city-state centre was short, since Dionysius refounded Messene the same year,[54] but other cities remained unfounded much longer.

Reaction and recovery in Sicily

P. Orlandini's study of Gela between 405 and 282 notes that on the hilltop of Gela, explored and excavated in every part, no object datable between 405 and 383 has been found. There were three small finds of objects datable between 380 and 350.[55] But, as Orlandini notes, contingents of Geloans served in the siege of Motya (397)[56] and in the campaign after Dion landed (357).[57] The explanation Orlandini cautiously adopts is that the Geloans who served in those campaigns were living in the hinterland and that the city had not yet been refounded.[58] The similarity of the cases of Camarina and Acragas suggests a parallel course of events in those cities.[59]

There were only isolated cases of attempts at establishing or re-establishing cities in the reigns of the Dionysii. Halaesa Archonidion and Mylae have been mentioned.[60] The other example of a foundation carried out in opposition to Dionysius I is that of Hipponium. The Carthaginians collected together all the exiles from this city in south Italy, taken by Dionysius in 388, whose population he had moved to Syracuse, and in 379 settled them back in their own city.[61] Their opposition to Dionysius, which had caused them to take an interest in Halaesa, must have been the Carthaginians' motive for taking care of the Hipponiates in this way; but a plague, Libyan and Sardinian rebellions, and disturbances in Carthage, were enough to distract the Carthaginians from whatever plan they had.[62] It is worth noting that not all Hipponiates were living as citizens in Syracuse nine years after the destruction of Hipponium: the wording of Diodorus' narrative of the refoundation ('the Carthaginians ... gathered up all the exiles ...', cf. n. 61 above) shows that a good many – enough to refound the place – had gone into exile *from Syracuse*. The revealing thing is that *all* the (Hipponiate) exiles are mentioned: this cannot mean 'all the Hipponiates who had gone from Hipponium to Syracuse' – first, because when they were living at Syracuse the Hipponiates were not exiles but Syracusan citizens, and, second, because, even if it were possible to regard the Hipponiates at Syracuse as exiles, it would have been impossible for the Carthaginians to recruit *all* of them in Syracuse under Dionysius' nose. The phrase implies that a proportion, at least, of the Hipponiates were outside Syracuse in 379. All three cases, Halaesa, Mylae and Hipponium, show that the very depressed condition of the Greek cities of Sicily in Dionysius' reign ensured that colonising enterprises would find willing participants. Nor was colonisation monopolised by Dionysius' enemies. Dionysius himself founded colonies: Messene, in Sicily, he peopled with Greeks from Italy; and 600 Messenians from the Peloponnese whom he settled at Tyndaris in 396 soon increased their number to over 5,000 by admitting new citizens.[63] But the recovery of the cities formerly surrendered to the Carthaginians, mentioned by Diodorus in the passage where he records these foundations, cannot have been more than partial; and the ruined condition of Greek Sicily was treated from a fairly early stage as a Panhellenic problem. The references in the Platonic letters to plans for colonising Sicily have been noted above,[64] but even as much as a generation earlier Lysias had alluded to the barbarisation of Sicily in the *Olympiacus*:[65]

> since one can see that Greece is in such bad condition – much of it under the power of barbarians and many cities ruined by tyrants – anyone who is a good man and a citizen worthy of his city must have matters of high policy on his mind.

A solution to this problem was achieved by Timoleon's expedition.

The beginning of Plutarch's *Timoleon* describes Syracuse itself as almost deserted because of the rapid exchange of tyrant for tyrant: this, as the reason given by Plutarch suggests, must have been a development which had come about since the times referred to in the Platonic letters – in the ten years or so before the coming of Timoleon. And in the same passage the rest of Sicily is described as 'now completely ruined and cityless because of the wars' and it is noted that the cities had been settled by 'half-breed barbarians and unemployed soldiers'.[66] Later, in the passage where he narrates how Timoleon sent to Corinth for settlers from Greece, Plutarch returns to the theme, mentioning grass growing in the market place of Syracuse, and deer and wild pigs living in the other cities. He describes the life of those living without a city-state centre:[67] 'none of the people who were living in the strong points and fortresses was subject to the government, and they did not even go down to the city, but they all lived in fear and hatred of market place and constitution and rostrum'. The cities, not entirely non-existent before refoundation, were too weak to be a focus of security and communal life.[68]

Timoleon's work in Sicily involved a vigorous reassertion of the conventional Greek pattern of settlement in the island. The movement of Greeks out of Sicily, which began before Dionysius I was tyrant, which had gained momentum as a result of his policies, and which had not been reversed in the period of Dionysius II and Dion, came to an end – and some Greeks returned from farther east than Italy. Towards the end of the *Timoleon* Plutarch mentions Acragas and Gela, noting how they had been ruined by the Carthaginians after the Attic war (the Sicilian expedition) and saying that in each case an expedition composed of former citizens (one with Megellus and Pheristus from Elaia or Elea,[69] the other, mentioned above,[70] with Gorgus from Cos) came from Greece to refound the cities.[71]

The resettlement of Sicily was clearly a widely and successfully publicised venture. At a period when the conventional Greek style of politics and diplomacy – not to say fighting – was doing badly against Philip of Macedon, Timoleon offered an appealing type of anti-monarchical way of doing things. According to Plutarch, the Corinthians had found that most of the Sicilian exiles were living in Asia and the islands, so they announced the impending colonisation in those places. But the results were disappointing, and even with volunteers from Corinth and the rest of Greece there were only 10,000.[72]

Further colonists gathered up from Italy and Sicily brought the total number of people newly settled in Italy by Timoleon up to 60,000.[73] Modern interpretations of these figures differ widely: J. Seibert's treatment of the migration from Italy as a *Rückwanderung*, a return of exiles to Sicily,[74] ignores Plutarch's statement about most of the exiles living in Asia and the islands; D. Asheri is certainly right to note that exiles formed only a small proportion of the total number of colonists,[75] but unfortunately he suggests no alternative reason why so many Greeks in the west were ready to follow Timoleon. It seems fair to suggest that the Greeks from Sicily who joined the colonising enterprise had been living in the hinterland of a ruined Greek city or as resident aliens in a Sicel or Greek city:[76] these were the people, or rather the descendants of the people, who had earlier lost their homes. Their return can be considered a *Rückwanderung*, since Timoleon brought them back into normal city life from outside it. But as for the Greeks from Italy he settled, it is impossible to be certain whether they included some descendants of Siceliots who had fled at the end of the fifth or in the early fourth century. Plutarch's statement about Asia and the islands could be reconciled with there being many such only on the hypothesis that, while those in Asia and the islands evidently kept their identity as Siceliots, those moving to Italy might have been more thoroughly absorbed.[77]

Greek setbacks in Italy

Wherever the migrants from Italy had originated 60 or more years earlier, their movement to Sicily about 340 must have meant a noticeable reduction in the Greek population of Italy.[78] When Dionysius II left Locri for Syracuse at the end of Dion's period of government, Syracusan influence in Italy collapsed. The Locrians threw out Dionysius' garrison and he failed to recapture the city.[79] Although Dionysius had refounded Rhegium (once set up, it was out of this control by 351)[80] and planted two cities in Apulia to secure safety against pirates in the Ionian sea,[81] he had not strengthened the Greeks enough to deter the Italic peoples from maintaining their pressure. And the vulnerability of the Italiot cities was obvious. They were geographically widespread – most were near the coast, and most were towards the south-east (though Neapolis was as far north as Campania) – and most of them had Italic neighbours. The larger cities are the only ones whose fortunes are even outlined in the extant historical record, but an odd comment of Strabo's illustrates the continual and wearing struggle smaller communities faced if they were to retain their Greekness. He notes that of the 13 Greek cities of Iapygia all except Taras and Brundisium were (by this time) only *polismatia*.[82]

Of the bigger towns, however, the Lucanians in the middle of the fourth century took Heraclea,[83] and the Bruttians Terina, Hipponium, Thurii and Sybaris.[84] Sybaris, founded by exiles on the river Traeis before the original Sybaris was absorbed in the foundation of Thurii,[85] was not refounded. According to Diodorus, its inhabitants were driven out by the Bruttians and killed.[86] But most of the other cities were retaken barely a generation later by Alexander of Epirus. In the case of Hipponium, since Livy does not mention it where he mentions the king's other successes,[87] the evidence of restoration to Greek control is the coin type: a new, determinedly non-Italic way of spelling the city's name, dated to the period of Alexander of Epirus,[88] suggests a reassertion of their Greekness by the inhabitants.[89] Terina, also captured by the Bruttians *c.* 350, is described by Livy as a Bruttian city (in the same breath as Consentia, the Bruttian capital) in the passage where he mentions its capture by Alexander of Epirus,[90] and since in the same sentence the other Greek city he mentions, Heraclea, is described as a colony of the Tarentines, it may be right to infer from his description of Terina that in the years since its capture it had begun to be de-Hellenised.

The struggle for survival by Greek communities in Italy, assisted briefly by Alexander of Epirus, had been in progress before he arrived in the cities he helped. Thurii seems to have recovered after being taken by the Bruttians – Timoleon's reinforcements from Corinth, stuck at Thurii, helped the citizens in a campaign against them – but was apparently taken by the Lucanians before coming under Tarentine control.[91] Roman influence in Magna Graecia shows in the alliance the Thurians made with Rome in freeing themselves of the Lucanians.[92] In a similar way Heraclea, recaptured from the Lucanians by Alexander of Epirus,[93] was fought over, in the fourth or third century, by the Tarentines and the Messapians.[94]

Neither Alexander of Epirus nor Archidamus, the king sent by Sparta to help the Tarentines in the middle 340s,[95] was able to produce a Greek renascence like the one induced by Timoleon in Sicily. Settlement, or resettlement, required a body of people who were uneasy enough where they were to go and try to live somewhere else. Timoleon scooped the pool, partly by using his connections at Corinth to attract settlers in Greece, and partly by drawing on Italy.

The late fourth century in west Greece

In the 320s Agathocles began to make his mark.[96] Brought to Italy as a chiliarch in the Syracusan army fighting for Croton against the Bruttians, he stayed there when his attempt to discredit Heracleides and Sostratus, the rulers of Syracuse, failed. He served as a mercenary at Taras until the Tarentines became suspicious of him.[97] Then he gathered 'the exiles in Italy' and went to help the Rhegines against Heracleides and Sostratus.[98] His activity as a mercenary leader in Italy was temporary, though: the regime in Syracuse fell, and he was able to return.[99] When he became an exile again, he repeated in Sicily what he had done in Italy, raising his own army in the inland areas.[100] But this exile too was short: he was soon back in

Syracuse, elected general.[101] It is no great surprise, perhaps, that an army could easily be raised in Italy by an experienced officer; but it may seem odd that Agathocles had the same success in Sicily, in the years of grain exports and general material revival.[102] It is worth noting that he went inland to raise this army, whereas the great Siceliot cities revived by Timoleon were on or near the coast.

For the first dozen years of Agathocles' reign as tyrant of Syracuse there was a body of Syracusan exiles ready to return if ever it had an opportunity. Six thousand had escaped to Acragas on the day of Agathocles' *coup d'état* in Syracuse,[103] and two years later at Messene some Syracusan exiles fought Agathocles until the Carthaginians successfully demanded peace for Messene from him.[104] Later Diodorus notes how all the exiles from Syracuse moved to Messene because all the other cities in Sicily had made peace with Agathocles,[105] and how when the Messenians, hoping for a peaceful settlement with the tyrant, sent them away[106] they tried (unsuccessfully) to take Centoripa,[107] and were then invited into Galeria.[108] At the same time they sought the Carthaginians' help, though the Carthaginians' actions against Agathocles in response to the exiles' request seem to have been of no direct use to the exiles.[109] By 307 they were at Acragas: it was probably where they went when Agathocles' generals Pasiphilus and Demophilus defeated them in 312, recapturing Galeria.[110]

It is particularly interesting to note how Deinocrates, the leader of the exiles, was able to gain control of Acragantine policy at the moment of the defeat of Xenodicus, the Acragantine general, in 307.[111] He was able to recruit a very large army: 20,000 foot soldiers and 1,500 cavalry, 'and all these had been in exile and were thoroughly used to hard work'.[112] This illustrates what effect ten years of Agathocles' rule had had on Sicily: political conditions had caused a fair number of men to leave their homes for some period. But the general prosperity of the country continued to increase.[113] A century earlier the Siceliots had feared and run from the Carthaginians; now the Carthaginians' alliance was regarded as a possible alternative to alliance with and domination by the Syracusans. The reason may have been Agathocles' practice of taking exceptionally cruel revenge on enemies;[114] or it may have been the Carthaginian policy of encouraging Greeks to live in Greek cities within their sphere of influence.[115]

In the last years of the fourth century the Tarentines, at war with the Lucanians and Romans, asked the Spartans again for help and for Cleonymus, the king, as a general.[116] His career in Italy was not distinguished, but two points stand out: first, that he could enlist as many mercenaries in Taras as at Taenarum in Laconia (it is not stated whether they were all Greeks);[117] second, that once the Lucanians (dismayed at the size of his army) had made peace he attacked the people of Metapontum, a Greek city, and planned to invade Sicily.[118] Where Alexander of Epirus had striven to regain cities and territory and to extend the sphere of Greek control north-westwards into Italy, Cleonymus treated Greek Italy not as an entity to be expanded at the expense of barbarians, but as a single unit in a projected personal kingdom. He and Agathocles, and, in the early third century, Pyrrhus of Epirus, illustrate how Hellenistic kingship took on a divergent form in west Greece, where it replaced the tyranny of the Dionysii. An all-Greek government was not the vigorous plant it proved to be farther east, and it was not to be long before Sicily was a Roman province.

The west Greek generals, from Cleonymus back via Agathocles, Timoleon and Dion to Dionysius I himself, all used armies of outsiders in areas where there was not a general surplus of Greeks, considering the land and resources available. The growth in numbers of outsiders reflected (most of the time) the general decline, sometimes deliberately induced, of the pattern of settlement in self-governing city-states. But in Greece and the east during the fourth century there was no such general decline. When there were moves to expel people from their cities the motive of concentrating strength against barbarians was not characteristically present. No one state could dominate the area in the way in which Syracuse dominated the Greek parts of Sicily and Italy.

Exiles, settlement and control in the periods of Spartan and Theban ascendancy

Manipulation of settlement and of outsiders was a means of imposing and retaining control that was used by dominant states from the end of the Peloponnesian war. Athens, as well as taking measures to inspire terror in potential enemies (as at Melos), had systematically settled Athenian citizens as cleruchs in places where their presence would aid control. After his victory at Aegospotami, Lysander sent the cleruchs back to Athens: the intention and effect were to worsen the famine during Sparta's siege.[119] Probably more than 10,000 people were moved.[120] The effect of the loss of the cleruchies was to make it impossible for Athens to achieve her former power, even when the Spartan alliance and the restrictions on the navy and the Long Walls had been shaken off. Sparta's refusal to destroy Athens, as Corinth and Thebes wished,[121] though prompted by worry about the potential power of those two cities, was based on a calculation – broadly accurate – of Athens' future prospects.

In the brief period of Sparta's clear supremacy action to expel the Messenians from Cephallenia and Naupactus[122] and the Oetaeans from Heraclea Trachinia[123] supported her security and prospects of control. In the first of these cases, while the Messenians dispersed to Sicily, Italy and Cyrene (where the Euesperites were inviting any Greek to join them),[124] Cephallenians and Ozolian Locrians were allowed to return to the places evacuated by the Messenians.[125] At Heraclea, where the Boeotians seized the city in 395 and put it in the hands of the people forced out four years before,[126] the difference between the sides was also ethnic. The policy was to turn Sparta's supporters into controllers of land and city resources while marginalising others (whether pro-Athenian or pro-Theban) by making them outsiders.

Fought to a standstill in the Corinthian war,[127] the Spartans found their capacity for intervention in the sphere of former Athenian power reduced. But in the Peloponnese, when Mantinea revolted, they achieved a similar marginalisation of their enemies by demolishing the walled city and making the people live in villages in Mantinean territory which, as well as being easier for the pro-Spartan oligarchs to dominate,[128] were treated as separate communities for army recruitment.[129] There is perhaps an echo of Gela here.[130] Even people still living in the territory a city had once held became in some measure outsiders when the state they had been part of lost its power.

Theban policy in Boeotia in the period of Thebes' rise and eventual hegemony illustrates how similar in effect the approach of destroying a city's buildings and scattering the inhabitants to the countryside was to expulsion of the inhabitants from the whole territory. Plataea and Thespiae, used by Sparta to keep up pressure on the Theban government after the expulsion of the Spartan garrison from the Cadmeia, were both destroyed by Thebes. So Theban control of Boeotia was consolidated. The Plataeans, who had brought the anger of the Thebans upon themselves by sending for Athenian soldiers,[131] were thrown out of Boeotia (those who were not captured by Theban cavalry);[132] but after the Thebans had demolished Plataea they merely sacked Thespiae,[133] and the Thespians at Xenophon, *Hell.* VI.3.1, may perhaps not have been living at Athens as the Plataeans were.[134] The evidence of Pausanias, writing about the battle of Leuctra,[135] shows that the Thespians stayed in the Thespian hinterland after the destruction of the city. This accounts for the fact that the plight of the Plataeans made a greater impact, if impressions at this distance can be trusted, on Greece than that of the Thespians.[136]

Theban power, as it grew, was reinforced by further attention to the weakening of the rest of Boeotia. (An oligarchic plot provided an excuse for demolishing Orchomenus and enslaving the Orchomenians, traditional enemies of Thebes.)[137] Understanding the importance of fortified cities in local politics, the Thebans imposed on Sparta the sort of balance of power they had themselves for the time being shaken off: Mantinea, though rebuilding began before the Thebans came,[138] almost certainly received support from Thebes;[129] Messene, when refounded, controlled half the territory the Spartans had had before Leuctra;[140] and Megalopolis was a fair attempt at giving Arcadia the strong centre neither Mantinea nor Tegea had been able to provide.[141]

Something is known about the founding of Megalopolis. Pausanias treats it in some detail, naming 41 cities which the Arcadians resolved to abandon in order to people the new city.[142] He describes how the inhabitants of four cities resisted and were compelled to move to Megalopolis,[143] but a reference elsewhere to Aliphera, one of the cities he mentions here, shows that the abandonment was not permanent: it is described as a small town because many of its inhabitants were removed by the synoecism of Megalopolis.[144] Probably Aliphera was small still in Pausanias' day (more than 500 years after the synoecism of Megalopolis), but since Pausanias' comments on the cults of Aliphera are explicitly noted as coming from local sources it is fair to think that his explanation for the smallness of Aliphera is based on a local tradition rather than merely on his own inference. So a certain amount of passive resistance to moving to Megalopolis can be inferred.

There were big changes in Arcadia in the 360s. As well as Mantinea and the 41 constituent communities of Megalopolis, Orchomenus and Euaimon decided on a synoecism. The Euaimonians moved to Orchomenus.[145] And in Messenia the return of exiled Messenians brought pressure to bear on Sparta from the other side. Epaminondas sent messengers round to bring them in:[146] even if they were Dorians *par excellence*, as Pausanias says,[147] the returners had never lived in the Peloponnese before. But former Helots must have been at least as important in the new community as returners.

Elsewhere, Athens was asserting herself. Possibly consciousness of Theban and Sicilian methods encouraged a reversion to fifth-century methods. In 365 an Athenian cleruchy was installed at Samos, and the Samian state was destroyed: the Samians lost their city and land for 43 years, until Perdiccas restored them in 322.[148] In his account of the events at Samos, S. Hornblower comments that[149] Samians who had been put on the streets of Greece by Athens were walking reminders of the power of Fortune, and that 'prudence should have counselled Athens against taking a step which was likely to alienate even opinion sympathetic to herself'. True, and borne out by the archive of Samian inscriptions, from the period of the restored city, in which the benefactors of the Samians in their wanderings are thanked.[150] But many states in the fourth century demonstrated that public opinion was no terror to those contemplating destroying a Greek city.

While the Theban hegemony was causing foundations and destructions of cities in the Peloponnese and central Greece, the Hecatomnid satraps in Caria were carrying out a programme of synoecisms and Hellenisation. This is fully investigated by S. Hornblower,[151] who pays considerable attention to the question of how far the eight communities drawn on for the synoecism of Halicarnassus continued to be inhabited.[152] His findings offer a little corroboration of the impression gained from the continued occupation of Aliphera that the inclusion of small communities in synoecised cities did not necessarily imply their abandonment.[153] But the objectives Mausolus and the other Hecatomnid satraps had in mind did not require the peopling of their cities with immigrant Greeks: the new citizens of Halicarnassus were Carians.[154]

Both Epaminondas and Mausolus synoecised cities in order to dominate more effectively. The other recorded synoecism of the 360s, that of Cos, occurred in an island to some extent isolated from the politics of Greece and Asia. But it gained enough attention to be recorded in Diodorus, and the fact that 'a multitude of men was gathered to this (city)'[155] makes it proper to mention the synoecism in this account of foundations and destructions. S. M. Sherwin-White discusses the synoecism, and the upheavals connected with it, at some length,[156] concluding that before 366 Cos was an island of more than one city. Showing that the synoecism was part of a Theban plan, Sherwin-White notes that the Coans gave Orchomenians citizenship after the destruction of Orchomenus by the Thebans in 364.[157] This shows that Diodorus' comment about a multitude of men being gathered refers to immigration from outside Cos into the new city, as well as to concentration of the island's existing population. And in Thessaly a new city, Metropolis, was founded in the 360s. Strabo gives a brief account of its foundation from three small settlements, which is given a *terminus ante quem* by the Delphi inscription *Syll.*[3] 239E.[158]

Greece and Macedonia in Philip II's reign

Further north, in Macedonia, Philip II in the middle of the fourth century made his people (or at least some of them) inhabitants of cities.[159] He founded some cities in Macedonia and Thrace,[160] including Philippi – which secured access to the gold mines.[161] But non-Macedonian Greeks had more occasion to notice how Philip destroyed cities. As early as 357 he had attacked and captured Potidaea. Diodorus notes that he did so as part of an agreement giving him alliance with Olynthus, and that Athens was Philip's rival for the alliance.[162] Cawkwell makes it explicit that Athens was unlikely to hand Potidaea over to the Olynthians;[163] but Philip, who let the Athenian garrison go (garrison is Diodorus' word, but there were cleruchs there from Athens too),[164] sold the citizens into slavery and gave the city (evidently still standing) and the land to the Olynthians. Beloch estimates the citizen population of Potidaea at 2,000–3,000,[165] so that the availability of the city and its territory offered the Olynthians an ideal opportunity for quick expansion.

In 354 Philip captured and destroyed Methone, allowing the inhabitants to leave with one garment each.[166] Cawkwell stresses the strategic importance of the capture of Methone (and the place, whose site is unknown, can only have been small),[167] but the distribution of the land to Macedonians is an example of how Macedonian expansion in north Greece under Philip was tending to limit the area in which non-Macedonian Greeks could live.

In the year in which Philip captured and destroyed Methone the Athenians' general, Chares, captured Sestos (which Athens had earlier lost[168]), killed the adult males and enslaved the others.[169] At the same time the Athenians, at Cersobleptes' invitation, sent out cleruchs to the cities of the Thracian Chersonese (except Cardia).[170] The inhabitants made room for the Athenian settlers, without compulsion, if the hypothesis of Demosthenes 8 (*Chersonese*) is to be believed.[171]

Philip captured Olynthus, where the party favourable to Macedon (which had secured the gaining of Potidaea) had lost power,[172] in 348. The year before, Philip had taken and razed Zereia in his campaign against the Chalcidic cities;[173] now he thoroughly carried out his Chalcidian policy. The inhabitants of Olynthus were enslaved.[174] 'The mass of the inhabitants,' Cawkwell says, 'were carried off to slavery in Macedonia itself.'[175] There are three references in the *Embassy* speech to Olynthians as slaves in Macedonia (in two cases they allude to Philip's being in control of them himself and setting them free or giving them away).[176] These references certainly indicate that Philip and his courtiers had taken a good many women and children with them (and probably a large proportion of the men had been killed, though Diodorus' account does not say so explicitly),[177] but it may not be possible to extend this automatically and conclude that *most* of the Olynthians had gone to serve Macedonian masters. Some Olynthians reached Athens and were granted *isoteleia* (probably, or possibly citizenship), and probably others stayed to work as slaves on the land they had formerly owned – at any rate this would seem a sensible inference from the absence of any suggestion that Cassander had difficulty later when he was gathering up the Olynthians.[178]

Here, as at Methone, Philip gave land to Macedonians. *Syll.*[3] 332,[179] a grant made by Cassander to Perdiccas, son of Coenus, confirms Perdiccas' possession of lands granted by Philip in the area of Potidaea to Perdiccas' grandfather and father. Here again Macedonians were taking the places formerly inhabited by Greeks from the world of the city-states. And not only from the Olynthians: besides Olynthus and Methone Demosthenes mentions 'Apollonia and thirty-two cities in Thrace, all of which he has so savagely wiped out that it would not be easy for one to say whether they had ever been inhabited'.[180] These can only have been small cities – what E. Ruschenbusch calls *Normalpoleis*[181] – but, with several hundred occupants each,[182] the destruction of more than 30 of them to make room for Macedonian settlers implies that, say, 10,000–20,000 Greeks were either enslaved or thrown out of their homes, besides those who were enslaved from Olynthus. Cawkwell calls the destruction of these cities 'by no means necessary', but draws attention to how many of Alexander's cavalry came from Lower Macedonia:[183] expanding the area of Macedonian settlement helped Macedon dominate the Greek – and the Near Eastern – world.

In southern Greece Philip gained a reputation for piety by defeating the Phocians in the third Sacred war and destroying the cities of Phocis, compelling the inhabitants to live in villages at least a stade apart, and containing no more than 50 houses.[184] At the same time he restored to his Theban allies the three Boeotian cities the Phocians had been holding: Coroneia, Corsiae and Orchomenus. Evidently the Phocians had rebuilt Orchomenus, since the three cities were fortified, but it was torn down again after the defeat of Phocis, at least to the extent of being unwalled.[185]

A few years earlier the Phocians had shown themselves capable of destroying other peoples' cities: in 352 Phayllus, attacking a Boeotian force which was retreating with booty from Phocis, succeeded in overrunning the Locrian city of Naryx, which a Phocian force had been besieging. It was plundered and demolished.[186]

After the destruction of their cities the Phocians lived a wretched life in Phocis, dwelt on by Demosthenes in the *Embassy* speech,[187] and some of them went to Athens.[188] Philip and the Amphictyons had succeeded in their aim of rendering Phocis defenceless.[189] But before Chaeronea the Athenians and Thebans brought the Phocians back to their cities,[190] rebuilding walls: Pausanias comments on the walls of Ambrossus, built at this period.[191] After Chaeronea, Philip's wish to have Thebes weak was probably his reason for not suppressing the Phocian cities again.

His positive measures to weaken Thebes included the refoundation of Plataea and Orchomenus.[192] These cities continued, it appears, to have Macedonian patronage after the death of Philip: one of Alexander's gestures on becoming king of Asia, according to Plutarch, was to send a message to the Plataeans that their city should be rebuilt – because their ancestors had provided their land for the Greeks to fight for freedom in.[193] The message need have no implication as to how much rebuilding still needed to be done by then: Alexander sent it as a public statement about himself. But it is not difficult to believe that there was still work to do in 336, after Thebes was destroyed.

Alexander the Great, in his father's lifetime, founded a city and called it Alexandropolis;[194] before he began his career of conquest in Asia he defeated the Theban rebellion and destroyed Thebes.[195] The decision was not, formally, his own,[196] but the allies' power derived from Alexander: he was responsible for the act. Diodorus records that 30,000 Thebans were sold as slaves:[197] here as elsewhere it seems best (bearing in mind later events) to suppose that more Thebans would have remained as slaves on the land of Thebes than would have been taken away. Even if Philip could have made a Theban revolt less likely by being kinder in 338 (as R. J. Lane Fox argues)[198] the parallel with the destruction of Olynthus is clear: the existence of a dangerous city was intolerable to both Macedonian kings.

Changes under Alexander

When Alexander crossed to Asia he turned his attention, as he moved onward, to patronage of cities in Asia Minor. S. Hornblower points out (arguing that Alexander was probably 'the central and decisive figure in the rebirth of Priene')[199] that 'if Alexander wanted to found cities in highly urbanised Asia Minor, such refoundations must, of virtual necessity, take the form of revivals – contrast central Asia'.[200] Besides Priene, Alexander may well have refounded Smyrna (an ancient city which had been disestablished through the earlier part of the century);[201] it is not possible to date his activities in these places, and it is quite likely that he did not give much personal attention to each city. He had people who could manage that sort of thing. The pattern shown in the foundation of the eastern Alexandrias was probably applied, particularly since it can be seen being developed in the foundation of Alexandria by Egypt.

This foundation is well documented. Returning from Memphis in

331, Alexander (according to Arrian) came to Canobus, and sailed round lake Maria, disembarking on the site of Alexandria:[202]

> ... and he thought the place was very suitable for the foundation and successful development of a city. A desire for the work seized him and he personally laid out the plans for the city: where they were going to build the market place; how many temples there would be and to what gods – the Greek gods and the Egyptian Isis; and where they were going to put the wall round. He made a sacrifice for the purpose, and the omens turned out good.

Verbal similarities to this account in passages in Arrian describing later foundations point to Alexander's consistent approach on separate occasions.[203]

Clearly Greeks did come to live in Alexandria. Fraser comments that 'the dominating problem in the first period is that of the source of the original population of the city',[204] but in view of the lack of source material it is unlikely ever to be possible to add much to Fraser's suggestions: Macedonians; people from the poorer regions of Greece (as later at Ptolemais:[205] but Fraser cautions that Alexander would probably not encourage the settlement of only needy persons as citizens); people from Cyrene (Fraser refers to evidence showing that Cyrenian exiles found asylum in Egypt in Ptolemy I's time, and that Cyrenians were the largest group of Greek settlers in the Fayyum in the third century);[206] argument from nomenclature (no great help, as only 300 names of Alexandrian demesmen are known from the 300 years of the Hellenistic period in Alexandria);[207] and the linguistic approach (not favoured by Fraser, though he comments that if it pointed anywhere it would point to Boeotia and Euboea).[208] Fraser adds, referring to a passage in Theocritus XV which would point to Syracuse as a source of population,[209] that 'it would require no great exercise of imagination to suppose that there were Syracusans in Alexandria, and that Magna Graecia provided some of the original inhabitants of the city'.[210]

Fraser's picture could perfectly well be consistent with settlement of stateless people (including stateless people from Alexander's mercenary forces) in Alexandria, though his warning that Alexander will not have been looking only for the poor as settlers is well offered. It should be added that here (as in later Alexandrias)[211] local people – non-Greeks – were required for the foundation. Curtis says,[212] 'He filled the new city with a great crowd commanded to migrate to Alexandria from the neighbouring cities.' Naturally the original full citizens will all have been Greeks: but a synoecism of existing communities was an element in the foundation of Alexandria (the pseudo-Callisthenes account of the establishment of the city names them),[213] so it is necessary to recognise the importance of non-Greeks in the plan for the city.[214]

The city was not completed in Alexander's lifetime. Tacitus notes that Ptolemy I was the first to wall it – evidently Alexander's marking-out of the walls, though effective as a statement of his intention to carry forward the foundation of Alexandria, did not at once lead to their construction. This feature is paralleled in Arrian's account of the foundation, in 329, of Alexandria Eschate (an account which shows other similarities to his account of the Egyptian foundation):[125]

> and he himself walled the city, which he was planning, in twenty days; and in it he settled some of the Greek mercenaries, and any of the neighbouring barbarians who was willing to participate in the settlement, and even some of the Macedonians from the camp – those who were invalided out of the army.

Twenty days is too short a period for the construction of city walls on a green-field site (even by Alexander): clearly he was doing what he had done in Egypt. The pattern is corroborated by the earlier passage in which Alexander's reaction to the site of this city is recorded:[216] 'for the place appeared to him suitable for the city to grow great and be established on a successful basis'. Here the similarity with the comment on the site of Alexandria shines through the change of vocabulary, which Arrian makes for literary reasons.[217] Comparable accounts showing points of similarity to the Egyptian account are those concerning Alexandria on the Caucasus, Alexandria Iomousa, the Indian and Sogdian Alexandrias, and the Alexandria at Pollacopa.[218] Since some of these include settlement of mercenaries and Macedonians, and show that it was part of Alexander's standard procedure, and since each account is brief and includes only a selection of possible elements, it can be said with near certainty that settlement of mercenaries and Macedonians was an element in the foundation of all Alexandrias, including the first.

G. T. Griffith computes how many mercenaries Alexander is known to have left behind him 'in garrisons or as settlers on the track of his advance to India',[219] and concludes that the number exceeded 36,100.[220] But most of the soldiers on Griffith's list were not in the Upper Satrapies, so he argues that the 26,000 Greeks from the Upper Satrapies who revolted after Alexander's death ought probably to be added to his other figure.[221] This is a more helpful datum, for the task of assessing what Alexander sought to achieve by way of foundations of Greek cities, than a list of names of cities (some disputed, some perhaps never finished).

His achievement was an abiding one at Alexandria in Egypt. Other Alexandrias survived the revolt of 323,[222] and the revolt of Greeks in the Upper Satrapies does not show that new cities were not needed – only that settling mercenaries (many without their families) in cities, outside the Greek world, which were not only unfinished when Alexander left them but indeed barely started, was not a technique leading to enough stability. He had shown the way for the settlement of Asia ('one of the most amazing works which the ancient world ever saw')[223] but, as W. W. Tarn comments,[224] 'the settlement of Asia as we know it was essentially Seleucid'.

A world for Hellenistic kings to live in

When Alexander the Great died he left plans behind him.[225] Put before a formal Macedonian assembly by Perdiccas, they were rejected as impracticable;[226] but they merit consideration here, not only as evidence of what Alexander had hoped to do with the world he had turned upside down, but as a prologue to the Successors' activities in that world.

Alexander had planned to continue doing what he had been doing since he acceded to the throne of Macedon. The plans divide into three parts: extension of conquest westwards; temple-building; synoecisms and resettlements.[227] Conquest was his speciality, and W. W. Tarn's argument purporting to show that he renounced it when he turned back from India is not convincing:[228] it is easy to believe that he intended to move west. Temples, too, were already an interest of his.[229] Similarly synoecisms and resettlements:[230] but as the other schemes were grander than Alexander's already completed achievements, so his plan for synoecisms and resettlements makes the great things he had done seem small. Diodorus explains the third part of the last plan in this way:[231]

> ... to make synoecisms of cities and transplants of population from Asia to Europe, and in the opposite direction from Europe to Asia, so that he could bring the greatest continents to a state of concord and family affection by intermarriage and settlement.

Here synoecisms and transplants of population, features of Alexander's past activity, are elaborated on through a plan to bring Asiatic people to Europe, as well as taking Europeans to Asia: the plan is based on what Alexander had done, and embroidered with what he would have liked to do.[232]

But whole populations had been moved from place to place in Philip II's time. Interesting, then, that the age of the Successors began with two such transplants of population – one actually carried out, the other only contemplated. The first was imposed on Athens at the end of the Lamian war: Antipater ordered that citizen rights should be based on a census of wealth.[233] Two thousand drachmas was the qualifying level: about 9,000 qualified, over 12,000 did not.[234] Diodorus says that the 12,000 were removed from the fatherland, but his account appears a little confused: in the previous sentence he has stated that Antipater gave land in Thrace for settlement – to those who wished. Plutarch's *Phocion* makes it clear that not all the disfranchised persons left the city.[235] The suggestion that Antipater gave the disfranchised Athenians a city as well as land is exclusive to the account in Plutarch. Diodorus mentions only 'land ... for settlement'.[236] But Plutarch's account is the more lucid in the matter of what the 12,000 disfranchised Athenians did. It is worth considering whether his testimony that Antipater gave the Athenians a city is of any value. There were good reasons for Antipater to have done so: Alexander's leaving Greeks behind in the Upper Satrapies without firmly founded cities had led to a dangerous revolt. Several thousand Athenians deciding to try to force their way to Attica from Thrace could have caused damage. Antipater must have done, or intended to do, something for them – and Plutarch makes it explicit that he did.[237] This gives rise to the question whether there is any evidence to suggest how Antipater provided for this need.

It is the kind of evidence which is often unavailable. But in this case a suggestion can be made. Cassander, Antipater's more famous son, had a less famous brother. His name was Alexarchus. Modern suggestions that he was mad are far from fully convincing.[238] He was the founder of Uranopolis, on the Athos peninsula. It was a city which became well enough established to be mentioned in Strabo (who quotes Demetrius of Scepsis, first for his opinions about Xerxes' canal, near which the city stood, then as saying that Alexarchus laid the foundations of Uranopolis, which had a circuit of 30 stades)[239] and in Pliny the Elder.[240] The name is odd (as Tscherikower comments),[241] but it is quite likely to be merely an indication of a relatively early date (at which Antipater would not have named a city after himself). Philip II's policy of founding cities in Thrace had ceased by this time, its aim achieved: so if Antipater's son founded a city in Thrace, there was probably a definite reason for him to do so. It is not far-fetched to think that the reason may have been the need to provide a city for the thousands of Athenians moving to Thrace in 322. The hypothesis cannot be proved, but it has a good deal in its favour.

In 319 the disfranchised Athenians were able to return from Thrace. It is no argument against the connection of Uranopolis with their migration that it survived their return: volunteers from the floating population could have been found to live there, specially when three years' building work had already been done. Polyperchon, Antipater's designated successor,[242] issued an Exiles' Decree on the model of Alexander's.[243] The constitutions under Philip II and Alexander the Great were restored in the cities.[244] Alexander son of Polyperchon arrived in Attica with a force; the exiles joined him in attacking and were soon in the town, where they, the disfranchised persons and (Plutarch says) foreigners formed an assembly, deposed Phocion as general and chose others.[245] The exiles' sojourn in Thrace had proved temporary.

Antipater's scheme to move the Aetolians to the farthest desert of Asia did not reach even temporary fulfilment. He and Craterus made the plan in 322/321, when circumstances forced them to make a treaty with the Aetolians, and they wrote a decree embodying it.[246] The revolt of the Greeks in the Upper Satrapies, and their leaving their settlements,[247] was presumably what led Antipater to refer to 'the farthest desert of Asia'; at this date Alexander's empire was still a unit (though the Successors were at each other's throats), so Antipater perceived no need to make his plans parochial.

There were no other transplants of population. But the age of the Successors was not many years old before attention was turned to making synoecisms. S. Hornblower is right to stress that synoecism is strength;[248] he adds that 'the maxim, synoikism is strength, will explain both the Classical synoikisms (where political motives are usually uppermost) and the great Hellenistic synoikisms, which are best interpreted as an accumulation of physical resources, in an attempt to remedy the chronic poverty of the states concerned'. This analysis is particularly useful in the case of the first Hellenistic years, the years before Ipsus, in which it is possible to trace continuity with the Classical age which ended with Alexander. But one very early, and most interesting, Hellenistic synoecism achieved its connection with the Classical Age through the undoing of Alexander's work: the restoration of Thebes.

The Boeotians had supported the Macedonians at the time of the Lamian war, because they had received from Alexander the Thebans' land (and were now gaining large revenues from it); they knew that if the Athenians were successful they would give back city and land to the Thebans.[249] But in 316 Cassander, marching south from Macedonia in order to throw Alexander son of Polyperchon out of the Peloponnese, forced a passage of Thermopylae, and then[250] 'summoning from everywhere the surviving Thebans, he started resetting the city, thinking it a very good opportunity to re-establish a famous city and to get an immortal reputation by this benefaction'. His motive, and the occasion of the refoundation, attract attention.

He wanted to outdo Polyperchon, and his son Alexander, who had brought back the exiles to Athens. He persuaded the Boeotians,[251] who, given the presence of a Macedonian army, may have felt that gracious and speedy consent was the wisest course to follow. Probably most of the Theban survivors were living in the country: Cassander had sent for them after passing Thermopylae,[252] rather than bringing them from Macedon, and the Athenians' presumed intention in 323 of giving back city and land to the Thebans also suggests that the Thebans in question were living on the land, rather than that they were going to be brought out of Macedon.[253] Cassander had the help of 'many of the Greek cities', including Athens,[254] which by 316 was under the oligarchic constitution presided over by Cassander's man Demetrius of Phalerum, instead of the democratic constitution which had been restored by Polyperchon.[255]

Cassander synoecised other cities. The importance of synoecisms in providing individual Successors with strong centres of support in particular areas is well illustrated by Cassander's activity in Acarnania in 314. He took a large army to Aetolia (the Aetolians, who supported Antigonus, were fighting a border war with the Acarnanians) and persuaded the Acarnanians[256] to 'move to a few cities out of their vulnerable small settlements'. Most of the Acarnanians, according to Diodorus, moved into Stratus; the Oeniadae into Sauria, the Derieis into Agrinium.[257] Cassander left a force behind in Acarnania, but the Aetolians attacked: 3,000 of them besieged Agrinium and forced the inhabitants to surrender.[258] This shows that Agrinium was a small city, and though it had had Cassander's support it may not have been well walled yet. None the less Cassander's men continued, despite this setback, to hold Acarnania.[259]

Cassandreia was synoecised in 316. Cassander settled in it the Olynthians who survived,[260] and there were many of them: and since a large amount of good land had been marked off for the Cassandreians, and Cassander was keen on his city's expansion, Cassandreia became the strongest city in Macedonia.[261] It was a centre of support, such as Cassander tried from 314 to create in Acarnania, but it was more than that: it was the first of the 'capital cities' founded by the Successors and named after themselves. Some of the Successors founded more than one city of this type, and they did not treat them as the administrative or diplomatic centre of their realm unless they happened to be in residence in them. Their strength as centres of support is the feature which they chiefly have in common, and which (together with prestige) must have given the Successors most encouragement in founding them. Suddenly population – Greeks of any kind – was needed. In a single year Cassander resettled the two largest outstanding groups of Greeks without cities in mainland Greece.[262]

No information is available about whether the other cities founded by the Successors had settlers who had been without cities. An inscription relating to action by a king of Egypt to add further settlers to Ptolemais, the Greek city founded by Ptolemy Soter in the Thebaid, records the provenance of the supplementary settlers (Argos and Thessaly are mentioned, together with other place names now lost),[263] but this third-century or later evidence, though it is an interesting indication of how their patrons sought out Greeks to people Hellenistic foundations, is only a vague indication of what fourth-century conditions may have been like. A text to contrast with this is D.S. XIX.85.4, where after the battle of Gaza Ptolemy sent those of Demetrius' troops whom he had captured to be divided among the nomes in Egypt.[264] This was a forcible settlement, and not into cities (most of the Greeks of Egypt lived in villages: few cities were ever founded), though Ptolemais was probably founded not much later than 312.[265]

It was probably typical in the age of the Successors that newly synoecised cities had elements added to the populations of the communities used in the synoecisms. This was so at Cassandreia,[266] and Cassander would have transplanted some populations into Phthiotic Thebae in 302 had Demetrius not prevented him.[267] It was probably so at Thessalonice and Lysimacheia. Thessalonice, the metropolis of the Macedonia of Strabo's time,[268] was synoecised by Cassander, who demolished 26 towns in Crousis and on the Thermaic Gulf in the process. Strabo names six of them,[269] but presumably the other 20 were very small communities indeed; Lysimacheia was founded with the destruction of Cardia.[270] In both cases, prestige depended on the new cities' being imposing, strong and large: Cassander would not have wished to found a city which was *not* going to be the metropolis of Macedonia; nor would Lysimacheia have been any good to Lysimachus if it had not been a better bulwark against the Thracians than Cardia could have been.[271] There is a strong case for the supposition that Successors must have been ready to recruit available Greeks, including those without Greek cities, into their synoecised cities.[272]

The great expansion of Greek colonisation into Asia which was begun by Seleucus I mostly falls outside the scope of this study, since the greater proportion of the colonisation attested by Appian occurred after the battle of Ipsus. But two great foundations in what was to be the Seleucid empire occurred in the period under consideration here, and are comparable, from the point of view of their intended function, with the other foundations of the last quarter of the fourth century. It was probably soon after 311 (after Cassandreia, before Lysimacheia) when Seleuceia on the Tigris was founded;[273] and though V. Tscherikower's argument that Seleuceia was 'the old Babylonian Opis refounded by Seleucus' is sound and convincing,[274] it should not be allowed to obscure the newly Greek city's role in the years before the foundation of the great Antioch of Syria as the capital of Seleucus' domains,[275] designed to eclipse Babylon.[276] Josephus, *AJ* XVIII.372, telling the story of how Jews fled to Seleuceia in the late 30s AD to escape persecution by Babylonians, comments on how 'many of the Macedonians, very many Greeks, and no small number of Syrians' formed the civic body when Seleucus founded the city. It may be noted that in Mesopotamia and Babylonia in 312 he was able to recruit Macedonians (who were settled already at Carrhae)[277] and soldiers (Greek mercenaries?);[278] it may also be suggested that Seleucus did what Xenophon had hoped to do, ending his 'anabasis' into Asia by making at least some of his army a Greek city.[279]

Antigonus did the same sort of thing in 307, founding Antigonia on the river Orontes. Diodorus' statement that the city did not survive very long, but was dismantled and moved to Seleuceia,[280] is perhaps not misleading politically (Seleucus made sure that his own foundations were the only ones of importance) but is shown to be a little inaccurate by the evidence in Cassius Dio that the city still existed in 51 BC.[281] Its site was well chosen, it was expensively built, and evidently it was set up with the intention that it should serve as a centre of control – at least a local capital for Antigonus. Here again the settlers must have been drawn in the first place from Antigonus' army,[282] but it is worth noting that in 302 Antigonus held games and a festival at Antigonia, bringing athletes and artists from everywhere:[283] a piece of deliberate publicisation of the existence of Antigonia which would seem strange if the city were being built up only from his supply of time-expired soldiers. The gesture stresses Antigonia's membership of the Hellenic world, rather than her identity as a Macedonian outpost. An action of this kind would be consistent with Antigonus' having brought Greeks into his new city, as he did into his other great foundation, the Antigonia in Bithynia which was later to be renamed Nicaea.[284]

A well-defined picture emerges. Jones questions whether most of the Successors had any very genuine enthusiasm for the political side of Greek culture,[285] but there can be no doubt that they had all the enthusiasm of outsiders who hoped to find in the Greek city a means of controlling their Greek and Asian dominions and a way of associating their own names with the cultural and military achievement which the foundation of a city represented. Cities outside formerly Greek areas required settlers from armies – these will have included Greek mercenaries as well as Macedonians, because the Successors' armies included Greek mercenaries as well as Macedonians;[286] and the Successors' activities in cities established in Greek areas (Athens as well as the more complete refoundations) required from time to time large numbers of Greeks as settlers.

Throughout the Greek world the tendency as the fourth century progressed had been towards larger-scale and more deliberate intervention by rulers to manipulate patterns of settlement and exploit the possibilities available when people had no settled homes. As cities came to have less power and monarchs to have more, the monarchs used foundations or refoundations not only to give themselves centres of support but also as a source of legitimation. By founding cities they incorporated a key element of the political organisation of classical (free) Greece into the structure of their personal power.

Notes

1 E. Ruschenbusch, 'Zur Wirtschaft- und Sozialstruktur der Normalpolis', *ASNP*, Ser. III, 13.1 (1983), pp. 171–94, at p. 171.

2 Thebes, for instance, absorbed some small neighbouring communities during the fifth century: *Hell. Oxy.* 16.

3 See chapters 4 and 5 below.

4 D.S. XIII.62.4.

5 D.S. XIII.80.1: the successes at the sieges of Selinus and Himera may have suggested to the Carthaginians that their siege techniques, not seen before in the Greek world (cf. Y. Garlan, *Recherches de Poliorcétique grecque*, Bibliotheque des écoles françaises d'Athènes et de Rome, fasc. 123, 1974, pp. 156–7), could make the conquest of Sicily a practical possibility (I owe this point to P. M. Tickler). C. R. Whittaker appears to misunderstand this passage when he comments that events before 406 showed 'nothing to justify Diodorus' words that Carthaginians were "eager to be overlords of the island"' (P. D. A. Garnsey and C. R. Whittaker, *Imperialism in the Ancient World*, Cambridge, 1978, p. 66). Diodorus does not comment here on Carthaginian motives *before* 406, but says that '*about these times*', after the more modest activity of previous years, they were 'eager to be overlords of the island'. The nuisance caused by Hermocrates may also have had something to do with the decision of 406: but the expedition was too large to be aimed merely at suppressing or punishing him.

6 D.S. XII.58.3–4.

7 D.S. XIII.81.4–84.7.

8 In four stages, after the measures taken in 404 to consolidate the tyranny: (*a*) the absorption of the population of Leontini (403; there

were at Leontini the survivors from Acragas, Gela and Camarina. These were now brought to Syracuse. D.S. XIV.15.4); (*b*) the fortification of Epipolae (401; D.S. XIV.18.2–8); (*c*) the great rearmament (399; D.S. XIV.41.3–43.4) and (*d*) the absorption of the populations of Caulonia and Hipponium, followed by the building of dockyards, a new circuit wall, gymnasia, temples and other public buildings (the early 380s; D.S. XIV.106.3, XIV.107.2 and XV.13.5). So Dionysius planned and carried out development in three areas: population, military strength and building.

9 Plutarch, *Timoleon* 22.3, where the comment about the citizens going into exile can be taken to refer mainly to the years after 367.

10 Plato, *Ep.* III.315b6–7. A further denial at *Ep.* III. 319c7–d2.

11 Plato, *Ep.* VIII 353a4–8.

12 D.S. XI.21.1–22.6 and 26.7.

13 D.S. XI.38.1.

14 Herodotus, VII.156.1–3. Cf. T. J. Dunbabin, *The Western Greeks* (Oxford, 1948), pp. 416–18.

15 D.S. XI.49.2.

16 D.S. XI.49.1.

17 D.S. XI.49.3.

18 D.S. XIII.91.1.

19 Timaeus' figures passed on by Diodorus (see D.S. XIII.82.6 and 7; the material forms, *FGrHist* 566 F 26a) suggest that there were 20,000 Acragantines and, 'counting the foreign settlers', no fewer than 200,000 inhabitants. The figure of 800,000 at Diogenes Laertius VIII.63 seems to be a multiplication of this by four (Beloch, *Bevölkerung*, p. 281 n. 3). J. A. de Waele, 'La popolazione di Akragas antica', *Philias charin: Miscellanea di studi classici in onore di Eugenio Manni* III (Rome, 1979), pp. 747–60, uses an archaeological argument, based on the aerial photography and excavation work of G. Schmiedt and P. Griffo, to suggest that 16,000–18,000 people could have lived in Acragas, so that while the figure of 20,000 is credible, since people had come in from the countryside during the siege, the figure of 200,000 is incredible. But de Waele's exegesis of 'counting the foreign settlers' (p. 751) as referring to metics and slaves normally resident in Acragas is not satisfactory – not only because it would seem odd to call a slave 'foreign' (*xenos*), but also in view of the position of Acragas as the first fortified city in the Carthaginians' westward path in 406/405. Non-Acragantines as well as country-dwelling Acragantines must have fled inside the walls of Acragas in that year.

20 D.S. XIII.89.4.

21 D.S. XIII.92.6.

22 See above, pp. 16–17.

23 D.S. XIII.109.1–111.3.

24 D.S. XIII.111.3.

25 D.S. XIII.113.4.

26 Leontini had become the focus of opposition to Dionysius in 405 when the evacuated Geloans and Camarinaeans had gone there (D.S.

XIII.113.4). Diodorus' account of the surrender of Leontini ends with
the statement that the Leontines migrated to Syracuse (D.S.
XIV.15.4), but apparently not all did – some joined Archonides'
colonising venture from Herbite, a city which had withstood
Dionysius' attack on it earlier in the year (D.S. XIV.14.1). The
colonists were mercenaries, 'a motley crowd which had streamed into
the city because of the war with Dionysius', and poor Herbitaeans
(D.S. XIV.16.1–2). The colony, Halaesa Archonidion, survived –
probably with Carthaginian support: Diodorus notes that some say
that Halaesa was founded by Himilco at the time of the treaty (D.S.
XIV.16.4). Archonides and his father of the same name were friends of
Athens and so enemies of Syracuse from the time of the
Peloponnesian war (*IG* I³ 228, lines 6–25, cf. *HCT ad* Thucydides
VII.1.4). Good relations with Carthage would seem logical.

27 Strabo VI.1.2 (=253).
28 D.S. XIV.91.1.
29 D.S. XIV.87.1: 'the survivors of the Naxians and Catanians'.
30 D.S. XIV.15.2–3.
31 D.S. XIV.87.3.
32 Polybius II.39.1–6.
33 J. A. O. Larsen, *Greek Federal States* (Oxford, 1968), pp. 95–7.
34 D.S. XIV.90.4–7.
35 G. Pugliese Carratelli, 'Sanniti, Lucani, Brettii e italioti dal secolo IV
    a. C.', *Convegno di studi sulla Magna Grecia* 11 (1971), pp. 37–55. In
    general, Pugliese Carratelli comments on the degree of Hellenisation
    among the Bruttians and Lucanians, noting, for instance (p. 48), their
    adoption of Greek civic forms. He explains how this Hellenisation later
    became part of anti-Roman sentiment. J. de la Genière ('C'è un
    "modello" Amendolara?', *ASNP*, Ser. III, 8.2, 1978, pp. 335–54)
    makes the point that after severe dislocation of existing populations by
    the foundation of Sybaris (pp. 344–7) an economic pattern was
    established whereby the Italic inhabitants of Amendolara probably
    produced manufactured goods for the Sybarites (pp. 348–51). So as
    early as the seventh century relations between Greeks and non-Greeks
    might be not merely of peace but even of economic interdependence.
36 D.S. XIV.100.5: sections 1–5 of this chapter deal with Dionysius'
    second attack on Rhegium (390).
37 D.S. XIV.101.1.
38 D.S. XIV.102.3.
39 D.S. XIV.100.1–102.3.
40 D.S. XIV.103.1–106.3. Cf. L. Moretti, *Olympionikai, i vincitori negli
    antichi agoni olimpici* (Rome, 1957), No. 379 (cf. Nos. 388–9), on
    Dicon son of Caulonia, who won the boys' *stadium* in 392 as a
    Cauloniate, and was called a Syracusan on the occasions of his two
    later victories (388 and 384), not corruptly as Pausanius VI.3.11
    alleges, but because the Cauloniates were moved to Syracuse in 389.
41 D.S. XIV.107.2–108.6 and 111.1–4.
42 D.S. XIV.111.4.

43 Justin XX.1.1.
44 D.S. XIV.107.3.
45 At D.S. XV.15.2 there is a passing comment about Dionysius' army going to Italy in 383 in the two-front war against the Italiot–Carthaginian alliance, but there is nothing else.
46 The three references are: Livy XXIV.3.8, Justin XX.5.1 and Dionysius of Halicarnassus, *Excerpta* XX.7. From the third of these E. Ciaceri dates the fall of Croton to 379 (*Storia della Magna Grecia* II, Milan, Rome and Naples, 1927, pp. 432–3), but while this may be right it should be noted that the passage reads 'and he conquered the Crotoniates and the Rhegines and remained the tyrant of these cities for twelve years'; since Rhegium, captured in 387, remained in Dionysius' control for the rest of his life, the fact of its being mentioned here should induce some caution about the 'twelve years' in the passage. Ciaceri (*ibid.*) also takes Justin as implying that the conquest of Croton was incomplete, but the fact that nothing more is said about Croton after 'Dionysius tyrannus ... Crotonienses adgreditur' is most likely only a symptom of Justin's erratic epitomising: the passage in Livy says that the citadel of Croton was taken.
47 D.S. XIV.103.4.
48 Beloch, *Bevölkerung*, pp. 301–2.
49 The word *exeile* in D.H. *Excerpta* XX.7 (cf. above, n. 46) shows that Dionysius took the Crotoniates out of the city: but there is no indication of what happened next.
50 In 398 the Greek communities of Sicily did as Dionysius wished and expelled the Carthaginians in them, seizing their property. D.S. XIV.46.2 attributes this action not to Dionysius' popularity but to the Carthaginians' cruel character. Not that the Siceliots were less cruel when they had the chance – cf. D.S. XIV.51.4 and 53.2.
51 Cf. D.S. XIV.41.1–2. P. M. Tickler points out to me that the relevant part of section 1 should be rendered 'running away to the domain of the Carthaginians and *receiving back* their cities and possessions' (cf. D.S. XIV.78.4). Presumably the inhabitants of the Greek cities ceded to the Carthaginians in 405 are being referred to here (cf. D.S. XIII.114.1). D.S. XIV.75.3 explicitly notes that Dionysius made use of the Greeks' fear of the Carthaginians; presumably Timaeus is the source of this comment (K. Meister, 'Die Sizilische Geschichte bei Diodor von den Anfängen bis zum Tod des Agathokles', diss., Munich, 1967, p. 94, uses it as evidence that the whole passage from 70.4 to 75.6 derives from Timaeus), which is well borne out by the narrative in general.
52 D.S. XIV.57.3 and 58.3–4.
53 D.S. XIV.57.4.
54 D.S. XIV.78.4–5. Section 5 concentrates on Dionysius' new colonists in Messene; but the comment in section 4 about survivors 'getting back their fatherlands' is without point unless it is recognised that Messenian survivors joined in the refoundation (a point not noted at

Beloch, *Bevölkerung*, pp. 288–9).
55 P. Orlandini, 'Storia e topografia di Gela dal 405 al 282 a.C. alla luce delle nuove scoperte archaeologiche', *Kokalos* 2 (1956), p. 162.
56 D. S. XIV.47.6. Note that Dionysius received contingents from Camarina, Gela, Acragas, Himera and Selinus: the very cities overthrown between 409 and 405. The author of the account on which Diodorus' is based (Meister, 'Sizilische Geschichte', p. 89 and n. 66, argues against the view that the source here is Ephorus, and suggests Timaeus) was making a point by bringing in these names during the advance on Motya. The fact that they are named does not, therefore, imply that they were able to send large contingents: it does symbolise the Siceliot *revanche*.
57 D.S. XIV.9.5 and Plutarch, *Dion* 26.1.
58 Orlandini, 'Gela', p. 161: 'Geloi residenti nel retroterra e non gli abitanti di una polis ricostuita.' Orlandini (ibid.) notes D.S. XIV.68.2, where Theodorus of Syracuse, speaking in 396, refers to Gela and Camarina as *aoiketous*.
59 D.S. XIV.102.3. G. Navarra, 'E Gela e Katagela', *Rom. Mitt.* 82 (1975), pp. 21–82, contends that Orlandini has identified the site in question wrongly and that it is the Phintias founded in the third century after the destruction of the first Gela. But his insistence (p. 71) that the historical sources speak only of *ripopolamento* of Sicilian cities in the Timoleontic period and not of *fondazioni o ricostruzioni* is undermined by *SEG* XII.379 and 380, where Coans (cf. Plutarch, *Timoleon* 35.2) are referred to as 'co-founders' of Camarina and Gela respectively.
60 Cf. pp. 36–7 nn. 26 and 29–31 above.
61 Capture of Hipponium and removal to Syracuse: D.S. XIV.107.2; refoundation: D.S. XV.24.1.
62 D.S. XV.24.2–3.
63 D.S. XIV.78.4–6. The Italiots were from Locri (1,000) and its colony, Medma (4,000) (section 4).
64 Above, p. 35.
65 Lysias XXXIII(*Olympiacus*).3. It is scarcely necessary to argue that this generalisation is intended to make the hearer or reader think of Sicily: note that Lysias, who refers to himself as a 'good man and a citizen worthy of his city', was a citizen not of Athens (where he lived), but of Syracuse (D.H. *Lysias* 1). Sicily must have been close to his heart. Naturally the reference is also general (as appropriate to an Olympic speech) and encompasses the state of Asia Minor.
66 Plutarch, *Timoleon* 1.1–2.
67 Plutarch, *Timoleon* 22.3–4.
68 D.S. XIV.107.2–108.6 and 111.1–4: cf. Nepos, *Timoleon* 1.1 and 3.2.
69 Plutarch, *Timoleon* 35.2. G. Manganaro was first to suggest following the manuscripts (all except one) which give the reading *Elaias*, and believing that the Epirote city Elaea was the source of these colonists (in the debate after P. Lévêque's paper 'De Timoléon à Pyrrhos', *Kokalos* 14–15, 1968–9, pp. 135–51 (debate at pp. 151–6), at pp. 155–

6.) R. J. A. Talbert, *Timoleon and the Revival of Greek Sicily, 344–317 BC* (Cambridge, 1974), pp. 204–5, thinks it puzzling that Plutarch should not have clarified his meaning 'to prevent confusion with more famous cities of very similar name'; this is a fair point, but it ought to be noted that the names were not all that similar, except on paper – the name of Elea, the Lucanian city, began with a 'W' sound which was not marked in the Atticised spelling of the word. Its Roman name was Velia. Talbert, *Timoleon*, is sceptical about D. Asheri's suggestion that the lack of any Ionian influence in fourth-century Acragas tends to make the Dorian city in Epirus seem a more likely source of settlers than the Ionian city in Lucania ('I coloni elei ad Agrigento', *Kokalos* 16, 1970, pp. 79–88). Talbert may be right to say that it cannot be considered definitely proved, but it is only just to add that Manganaro's and Asheri's respective contributions are quite persuasive. On the other hand no *Thearodokoi* from Elea are recorded in *IG* IV² 95 among the contributors to the Epidaurian Asclepieum. This (D. M. Lewis suggests to me) does not inspire great confidence in Elea (cf. N. G. L. Hammond, *Epirus*, Oxford, 1967, pp. 517–18). The conclusion is that there is no conclusion, as yet.

70 Above, n. 59.
71 Plutarch, *Timoleon* 35.2.
72 Plutarch, *Timoleon* 23.3.
73 Plutarch, *Timoleon* 23.4, quoting Athanis. The figure in Diodorus which appears to correspond to this is 50,000 (D.S. XVI.82.5). 'Appears to', because Athanis' figure may perhaps include settlers who settled elsewhere than at Syracuse and nearby Agyrium.
74 Seibert, *Flüchtlinge*, p. 257.
75 D. Asheri, *Distribuzioni di terre nell'antica Grecia* (Turin, 1966), p. 29.
76 Carcinus, the father of Agathocles, does not quite conform to this pattern. He was an exile from Rhegium who settled at Therma in the Carthaginian sphere in Sicily (D.S. XIX.2.2). He later moved to Syracuse (2.7) and became a citizen under Timoleon (2.8). He had migrated before Timoleon's appeals for settlers. But he was probably a man of importance: reduced circumstances may have turned him to being a potter (2.7), but while at Therma he was able to give 'commands' to Carthaginian envoys (2.3) to question the Delphic oracle for him.
77 This may have been the case if Alcibiades' comments on Sicily (cf. above, p. 36) could have been applied also to Italy.
78 Cf. below, n. 82, for P. A. Brunt's estimate of the Greek population of Italy in 225 at 210,000. Even assuming that the population had declined over the previous century or so, the loss of colonists to Sicily soon after 340 must have had an impact unless Italiots formed only a small proportion of the 50,000.
79 Strabo VI.1.8 (=259–60).
80 D.S. XVI.45.9.
81 D.S. XVI.5.2.
82 Strabo VI.3.5 (=281). 'That's how bad things were,' Strabo explains.

P. A. Brunt, *Italian Manpower 225 B.C.–A.D. 14* (Oxford, 1971), does not discuss this passage, but it is apparent that he finds no reason to think of the Greeks as having formed a sizeable proportion of the population of Iapygia/Apulia in 225 BC: he deduces a population of 284,000 (Italic) Apulians (p. 54), but puts the population of Greeks *in all Italy* at only 210,000 (p. 59). Therefore it seems best to put the gradual decline of the eleven cities of Apulia as far back as the fourth and earlier third centuries.

83 Livy VIII.24.4 is the account of its recapture from the Lucanians. There is no direct testimony to its capture by them.

84 D.S. XVI.15.2. Sybaris: D.S. XII.22.1.

85 D.S. XII.9.1–11.3; cf. Strabo VI.1.13 (=263) and D.S. XII.22.1.

86 D.S. XII.22.1.

87 Livy VIII.24.4.

88 B. V. Head, *Historia Numorum* (second edition, Oxford, 1911), pp. 100–1: the series dated between 379 and 350 is marked [EI or [EIΓ (the letter [being a digamma, cf. the city's Roman name, Vibo Valentia), but the later coins are marked EIΓΩΝΙΕΩΝ.

89 Here cf. C. M. Kraay, *Archaic and Classical Greek Coins* (London, 1976), p. 189, where it is noted that the dominant theme in fourth-century Italiot coinage is that of increasing pressure on Greek cities and of the Greeks' efforts to resist it.

90 Livy VIII.24.4.

91 The key passage is Strabo VI.1.13 (=263): 'The Thurians, after a long period of success, were enslaved by the Lucanians. When the Tarentines had thrown the Lucanians out the Thurians took refuge with the Romans. They sent settlers to the Thurians, who were underpopulated, and changed the name of the city to Copiae.' The question is whether, when he mentions the Tarentines, Strabo is referring to the time of Alexander of Epirus or to the time of Pyrrhus. The Romans fought for the Thurians at the time of Pyrrhus, but not against the Tarentines: the enemies besieging Thurrii then were Samnites, Lucanians and Bruttians (D.H. *Excerpta* XIX.13); but after the death of Alexander of Epirus there was a Roman–Tarentine war (326: Livy VIII.27.1–11), and though Livy's explanation of its causes does not mention a request from Thurii (since Livy here aims to characterise the Tarentines as *cupidos rerum novandarum*), this war fits Strabo's comment much better than the other.

92 See above, n. 91. Cf. also Livy IX.19.4, which lists the 'seaboard of the Greeks of the southern sea from Thurii to Neapolis and Cumae' among the 'strong allies or broken enemies of the Romans' at the time of Alexander the Great. The Thurians had apparently never been enemies of the Romans, so this is a reference to the alliance.

93 Livy VIII.24.4.

94 Strabo VI.3.4. (=281).

95 D.S. XVI.62.4–63.1. This is recorded under 346/345, but it is not made clear how long Archidamus' Cretan campaign took before the departure to Italy.

96 M. Goldsberry, 'Sicily and its cities in Hellenistic and Roman times' (diss., University of North Carolina, Chapel Hill, 1973), p. 44 (with references to secondary sources), ascribes his service in the Crotoniate–Bruttian war to this date.
97 D.S. XIXI.3.3–4.1.
98 D.S. XIXI.4.2, which unfortunately gives no idea of the scale of this force.
99 D.S. XIXI.4.3.
100 D.S. XIX.5.4: 'he set up a private army in the inland area'.
101 D.S. XIX.5.5.
102 Goldsberry, 'Sicily and its cities', p. 10, deals with the evidence for grain exports from Sicily at this period; pp. 9–14 are a review of evidence for the late fourth-century revival throughout Sicily. Cf. also above, n. 59.
103 D.S. XIX.8.2.
104 D.S. XIX.65.4–5.
105 D.S. XIX.102.1.
106 D.S. XIX.102.4.
107 D.S. XIX.103.2–3.
108 D.S. XIX.104.1.
109 Request for help: D.S. XIX.103.1. The Carthaginians attacked Syracuse by sea (103.4–5) and took a hill called Ecnomus in Geloan territory (104.3–4). After defending this in battle against Agathocles in the next year (311), they were able to gain the alliance of most of the Siceliot cities and confine Agathocles to Syracuse (110.1–4).
110 D.S. XIX.104.2.
111 D.S. XX.57.1.
112 D.S. XX.57.2.
113 Talbert, *Timoleon*, p. 148, comments that '317, the year of Agathocles' seizure of power, only marked the end of Timoleon's political influence; the prosperity he set in motion continued to increase'.
114 D.S. XIX.1.8.
115 Entella, too, was a city in the Carthaginian sphere of influence (or at certain times only on the edge of it) which may have had help from the Carthaginians. The dossier of inscriptions relating to its destruction and refoundation, though, raises questions which are not yet fully settled (*SEG* XXX.1117–23 and, among other studies, a quantity of material by a range of authors at *ASNP*, Ser. III, 12.3 (1982), pp. 771–1103).
116 D.S. XX.104.1.
117 D.S. XX.104.2.
118 D.S. XX.104.3–4.
119 Xenophon, *Hell.* II.2.2.
120 Beloch, *Bevölkerung*, pp. 82–3. A. H. M. Jones, *Athenian Democracy* (Oxford, 1957), pp. 169–77, with a more detailed account of the evidence, would suggest a higher total: no estimate is offered for the total, though. C. Mossé, *Athens in Decline 404–86 B.C.* (London and Boston, Mass., 1973), p. 13, suggests that many Athenian cleruchs

must have given up their status as Athenians in order to keep their land. This speculation is highly problematic. Allowing these cleruchs to stay where they were would have conflicted with Lysander's policy of enforcing a quick surrender by causing famine in Athens. In any case, the idea that citizenship can be renounced by the holder is modern rather than ancient.

121 Xenophon, *Hell.* II.2.19–20.
122 D.S. XIV.34.1–2.
123 D.S. XIV.38.4–5.
124 D.S. XIV.34.1–2.
125 D.S. XIV.34.3–6; Pausanius IV.26.2. Note also that Pausanius IV.26.3–5 makes D.S. XIV.34.5., 'nearly all were killed', look tendentious: evidently the community of Messenians in Cyrene lasted until the refoundation of Messene. Cf. Seibert, *Flüchtlinge*, pp. 102–3.
126 D.S. XIV.82.6–7.
127 Xenophon, *Hell.* IV.2.1–4.1. At 4.1 Xenophon notes that the Athenians, Boeotians and Argives (*after* the defeats at Nemea and Coronea) continued operations from Corinth. The Corinthian war lasted eight years (D.S. XIV.86.6).
128 Xenophon, *Hell.* V.2.7.
129 D.S. XV.11.2: the move to villages and the destruction of the city; Xenophon, *Hell.* V.2.7., notes how the Spartans sent a recruiting officer to each village.
130 See above, pp. 39–41.
131 D.S. XV.46.4.
132 D.S. XV.46.5.
133 D.S. XV.46.6.
134 Seibert, *Flüchtlinge*, p. 118 and n. 939, takes it that they were living at Athens. This is possible, but not a necessary inference from what the text says: 'but the Athenians, seeing that their friends the Plataeans had been thrown out of Boeotia and had taken refuge with them, and that the Thespians were supplicating them not to overlook that they had become cityless, became less friendly with the Thebans'. It would be perfectly consistent with this to suppose that the Thespians had come from outside Athens to do their supplicating.
135 Pausanius IX.14.2, which is an awkward passage: '... but the Thespians decided to leave the city and flee to Ceressus. Ceressus is a strong point in Thespian territory.' This was after the Thespian contingent had left Epaminondas' army before Leuctra. Section 4 notes that Epaminondas flushed out the Thespians from Ceressus after the battle and before he proceeded into Arcadia. Xenophon, *Hell.* VI.3.1 (cf. above, n. 134), is positive that the Thespians were cityless, and Isocrates' comments at 6(*Archidamus*).27 support the idea that the city was ruined. But it is possible to imagine partial reoccupation of the site of the city by 371 – and indeed the withdrawal to Ceressus bears witness to the unwalled state of the settlement on the site of Thespiae. The Thespians left Epaminondas' army with permission, but the victor of Leuctra would not let them occupy a strong-point.

136 Isocrates wrote a *Plataicus*, not a *Thespiacus*; and there is an
   important point in it: Isocrates 14(*Plataicus*).9 argues (in the *persona*
   of the Plataeans) that when the Thebans could not get the Plataeans'
   consent, they should merely have compelled them to 'pay taxes to
   Thebes', as they did the Thespians and Tanagraeans. It is obvious now,
   Isocrates continues, that that was not what they wanted to accomplish,
   but that they coveted our land. The implication is that the Thebans
   had got the Plataeans' land, but not the Thespians'.
137 D.S. XV.79.3–5.
138 Xenophon, *Hell.* VI.5.3. Cf. M. Moggi, *I sinecismi interstatali greci*
   (Pisa, 1976), pp. 251–6.
139 Pausanius IX.4.4. Pausanias is mistaken to imply that Epaminondas
   marched straight from Leuctra to the Peloponnese: cf. Xenophon,
   Hell. VI.5.19 and 22–32, and also D.S. XV.62.3–5.
140 Though it was not a specially large city: cf. Beloch, *Bevölkerüng*,
   p. 486.
141 Megalopolis was substantially larger than either Tegea or Mantinea:
   cf. D.S. XVIII.70.1 and Beloch, *Bevölkerung*, p. 127. Beloch's
   comment that less than half the space within the walls was filled with
   houses appears to be an inference from Polybius IX.21.1–2, though he
   does not quote it: cf. W. Loring in E. A. Gardner *et al.*, *Excavations at
   Megalopolis 1890–1891* (London, 1892) at pp. 12–16 and Plate 1,
   which shows only a small area with finds, compared with the size of
   the area within the wall circuit.
142 Pausanius VIII.27.1–4. On Megalopolis cf. Moggi, *Sinecismi*, pp.
   293–5.
143 Pausanius VIII.27.5.
144 Pausanius VIII.26.5.
145 *IG* V (2) 343, lines 80–3. Cf. Moggi, *Sinecismi*, pp. 279–90.
146 Pausanius IV.26.5.
147 Pausanius IV.27.9–11.
148 D.S. XVIII.18.9. S. Hornblower, *Mausolus*, p. 199, doubts whether
   only the rich Samians were expelled.
149 S. Hornblower, *Mausolus*, p. 199. The account runs from p. 197 to p.
   200.
150 C. Habicht, 'Samische Volksbeschlussen der hellenistischen Zeit', *Ath.
   Mitt.* 72 (1957), pp. 152–237, is a collection of decrees, of which the
   following honour persons who had helped the exiled Samians: No. 2
   (Naosinicus son of Philoxenus of Sestos), No. 3 (Nicomedes son of
   Aris[tander of Cos]), No. 4 (Dionysius .../... ous, Macedonian, from
   Amphipolis), No. 13, No. 20 (Eurya[lus]), No. 21 (Dracon son of
   Straton of Cos), No. 22 (Hipparchus son of Heniochus of Cyrene),
   No. 23 (Epinoidas son of Eudemus of Heraclea), No. 24, No. 25
   (Agathocles), No. 26 (——s son of Melaenius [of Iasos?]), No. 27
   (——s son of Dionysius of ——) and No. 28; *id.*, 'Hellenistische
   Inschriften aus dem Heraion von Samos', *Ath. Mitt.* 87 (1972), pp.
   191–228, is a supplementary list: No. 2 (Hermonax son of Phi[listus of
   Erythrae?]), No. 3 (Nicias son of Demetrius of Heraclea) and No. 4

(Sosistratus son of Phanodicus of Miletus) honour helpers of the exiled Samians. This indicates a very wide dispersion of Samian exiles, and confirms the presumption that there were a good many of them.

151 S. Hornblower, *Mausolus*, pp. 78–105.
152 S. Hornblower, *Mausolus*, pp. 88–99.
153 Though S. Hornblower does not mention the parallel.
154 S. Hornblower, *Mausolus*, pp. 85–8.
155 D.S. XV.76.2. Strabo XIV.2.19 (=657) puts this in perspective by noting that the city is not large. Cf. G. E. Bean and J. M. Cook, 'The Carian coast III', *BSA* 52 (1957), pp. 58–146, at pp. 120–6.
156 S. M. Sherwin-White, *Ancient Cos* (Göttingen, 1978), pp. 43–81.
157 Sherwin-White, *Ancient Cos*, pp. 64–65, quoting the scholium on Theocritus VII.21a, which records a suggestion that the Simichidas in Theocritus' poem was descended from another (presumably well-known) Simichidas. Sherwin-White's n. 185 on p. 65 points to a possible Coan source for this scholium. In the same note A. S. F. Gow, *Theocritus* II (Cambridge, 1950), p. 128 n. 3, which records possible emendations of the unsatisfactory text (but gives no opinion on them), is mentioned.
158 Strabo IX.5.17 (=437–8), and *Syll.*³ 239E, lines 32–3. See Moggi, *Sinecismi*, pp. 244–51.
159 Philip's achievement recalled by Alexander at Arrian, *Anab.* VII.9.2. In this speech at Opis the life of homeless Greek wanderers seems to be the model envisaged for the life of Macedonians before Philip, which is probably not an appropriate picture, factually. But apparently it has been put into the speech with a view to making it sound convincing as part of the fourth-century scene.
160 Cawkwell, *Philip of Macedon*, pp. 39–44: cf. J. R. Ellis, 'Population transplants under Philip II', *Makedonika* 9 (1969), pp. 9–17, at p. 15.
161 D.S. XVI.8.6–7.
162 D.S. XVI.8.3–4.
163 Cawkwell, *Philip of Macedon*, p. 84.
164 D.S. XVI.8.5: cf. Tod II.146.
165 Beloch, *Bevölkerung*, p. 203.
166 D.S. XVI.34.4–5.
167 Cawkwell, *Philip of Macedon*, p. 37. D. M. Lewis points out that 'Methone is so near Pydna that absorption would be natural' (cf. Strabo VII, Fragment 20, and N. G. L. Hammond and G. T. Griffith, *A History of Macedonia* II (Oxford, 1979), pp. 256–8).
168 Demosthenes 23(*Aristocrates*).158.
169 D.S. XVI.34.3.
170 D.S. XVI.34.4.
171 Cf. U. Kahrstedt, *Beiträge zur Geschichte der thrakischen Chersones* (Baden-Baden, 1954), pp. 32–4.
172 Cf. M. Gude, *A History of Olynthus* (Baltimore, 1933), p. 35.
173 D.S. XVI.52.9.
174 D.S. XVI.53.2.
175 Cawkwell, *Philip of Macedon*, p. 90.

176 Demosthenes 19(*Embassy*).193–5 and Aeschines 2(*Embassy*).156; Demosthenes 19(*Embassy*).195–8 and 306.
177 D.S. XVI.53.3.
178 Athens: Harp., s.v. *Isoteles* (cf. Aeschines 2(*Embassy*).154) and *Suda*, s.v. *Karanos*. Cassander: cf. D.S. XIV.51.2.
179 *Syll.*³ 332 was found on the site of Cassandreia/Potidaea.
180 Demosthenes 9(*Philippic* III).26.
181 Ruschenbusch, *Untersuchungen*, pp. 3–9, presents evidence on the (large) number and (small) size of cities known to have existed. See also Ruschenbusch, 'Normalpolis' (1983), p. 171.
182 Ruschenbusch, *Untersuchungen*, p. 9, calculates that the *Normalpolis* had 450–1, 250 citizens (225–625 men).
183 Cawkwell, *Philip of Macedon*, p. 37 and n. 20 to p. 38.
184 Cf. Demosthenes. 19(*Embassy*).65.
185 D.S. XVI.60.1. Orchomenus was refounded by Philip after Chaeronea (see below, n. 192), so presumably at this stage the Thebans returned it to a state of ruin (cf. D.S. XV.79.3 on the traditional hatred between Thebes and Orchomenus).
186 D.S. XVI.38.3–5.
187 Demosthenes 19(*Embassy*).64–5 and 80.
188 Demosthenes 5(*Peace*).19, and here cf. Seibert, *Flüchtlinge*, pp. 138–40.
189 This is the point of the comment at Demosthenes 19(*Embassy*).141 that the Thebans have gained 'as much of the Phocians' land as they wanted'. Note also that payment of the fine to the Delphic Amphictyony commenced soon and continued for 26 instalments (Tod II 172): resistance to it was not made.
190 Pausanius X.3.3.
191 Pausanius X.36.3–4. X.3.3 shows that similar activity went on throughout Phocis.
192 Pausanius IV.27.10, IX.1–8 and 37.8.
193 Plutarch, *Alexander* 34. The Eudemus of Plataea who contributed a thousand yoke of oxen to Athenian building efforts in 329 (Tod II 198) was presumably active on a large scale in the refoundation of Plataea.
194 Plutarch, *Alexander* 9.1.
195 Arrian, *Anab.* I.7.7–9.10; D.S. XVII.8.2–14.4; Justin XI.3.7–4.8.
196 Arrian, *Anab.* I.9.9.
197 D.S. XVII.14.1 and 4.
198 R. J. Lane Fox, *Alexander the Great* (London, 1973), pp. 86–9.
199 S. Hornblower, *Mausolus*, p. 330.
200 S. Hornblower, *Mausolus*, p. 399.
201 S. Hornblower, *Mausolus*, p. 321; cf. J. M. Cook, 'Old Smyrna, 1948–1951', *BSA* 53 (1958), pp. 1–34, at p. 34.
202 Arrian, *Anab.* III.1.5.
203 See below, n. 218.
204 P. M. Fraser, *Ptolemaic Alexandria* (Oxford, 1972), p. 62.
205 Fraser, *Ptolemaic Alexandria*, p. 63, and cf. p. 62 on Ptolemais (with below, p. 58 and n. 265).

206 Fraser, *Ptolemaic Alexandria*, p. 63.
207 Ibid.
208 Fraser, *Ptolemaic Alexandria*, p. 64.
209 Fraser, *Ptolemaic Alexandria*, p. 65; cf. Theocritus XV.87–93 (reprinted in Fraser's n. 200). Fraser describes this as 'the only direct literary evidence concerning the population of Alexandria' at this early period, but he points out that there is no knowing whether Theocritus means his readers to imagine the Syracusan ladies in the crowd as permanent residents or visitors to the city.
210 Fraser, *Ptolemaic Alexandria*, p. 65.
211 Cf. Arrian, *Anab.* IV.4.1; IV.22.4, IV.24.7 and V.29.3. Cf. also below, n. 218.
212 Q. Curtius Rufus IV.8.5.
213 Pseudo-Callisthenes I.31.2. Fraser, *Ptolemaic Alexandria*, p. 4, notes that 'there are considerable sections of pseudo-Callisthenes which are of Hellenistic origin', and argues that when dealing with the city of Alexandria the author's account should be treated 'with care, even with respect'.
214 P. Briant in two papers ('Colonisation hellénistique et populations indigènes. La phase d'installation', *Klio* 60, 1978, pp. 57–92, and 'Colonisation hellénistique et populations indigènes II. Renforts grecs dans les cités hellénistiques d'Orient', *Klio* 64, 1982, pp. 83–98) argues that Near Eastern peoples were introduced into foundations of this sort in a dependent position in the countryside and suggests that the Greco-Macedonian class continued in a position of dominance. On this point Arrian's account, derived from Ptolemy, amounts to a kind of Authorised Version: this should be borne in mind.
215 Arrian, *Anab.* IV.4.1.
216 Arrian, *Anab.* IV.1.3.
217 The other passage is Arrian, *Anab.* III.1.5. Correspondences are almost exact.
218 (*a*) Arrian, *Anab.* III.28.4; (*b*) V.29.3; (*c*) VI.15.2 and (*d*) 4; (*e*) VII.21.7. (*a*) has Alexander sacrificing, as at the foundation of the Egyptian city; (*b*) has settlement of mercenaries and locals; (*c*) has a comment on hope of future prosperity; (*d*) has a comment on wall-building and (*e*) has comments on the good site and the settlement of mercenaries. These accounts and the accounts of the foundations of the Egyptian and Farthest Alexandrias share seven elements (the Egyptian has five, the Farthest six of them): site, sacrifices, walls; mercenaries, Macedonians, locals; future prosperity.
219 Griffith, *Mercenaries*, p. 21.
220 Griffith, *Mercenaries*, pp. 22–3.
221 Griffith, *Mercenaries*, p. 23. Griffith says, 'no fewer than 26,000', but D.S. XVIII.7.2. speaks of more than 20,000 infantry and 3,000 cavalry.
222 W. W. Tarn, *Alexander the Great* II (Cambridge, 1948), pp. 234–7, summarises which Alexandrias are represented by modern towns, and which existed well down into Greek history.

223 W. W. Tarn, *The Greeks in Bactria and India* (second edition, Cambridge, 1951), p. 5.
224 Tarn, *Greeks*, p. 35.
225 D.S. XVIII.4.4. Tarn's elaborate rejection of D.S. XVIII.4.1–6 (*Alexander* II, pp. 398 and 427–9) is definitively refuted by E. Badian ('A king's notebooks', *HSCP* 72, 1967, pp. 183–204), adding to the earlier work of F. Schachermeyr, 'Die letzten Pläne Alexanders des Grossen', *JÖAI* 41 (1954), pp. 118–40. But cf. below, n. 227.
226 D.S. XVIII.4.6.
227 D.S. XVIII.4.4. The central suggestion of Badian, 'King's notebooks', is that Perdiccas read to the Macedonians a version of the plans which he had edited with a view to getting them rejected and to obviating the possibility that a document purporting to convey Alexander's last plans might later be produced by someone wanting to upset the settlement made after the king's death. (R. M. Errington, in 'From Babylon to Triparadeisos, 323–320 BC', *JHS* 90, 1970, pp. 49–77, at p. 59, with n. 75, claims to follow Badian's general interpretation but does not mention his idea that Perdiccas edited the plans.) The edited version would be the one available to Diodorus' source (tentatively, Badian, 'King's notebooks', favours Hieronymus of Cardia: p. 199, 'our reliable author – let us without prejudice call him Hieronymus –'; but J. Hornblower, *Hieronymus of Cardia*, Oxford, 1982, pp. 89–97, argues against derivation of D.S. XVIII.4 from Hieronymus), so that Diodorus' version of the plans would bear no close relationship to what Alexander had had in mind. The conclusion is (Badian, 'King's notebooks', p. 201) that 'concentration on the analysis of the actual *hypomnemata* . . . is merely a way of elaborately missing the point'. This argument is over-refined. If Perdiccas had edited out items likely to attract the army's support, there was nothing to stop any of the Successors, who (on Badian's hypothesis) knew what was in the *hypomnemata*, from publicising these items later in order to gain popularity. So there is no particular reason to think D. S. XVIII.4.4–5 misleading. It is a selection, certainly: but the scale of the projects mentioned in it can only suggest that the selection was made on the criterion set out at XVIII.4.4 ('the most important and memorable parts of the notes were these'). More likely, surely, that this selection was made by a historian (Diodorus or his source) than by Perdiccas. It is certainly possible to treat the plans as a fair reflection of what Alexander had in mind.
228 Tarn, *Alexander* II, pp. 394–7.
229 Strabo XIII.1.26 (=593); IPriene 156.
230 Cf. above, pp. 51–4.
231 D.S. XVIII.4.4.
232 Cf., for example, Alexander's sending Miccalus of Clazomenae to Phoenice and Syria with 500 talents to collect seafaring people with a view to settling them on the Persian Gulf. Arrian, *Anab.* VIII.19.5–6. S. M. Stern (*Aristotle and the World-State*, Oxford, 1968) discusses a letter attributed to Aristotle and preserved in an Arabic source. It is

clear that the Arabic is a translation of a Greek original (e.g. pp. 21–2). Stern gives the Arabic on pp. 8–10, and an English translation on pp. 3–8. Stern argues (pp. 28–32) that the text was composed at the time of Alexander, though not certainly by Aristotle. The first part of the text (pp. 3–5) advises Alexander to remove the inhabitants of Persia from their places (p. 4: 'If this cannot be done with all of them, do it at least with a great number, including the ruling class, and settle them in Greece and Europe. This will be acting justly towards them, since it just according to the law of Rhadamanthys to do to a man as he had done'). Stern (pp. 33–4) points out the difference between this and the plan in the *hypomnemata*: that this plan is punitive, and the other would have been intended as an integrative measure. It is interesting, then, that the two transplants of population discussed in this inquiry had a punitive purpose, at least in part.

233 D.S. XVIII.18.4.
234 D.S. XVIII.18.5.
235 Plutarch, *Phocion* 28.3.
236 D.S. XVIII.18.4.
237 Modern treatments display little interest in this point. Seibert, *Flüchtlinge*, p. 165 n. 1296, comments that 'jeder, der es wünschte, sollte in Thrakien Land erhalten, d. h. es handelte sich nicht um eine systematische Zwangsumsiedlung' ('anyone who wanted was to be given land in Thrace – that is, it was not a matter of a systematic migration'): this is not a legitimate inference, since a highly organised migration might begin from an announcement inviting those who wished to participate (Seibert is right to note that Alexander had looked forward to transplants of this kind in the *hypomnemata* (D.S. XVIII.4.4) – and it would be wrong to think that Alexander's transplants of population had been going to be unsystematic).
238 E.g. V. Tscherikower, *Die hellenistischen Städtegründungen von Alexander dem Grossen bis auf die Römerzeit* (Leipzig, 1927) p. 3, and Lane Fox, *Alexander*, p. 475. The idea of his madness arises from Athenaeus III.98d–f. This text concerns literary jokes, not schizophrenia.
239 Strabo VII, Fragment 35.
240 Pliny, *NH* IV.10.37.
241 Tscherikower, *Städtegründungen*, p. 3.
242 D.S. XVIII.48.4.
243 D.S. XVIII.56.1–8.
244 D.S. XVIII.56.3.
245 Plutarch, *Phocion* 33.1. Seibert, *Flüchtlinge*, p. 168, draws the necessary inference that the exiles were in Alexander's following (*Gefolge*). The distinction between 'exiles' and 'disenfranchised persons' here refers back to 28.3, where the distinction between those who stayed and those who left is first drawn. Alexander had brought the disfranchised Athenians back from Thrace. Ever since Polyperchon had passed his decree, they and the disfranchised democrats still at Athens had been his natural supporters (here cf. Nepos, *Phocion* 3.1.).

246 D.S. XVIII.25.3–5. The decree was presumably the source of Diodorus' source's information.
247 Q. Curtius Rufus IX.7.1–11; D.S. XVII.99.5–6; D.S. XVIII.4.8 and 7.1–9.
248 S. Hornblower, *Mausolus*, p. 81 with n. 22. Moggi, *Sinecismi*, is a collection of synoecisms, a fair number of which do not concern this inquiry because of their character as unions at the political level only, e.g. the union of Corinth and Argos (*Sinecismi*, pp. 242–51), the incorporation of Dium in the state of the Histiaeans (pp. 290–2), the political unification of Ceos (pp. 333–41) and the incorporation of Proconnesus in Cyzicus (pp. 341–4).
249 D.S. XVIII.11.3–4.
250 D.S. XIX.53.2.
251 D.S. XIX.54.1.
252 D.S. XIX.53.1–2.
253 Macedonia was the most likely destination of those who were carried off as slaves in 335 (as at Olynthos: cf. above, p. 49 and n. 175). But the Athenians were resisting Antipater in Greece: they were not going to attack Macedon.
254 D. S. XIX.54.2–3. Chiefly Athens, according to Pausanius IX.7.1. *Syll.*³ 337 is a Theban inscription recording the names of contributors. The most remarkable section of it is at lines 31–41, where three 'kings', among them Demetrius Poliorcetes (line 31), are recorded to have given money. This section (as Dittenberger notes) must have been added after the Successors took their royal titles – more than ten years after Cassander's first initiative. Though the propaganda value of his Theban activities was intended by Cassander to be immediate, *Syll.*³ 337 is a useful reminder that neither Thebes nor any other of the synoecisms of this period was built in a day.
255 D.S. XVIII.74.1–3.
256 D.S. XIX.67.304.
257 D.S. XIX.67.4. It is likely that this attempt by Cassander to concentrate the population of Acarnania in fewer centres had no permanent effect. A list of *theorodokoi* found in the Nemea excavations in 1978 gives the names of persons connected with the Nemean games in 13 Acarnanian cities: Palaerus, Anactorium, Echinus, Thyrrheium, Euripus, Limna, Oeniadae, Stratus, Pherium, Medion, Phoetia, Corontae, Astacus. I owe this list to D. M. Lewis, since the inscription is published only as a photograph: S. G. Miller, 'Excavations at Nemea, 1978' *Hesp.* 48 (1979), pp. 73–103, at pp. 78–80 and pl. 22c; since the list was revised in 311/310 (p. 79), it is evident that the reorganisation of 314 had made little impression. The names *Sauria* and *Agrinium* are not in the list – presumably Cassander's men intended (and failed) to build these from scratch.
258 D.S. XIX.67.5–68.1.
259 D.S. XIX.74.3–6 (313), and D.S. XIX.88.1–89.1 (312).
260 Cf. above, pp. 49–50 and n. 178.
261 D.S. XIX.53.2–3: the Olynthians were added to the people of Potidaea

and of the 'cities of the Chersonese', who were gathered up into the one new city. D. M. Lewis comments, 'it would seem natural to suppose that this Chersonese is simply Pallene'. Livy XXXI.45.14 (narrating events of 200) mentions *Mendaeum* as a *maritimus vicus* of Cassandreia: Mende and Scione seem to have been absorbed in the new city.

262 Cf. above, n. 250.
263 P. M. Fraser, 'Inscriptions from Ptolemaic Egypt', *Berytus* 13 (1960), pp. 123–61, No. 1, at pp. 123–33; cf. *SEG* XX.665. It runs: 'Decree of the council and people ... the Saviour God [founded] a Greek city in [the Thebaid] ... making its name Ptolemais [from himself, and becoming its patron.] To it the king sent [additional settlers from ...] and from Argos [and from ... and from Lacedaemo]n and from Thes[saly?] and from ... the [Council and people] decreed [to ...]', etc. Fraser argues (p. 127) that the king is not the same person as the Saviour God, 'since the same person would not be described in two different ways within two lines'. He adds (p. 130), 'lines 4–6 contain an obvious reference to the introduction of fresh population to the city. The reference to the foundation by Soter, followed by the action of "the king", indicates that this event occurred after the original foundation and was not part of it.' The stone appears (p. 125) to be a copy, inscribed at a Hadrianic or later date.
264 Accepting Wesseling's emendation of *nomarchias* for *nauarchias*.
265 There is no direct evidence for the date of this foundation. It would seem likely to have been after 312 because of the new attitude which according to Diodorus prevailed among the Successors after the treaty of 311 (D.S. XIX.105.1), whereby each began to treat his own territory 'like a spear-won kingdom' (D.S. XIX.105.4). E. Plaumann, *Ptolemais in Oberägypten* (Leipzig, 1910), makes no comment on the dating of the foundation. In D.L. II.86 one Aethiops of Ptolemais is listed among the pupils of Aristippus of Cyrene. Aristippus, a mature money-earning philosopher as early as when Socrates was still alive (D.L. II.65) can hardly have survived much beyond 350; so any pupil of his must have been born by 375 or not long after. It would have to be presumed that Aethiops was a Cyrenian when Aristippus taught him, but it could then be suggested that he went to Ptolemais with the first settlers and became a citizen there in his 60s or 70s. This argument would make a foundation soon after 312 seem likely, and one after about 300 distinctly improbable, especially since, in order to become known to posterity as a Ptolemaite, Aethiops must almost certainly have spent several years philosophising in Ptolemais before his death. E. Turner in *CAH* VII.1² (Cambridge, 1984), at p. 127, puts the foundation of Ptolemais well before 297, but does not present arguments for this dating.
266 D.S. XIX.52.2.
267 D.S. XX.110.3. The text gives Dium and Orchomenus as the places whose populations would have been moved. Fischer in the *apparatus criticus* of the Teubner edition (Leipzig, 1906) shows the impossibility

of the names, and suggests correcting the text from Strabo IX.5.15 (=436), which names Nelia, Pagasae and Ormenium as having been synoecised into Demetrias by Demetrius.

268 Strabo VII, Fragment 21.
269 Ibid. Apollonia, Chalastra, Garescus, Aenea and Cissus.
270 Pausanius I.9.8.
271 Cf. Appian, *Syriaca* 1; but Appian is wrong to say that Lysimacheia was destroyed as soon as Lysimachus died: cf. Tscherikower, *Städtegründungen*, pp. 1–2.
272 A case supported in general terms by Dio Chrysostom 39.1, where the orator speaks of Nicaea as 'a city which in strength and size is second to no city which anywhere is famous for the nobility of its line and the settlement of a great number of the most distinguished lines: not a few poor ones dragged in from here and there, but the most outstanding Greeks and Macedonians.' Jones, *The Greek City*, p. 7, suggests that this may mean that drafts from cities under Antigonus' control were sent to Nicaea (Antigonia, until renamed by Lysimachus – cf. Tscherikower, *Städtegründungen*, pp. 46–7). This is acceptable, though a little caution is induced by the fact that Dio Chrysostom's comments on Nicaea's past draw on a catholic mixture of history and myth; the section quoted here continues: 'and in particular, it had heroes and gods as its founders'. Cf. also section 8.
273 Strabo XVI.1.5 (=738). K. J. Beloch, *Griechische Geschichte* IV (1) (second edition, Berlin and Leipzig, 1925), p. 136 n. 2, argues that the name of Seleuceia shows that it must have been meant as Seleucus' capital. So he puts its foundation before that of Antioch on the Orontes.
274 Tscherikower, *Städtegründungen*, pp. 90–1.
275 Cf. above, n. 273.
276 Strabo XVI.1.5 (=738).
277 D.S. XIX.91.1. Presumably Carrhai.
278 D.S. XIX.91.5. 'Soldiers' in the Hellenistic context are not inevitably mercenaries: cf. Griffith, *Mercenaries*, pp. 84–5, 126, 132–5. None the less it is likely enough that there were mercenaries, especially since Seleucus bought up horses and distributed them to competent persons (in order to have a cavalry element).
279 The 'Anabasis' of Seleucus: referred to as such (in Nicanor's letter to Antigonus) at D.S. XIX.100.3.
280 D.S. XX.47.5–6.
281 D.C. XL.29.1. On Seleucus I's aims in founding cities cf. G. M. Cohen, *The Seleucid Colonies* (Wiesbaden, 1978), pp. 11–12.
282 Cf. Griffith, *Mercenaries*, pp. 149–51, who justly compares Antigonia on the Orontes to Antigonus' military settlements.
283 D.S. XX.108.1. This extravaganza gained, through Hieronymus and Diodorus, its place in the historical tradition. Foundations of military colonies, even the foundation of Nicaea of Bithynia (cf. Tscherikower, *Städtegründungen*, pp. 46–7), did not, in spite of Diodorus' concentration on Antigonus and Demetrius (cf. J. Hornblower,

Hieronymus of Cardia, p. 36). It is fair to infer that Antigonus had higher ambitions for his capital city than for his lesser settlements.

284 Cf. above, n. 265.
285 Jones, *The Greek City*, p. 6.
286 Griffith, *Mercenaries*, pp. 317–18, gives a convenient summary.

4

Mercenary soldiers and life outside the cities

Of occupations followed outside cities by Greeks in the fourth century BC, the most accessible was mercenary service. Doctors, philosophers and the friends of kings needed a long training before they could expect to earn a living from their respective skills. Traders needed some capital as well as practical know-how. But the paradox of serving as a mercenary was that it involved the application of skills characteristic of city life. The city-states were the places where young men would learn how to take their place in a hoplite army.

After Cyrus' expedition, and as the fourth century progressed, mercenary service came to have a military and social importance which it had not previously enjoyed. Except when the mercenary came from a destroyed city, though, it might be considered debatable how far any particular mercenary fitted into the category of 'outsider'. A man who left his home to serve for money and returned when his tour of duty ended would be someone with a place in city-state society, even while he was on campaign. Yet the army in which he served would itself be an element in the trend towards a significant number of outsiders. A. Fuks argues that 'people of long military service would become technically, or in fact, *apolides*',[1] but 'technically, or in fact ...' is a phrase which does not offer much precision. Though there were fully settled farmers and fully professional wandering soldiers, there must have been a range of people who were neither quite one thing nor the other – or whose circumstances pushed them in one direction or the other at varying points in their lives.

Given that there were more Greeks living outside the cities than before,[2] it would seem natural (even without Isocrates' opinionated comments)[3] to suppose that some of the homeless and destitute took to serving as mercenaries. Yet there are difficulties with the supposition. Hoplites in city armies owned their own armour: if such was also the case in mercenary armies, then the poorest or most destitute outsiders cannot have qualified. It is necessary to examine what sort of men could become mercenaries, what provision employers might make to enable poor men to serve, how mercenaries were recruited, and what their conditions of service would be like.

Who were the mercenaries?

The expedition of Cyrus is an interesting point at which to start examining what sort of man became a mercenary, and what sort of men mercenaries became. H. W. Parke traces the history of the remnant of the Cyreians from the time when they joined Thibron (399) as far as the battle of Coronea (394) and even beyond.[4] Certainly seven years after the march with Cyrus these remaining soldiers were living outside their cities. In fact once those who wished to had sailed away, or settled in the cities near Byzantium,[5] it could be said that the remainder had chosen the wandering life, that the army itself had become (now by choice, though previously by chance), in Isocrates' phrase, a 'wandering army'.[6] What makes this particularly interesting is Xenophon's insistence that the soldiers were mostly not on the expedition for lack of a livelihood, that on the contrary some had brought slaves, others had spent money on coming, and that others still had left fathers and mothers or children, and were hoping to make money and go home.[7] The details of this explanation are intended to assure the reader of the *Anabasis* of two points: the first and more obvious, that the soldiers were not the poorest of the poor; the second, that they were not rootless by virtue of having no relatives living. Isocrates presents another picture of the Cyreians,[8] but, for the reasons given by Parke, Xenophon's version, if rather exaggerated, is in general preferable.[9] The uniquely well-documented case of the army of Cyrus is an example of a mercenary army, recruited from city-dwelling and not unrespectable Greeks, eventually choosing to live by wandering – needing nothing from a city, because self-sufficient; desirers of war.[10]

This instance shows how mistaken it would be to assume that all mercenaries were destitute and unable to invest in becoming professional soldiers; or that all who could spend money on starting up as mercenaries would resume city life when the opportunity arose. In this context the relevance of the cost of armour and weapons is clear.

Ownership of armour and weapons

Modern writers have not explored the question of who provided the armour which the soldiers wore.[11] But a moment's consideration reveals its importance. If mercenaries usually provided their own armour, then outsiders who did not have capital assets to the value of at least 100 drachmas could only exceptionally turn to mercenary soldiering, at least in the hoplite role.[12] In this section the known instances of provision of armour and weapons will be examined with a view to determining what expectations employers and mercenaries would have.

After Tissaphernes had murdered the generals at the parley to which he invited them following the battle of Cunaxa, three former friends of Cyrus, Ariaeus, Artaozus and Mithradates, came to the Greek camp.[13] Ariaeus' line, with a view to inducing the Greeks to surrender their arms, was that they were the property of the king, having belonged to his slave Cyrus:[14] 'the king demands your armour from you. He says it is his, since it belonged to Cyrus, his slave.' This brief passage raises a number of difficulties. It must be examined carefully. If taken at face value, it implies that Cyrus provided armour for all his Greek mercenaries.

No other statement in the *Anabasis* directly confirms this. The Greeks had armour which was to some extent standard: I.2.16 says that they all had helmet, shield and greaves as well as a red tunic. The hoplites – that is, most of the Greeks – must have had thoraxes as well.[15] Cyrus had a personal cavalry troop armed in the Hellenic manner, and one presumes that he had given them their arms, but one cannot generalise from that (I.8.6–7). The king's and Tissaphernes' first embassy demanded (II.1.8) that the Hellenes give up their arms, but in the circumstances that is not at all surprising – it would have been a gesture of surrender rather than an acknowledgement of the king's right to them as *de iure* owner.

In the debates on whether to follow Cyrus, and on the occasions when the pay goes up, the terms of the issue of armour are not mentioned. Certainly it is clear that the soldiers had joined Cyrus on some terms, whether set forth explicitly or understood (I.3.1.); if the implication of II.5.38 is accepted, then it can probably be taken that the position as regards armour was stated from the first. It may simply have seemed unnecessary to revise it. The armour may have been a gift from the first: Cyrus' expedition was for death or the kingship of Persia: whichever the outcome, the cost of 13,000 suits of armour was not going to be a matter of concern to him afterwards.

It may be worth drawing an analogy to suggest why the matter of the armour was not raised in Cyrus' negotiations with his men *en route*. If an employee complains that his work is dangerous, he is more likely to be conciliated by an increase in pay than by being made a present of the protective clothing he already wears. 'Danger money' is surely the issue at I.4.12.

A particular difficulty is the fact that there is no obvious parallel for Ariaeus' statement at II.5.38 that the property of the king's slaves is the king's.[16] On the other hand, while the word *doulos* can be used by a Greek author of a person whom a modern reader might just call a subject,[17] it must be regarded as most implausible that it could ever 'mean' *subject* in anything approaching a neutral sense.[18] The Persians in Aeschylus were trying to 'throw the yoke of slavery over Hellas' (*Pers.* 50) – which illustrates what the Greeks thought being subject to the king was. It may be the case that Ariaeus was being particularly crafty and suggesting that, because the Greek word describing any subject of the king was *doulos*, the Greek practice with regard to property of a *doulos* was applicable to a Persian subject (as an ancient historian might call a helot a *serf*, then misapply to him some characteristics of feudal serfs). In that case what he said would probably fool the Greeks on the point of Persian custom, but would not affect his statement about the armour having belonged to Cyrus.

At the same period in Sicily, where Dionysius I had made himself tyrant of Syracuse, complicated events were going on. The question of arms and mercenaries here is complicated by the tyrants' practice of confiscating the citizens' own arms.[19] This meant that there was a stockpile of arms[20] which could, in theory at least, be distributed to mercenaries: in D.S. XIV.10.4 Dionysius I hires a crowd of mercenaries after seizing the citizens' arms. In view especially of his later activity in manufacturing armour, it would be perverse to doubt that on this occasion he gave out his stock of arms to the mercenaries.

But earlier Sicilian history should be recalled here. Hermocrates' advice to the Syracusans at Thucydides VI.72.4 includes the suggestion that the Syracusans' recent defeat could have been avoided if (among other things) armour had been handed out to those who had none: the implication is that even under democracy Syracuse could (given good management) issue arms to citizens to maximise hoplite strength in the field.[21]

Later Dionysius I instigated a programme of munitions manufacture.[22] His intention was to prepare an enormous quantity of arms, and missiles of all sorts, and the context makes it clear that they were for the mercenaries whom he gathered from many nations:[23] indeed, he took steps to ensure that they all had the armour they were used to.[24] His barbarian mercenaries cannot necessarily be assumed to have joined him on what Greeks might have considered the usual terms, so the fact of his making armour for them may seem of little significance for present purposes; but the list of the arms[25] not only shows the enormous scale of the programme, it also implies that the bulk of it was concerned with producing

Hellenic arms. There were 140,000 shields, and as many short swords and helmets; then there were 14,000 breastplates, for the cavalry, the infantry officers, and the mercenary bodyguards. The infantry officers were evidently to have full Greek panoply, while their followers were to be lightly armed. While the breastplates were to be 'of all types', there is no indication that the other arms were not of a standard pattern. The inference that Dionysius preferred to keep his barbarian mercenaries as his own bodyguard is reasonable, and fits in with D.S. XIV.8.4–6, where he hires Campanians when deserted by his other mercenaries.

In any case the largest single part of his army of 80,000[26] was certainly the citizen component,[27] and doubtless he meant to take their arms away again afterwards – though the second campaign after the making of the armour saw a good many Siceliots desert during the retreat, presumably taking the equipment with them. Evidently Dionysius had an adequate stock of armour in store for some time afterwards: when in 385 he concluded an alliance with Alcetas the Molossian, he sent him 500 Hellenic panoplies along with the 2,000 soldiers.[28] In conclusion, the production of 140,000 sets of arms was clearly intended as a once-only event. (Dionysius was planning a big war,[29] and the trouble taken in collecting skilled workers suggests that, as a very large quantity of equipment indeed must have been involved, the figure 140,000 is very likely of the right order for the quantity produced of each item.) It produced a reserve which was much larger than could be used in one campaign, so that it would seem sensible to conjecture that Dionysius envisaged giving some of it away (not to Syracusans). Such were probably the terms on which he hired men; like Cyrus, he was playing for high stakes (invasion of Libya was not unthinkable):[30] success against Carthage would make it unnecessary to worry about the cost of arms, failure would only increase the need for as many mercenaries as possible.

Later, in the 350s, Dion's decision to take arms to Syracuse[31] was influenced by the knowledge that the Syracusans' arms had been confiscated. His 5,000 panoplies were not for mercenaries but for the unarmed citizens who joined him at the borders of Syracusan territory.[32] Plutarch has a different picture, but it makes less sense: he shows Dion leaving his spare armour behind on landing, then having 5,000 ill-armed men whose 'keenness made up the deficiency of their equipment'.[33]

Dionysius II and his men evidently had a centralised supply organisation: so the list of his resources at D.S. XVI.9.2 implies. Presumably all his army, citizen and mercenary, was supplied with arms and other equipment.

Instances of arms being provided to mercenaries in mainland

Greece are less well attested. In 391 Evagoras of Cyprus sent envoys to Athens to ask the state for help and recruit some mercenaries;[34] peltast equipment was provided for the (relatively few) men recruited.[35] As this expedition was on a small scale, it is probably unfair to assume that the provision of arms was typical of mercenary recruitment.

There is, though, an interesting stratagem in Polyaenus, in which Iphicrates deals with some units whose captains have turned traitor.[36] The fact that Iphicrates seizes the men's armour before driving them out of the camp may (or, again, may not) suggest that it was not their own property. It would not be quite adequate to say that they were disarmed in order to prevent them turning traitors as their captains had: to make them harmless to his army, Iphicrates need only have taken their offensive weapons, but in fact they left the camp 'stripped'. Parke[37] assumes that the armour was their own and that the point of the punishment was (*a*) to prevent desertion to the enemy, (*b*) to prevent mercenaries from soldiering until they could buy new arms. This too is unsatisfactory: they would have had to travel several hundred miles to find an enemy to desert to.[38] The least that can be said is that Iphicrates probably found the confiscated armour useful – the king could surely find some men to wear it – so that the main point of the punishment was that the men were dismissed without the army losing strength as a result.

Another of Polyaenus' strategems says that Alexander gave some of his soldiers half-thoraxes instead of thoraxes.[39] This may (or may not) suggest that he had given them the thoraxes in the first place. 'Soldiers' could be either Macedonians or mercenaries.

A piece of third-century evidence adds a little more to the picture, and is not too far removed from the fourth-century context to be of interest. It points in the same direction as the story of Dion's landing in Sicily.[40] Archinus of Argos, put in charge of those fulfilling a contract to make new armour at the public expense, took the old armour from the citizens 'so as to dedicate it to the gods' (in accordance with the people's decision).[41] In sole control of everyone's old armour, he armed '*xenoi* and metics and disenfranchised people and the poor' and so seized the tyranny over the Argives. *Xenoi* is a standard word for 'mercenaries', and given the context it does not seem likely here to mean simply 'aliens' without suggesting that they were professional soldiers. As for the other sorts of people armed by Archinus, they are the groups who might want to start a revolution; Aeneas Tacticus warns against allowing them to get hold of arms.[42] The picture is of Archinus being able to recruit mercenaries (and discontented people from Argos) once he had armour to supply them with.

Epigraphical evidence shows how stocks of *matériel* were kept at Athens. *IG* II² 1424a, a long inventory prepared by the treasurers of Athene and the other gods in 371/370, records the continued presence in store of 778 of the 1,000 shields which the banker Pasion gave the city,[43] and mentions stockpiles of other kinds of weapons, mostly in the Chalcothece: 1,433 bronze helms,[44] for instance, 626 greaves[45] and 250 spear-butt spikes.[46] Less well preserved texts from other dates show that the city checked stocks regularly.[47] But it is difficult to tell what might have been used and what was (for religious or practical reasons) not available.[48] The 300 panoplies placed in Attic temples by Demosthenes in 425 seem not to be thought of by Thucydides as available,[49] but the shields given by Lysias to the Athenian Demos in 403 were for immediate use,[50] and one of the decrees given at the end of the *Lives of the Ten Orators*, speaking of Lycurgus' achievements, mentions that,[51] 'elected to take charge of war preparation, he brought up much armour and 50,000 missiles to the acropolis, and he prepared 400 seaworthy triremes', so it is clear that in some circumstances stockpiling weapons on the Acropolis could form a normal part of preparation for war. Clearly the purpose of collecting it was to hand it out, whether to citizens or to mercenaries.

The conclusion overall must be that there is enough evidence to suggest that persons and states wanting to raise an army would often start by collecting arms and armour, and that when they raised mercenaries they would often – perhaps even usually – equip them. Attention will now turn to aspects of the fourth-century practice of mercenary recruitment.

Mercenary leaders

Isocrates was disturbed by the existence of mercenaries:[52]

Greeks who share our language but live like barbarians. If we had any sense we should not overlook them gathering together under the generalship of any chance fellow – nor would we overlook the fact that larger and stronger armies come into being from the wanderers than from those who live in cities.

The way in which these armies were recruited from the wandering people, the Greeks outside the cities, will be examined in this section. Unfortunately there are not very many relevant texts.[53] Parke quotes one of them at the head of his chapter 'Other tyrants and autocrats'[54] – inappropriately, because the chapter is not at all concerned with the sort of mercenary army and mercenary commander the quotation refers to.[55] 'You know this (don't you?) – all these mercenary leaders are trying to seize and rule Greek cities. They are the enemies of everyone who wants to live as a free man under the law in his own country. That is the truth of it.' Demosthenes is characterising Charidemus (the whole speech is against an attempt to pass a decree in his favour) as a mercenary commander of the sort who travel around every land looking for a city to seize. Parke deals in detail with Clearchus of Heraclea and Jason of Pherae, and in a footnote names nine other autocrats, giving references.[56] Of the eleven, only Charidemus himself definitely answers Demosthenes' description.[57] The rest are mostly citizens who became tyrants of their own cities, though some – for example, Python the Clazomenian[58] – did so with the help of mercenaries. An exception is Hermias of Atarneus, slave, later partner, eventually heir of a banker who had attacked the places near Atarneus and Assus and become tyrant.[59] The beginning of this tyranny is hidden, though its end is known.[60]

Nevertheless examples of others besides Charidemus who fitted Demosthenes' description can be found. One such is mentioned in chapter 2 above: the Pasinus who took Paros.[61] The exiles from Siphnos formed only part of his force, and the speaker's comment that 'we thought this was a particularly safe island' makes it almost certain, first, that Pasinus was not a leader of Parian exiles – specially since presumably the worry that the Siphnian exiles might attack Siphnos was what induced its owners to deposit the money in Paros – and, second, that the Parians were not expecting any attack. The brevity of the remarks in the *Aegineticus* is the only difficulty which might make it prudent to hesitate before concluding that a mercenary commander could seize a Hellenic city more than 40 years before the speech *Against Aristocrates* was written.[62]

Some other wandering commanders of mercenaries (though none, so far as is known, ever managed to seize a Hellenic city) are attested as having formed part of an Athenian army. Inveighing against the prodigality of Chares in the *de falsa legatione*, Aeschines accuses him of spending the Athenians' money not on the soldiers but on the 'boastfulnesses of commanders'.[63] The sum he is alleged to have spent on them is 1,500 talents. A brief description of the commanders in question – Deiares, Deipyrus and Polyphontes – follows: 'wandering men collected together out of Greece'. Now Aeschines surely could not ask an audience to believe that the commanders had been given such an immense amount of money to keep for themselves; what he *is* saying is that Chares had used the three as sub-contractors, paying each for the wages of his followers. This is what the Athenian audience would have assumed was behind the remark, though some would also have responded to the implication that Deiares and the rest spent the money on conspicuous consumption and not all on soldiers for Athens.

Aeschines goes on to complain about commanders 'who were exacting sixty talents a year from the wretched islanders, and were bringing ships and Greeks to land off the high seas. Instead of fame and pre-eminence in Greece, our city was being filled with the reputation of Myonnesus and the pirates.' The association of these quasi-independent forces with pirates is hardly accidental.[64] W. K. Pritchett's case in defence of Chares' loyalty to Athens can be accepted readily enough,[65] but Aeschines' point is that the commanders (not Chares) were responsible for the poor peace terms:[66] 'put the blame for the peace terms on the commanders of your forces – not on the envoys!' Demosthenes, whom Pritchett quotes,[67] confirms as much by saying that in his trials at Athens Chares had been found to have had failures 'because of the people who do harm for money' – and so (Pritchett rightly infers) had been acquitted. But by condensing Aeschines' description of these officers, quoted above, to 'vagabonds of Hellas' in his translated quotation[68] Pritchett makes it seem imprecise, merely a gratuitous insult, and so lets slip the point alluded to by both Aeschines and Demosthenes: that Chares had hired wandering commanders (with their followers) and so spent Athens's money on unpopular piratical activities.[69]

Again, while Timotheus was besieging Samos in 365, many mercenaries arrived, and were using up the stores, until the general devised a means of confining the supply of food to his own men.[70] Parke comments,[71] 'these were apparently not mercenaries enlisted for his service, but adventurers arrived on speculation'. What seems to have happened is that the news of a military operation attracted men to go and try to join up. This evidence tends to confirm that Aeschines and Isocrates' picture of armies 'coming into being from the wanderers' is accurate – even unbidden, the wanderers turned up for Timotheus' campaign.

So Demosthenes' sketch of the activities of the mercenary leaders is an important part of the context in which Isocrates' remarks to Archidamus about larger armies coming into being from the wanderers than from those who live in cities ought to be interpreted. Pasinus and Charidemus seized cities with their mercenary bands. Timotheus was almost overwhelmed with mercenary volunteers at an inconvenient time. Chares took on three wandering mercenary leaders with their troops. The reason why the individual wandering commanders matter so much throughout the fourth century, from the *Anabasis* onward,[72] is that groups of mercenaries were closely associated with their leader, who commanded more loyalty from them than could the general of the whole army. Parke comments on the incident of Iphicrates and the two treacherous captains at Acre:[73]

'it shows ... how completely the *lochos* was the unit of the mercenary army and how intimately the *lochitai* were bound up with their *lochagos*'. Indeed it does. And the degree of loyalty must surely suggest that the smaller unit, with its own leader, had existed longer than the army.

Further light is shed on the expected relationship between mercenary employer and troops hired by a passage in Diodorus.[74] Sailing to west Greece with Phalaecus, his soldiers expected to see officers from the prospective employers on board. As there were none, they became suspicious and combined to force Phalaecus to take them back to the Peloponnese. The troops' own officers took the lead in this incident. Later, back in the Peloponnese, the officers took part with Phalaecus in negotiation with the envoys from Cnossus who engaged the army for a campaign in Crete. It seems a fair conjecture that these officers may not have been Phocians: after all, the Phocians surrendered to Philip when their mercenary army and Phalaecus had come to terms and withdrawn.[75] Such a sell-out is more likely to have been arranged without, than with, the knowledge of any Phocians who had been holding a command in the army. So it is thoroughly plausible to suppose that the officers who expected to see their future employers' officers on shipboard with them were the men who were already the leaders of bodies of mercenaries when they were enrolled at the time that Phocis needed every soldier it could find.[76]

The pattern of recruitment in the cases of Chares' operations, of Iphicrates' muster at Ace and of Phalaecus' Phocian army, then, is of an overall commander having employed existing units. Naturally ready-made mercenary units could come from within a city as well as from outside.[77] But Isocrates' assertion in the *Philippus* that it was *easier* to raise a larger and stronger army from the wanderers than from those who lived in cities cannot be dismissed as mere exaggeration, as the point he goes on to make about the difference in conditions between 401 and 346 shows:[78] 'in those days there were no mercenary units, so that they were forced to recruit from the cities and had to spend more on the presents given to the recruiters than on the soldiers' wages'. Now, however, Isocrates asserts, Philip can raise 'readily' as many soldiers as he wants. Clearly in 55 years there had been an enormous expansion in the number of wanderers available to take service: clearly it was also preferable to recruit without the overhead costs Cyrus incurred by having to deal inside the cities. Wanderers charged no commission. Isocrates' evaluation of the situation in 346 is all the more worth thinking about if we remember that, writing for Philip, he could scarcely include in his reckoning, as potential recruits to the Macedonian side, Phalaecus' 8,000 mercenaries in the Peloponnese.[79]

Mercenary service

What Parke called 'the general circumstance of mercenary service'[80] must be taken into account with reference to wandering mercenaries. The crucial question is what level of prosperity they could expect from their wages, and how regularly they could hope to be employed.[81] While employed, ration money would provide for food needs. Levels of pay have been discussed by Parke and also by Griffith,[82] but there was certainly less of a depression of mercenary wages in the middle of the century than Parke supposes:[83] Demosthenes IV(*Philippic* I).20 is a text of small importance, as the plan it outlines was not carried out; on the other hand the fact that the Phocians recruited men at a premium in 355/354, 354/353 and 353/352 (on the last of these occasions Phayllus doubled 'the customary rates of pay', whatever they were) proves that even a fairly modest recruiting requirement could force wages up considerably, at least for a while.[84] Assuming with Griffith that the middle of the fourth century was the time of the 'four-obol man' mentioned in New Comedy,[85] this would imply that the level of pay in one army at least was restored for a time to one drachma, and even eight obols, per day. It is certainly most improbable that the four-obol rate attested in Menander represented a rise in daily pay in terms of cash from some lower level.[86]

Both Parke and Griffith take two obols per day as a sort of *existence-minimum* in the mid-fourth century.[87] Both state that a larger cash income would have been 'the smallest wage or salary on which a man could reasonably be expected to keep himself alive'[88] by the end of the century.[89] Menander, *Epitrepontes* 136–41, however, suggests that two obols was still a possible minimum for subsistence even at the end of the century:

> *Smicrines.* He gives the pimp twelve drachmas a day.
> *Chaerestratus.* Twelve! That guy's got his affairs well in order.
> *Smicrines.* A month's keep for a man, and six days over.
> *Chaerestratus.* Well worked out. Two obols a day! Enough if a
> chap only wants barley gruel.

This perhaps gives an idea of purchasing power to add to the two-obol figure which Griffith takes as a baseline.[90] At any rate, if one is seeking a *bare minimum* cash income per person per day for survival in the fourth century there is no need to adjust the figure of two obols upwards.

This calculation indicates how little an employer need have paid by way of food allowance. But it is another question what level of prosperity a mercenary's wages (when he received them) could secure. An interesting but enigmatic piece of evidence comes from the early fourth century. Two brothers, in a speech claiming an inheritance, describe how they took to the soldiering life:[91] 'so, gentlemen, we married off our sisters; and since we were the right age, we turned to soldiering and spent time abroad with Iphicrates in Thrace. There we achieved some recognition for our merits: we made some money and sailed back here ...'. At first sight this would seem to give some support to the expectations of Xenophon's comrades-in-arms that they would bring money home from Cyrus' campaign.[92] But there are limitations on its usefulness. The brothers were not necessarily serving as common soldiers: contrary to Parke's assertion that 'they had never been well-off',[93] they had been well-off enough to marry their sister into a liturgy-paying family.[94] Each of the two sisters was given a dowry of 2,000 drachmas.[95] Thus the brothers may have been able, because of their thoroughly respectable background, to reach a higher-paid rank quickly: perhaps 'we achieved some recognition for our merits' implies that they did. In which case the fact that they came home having made money may well not say anything about the general likelihood of being able to do so.

What seems likely is that one of the brothers subsequently settled at home in Athens, and the other continued in an occupation (probably soldiering) which kept him abroad regularly; but his travel was, in his own word, *apodemia*: he was back in Athens from time to time.[96] So though there is this piece of fourth-century evidence about the travelling life from the mercenary's own mouth, its unique testimony has to be treated with some caution.

The career of these brothers, then, does not show for the 380s anything contrary to Parke's conclusion for the second half of the century, that 'the general rate of pay ... is too low to leave any room for doubt that the profession [i.e. the mercenary profession] was unremunerative, and had mostly been adopted for want of a better'.[97] And indeed the evidence of the *Panegyricus* of Isocrates supports this extension: published about 380, it deplores the wars and civil strife among the Greeks which forced many for lack of daily necessities to serve as mercenaries.[98] Later, in the *Philippus*, Isocrates refers to the idea again, this time in a context which shows still more explicitly that the soldiering life was taken up in default of a sufficient livelihood: 'we', the author argues (undertaking to speak for himself, Philip and the settled people of Greece), 'have an obligation to provide the wanderers with an adequate livelihood, before they become a greater menace than the barbarians'.[99] This passage refers to wanderers banding together, as had Isocrates' letter to Archidamus ten years earlier,[100] so the definite assumption that the mercenary career was not an adequate livelihood cannot be thought of only as a response to the low wages, but should also be recognised as Isocrates' explanation of why wanderers tended to form mercenary (and brigand) units.

There must have been hopes of plunder on the part of some soldiers joining mercenary armies. On some occasions in the fourth century armies took very large quantities, some of which must have gone to the men.[101] But, except to naive recruits, such hopes are not likely to have formed a large part of the motive for joining up.

A very convenient overview of the use employers made of mercenaries for most of the fourth century can be gained from a look at Parke's table II.[102] He comments, 'table II ... shows that between 399 and 375 BC there were never less than 25,000 mercenaries in service, and later the average number must have remained about 50,000. Wherever hired fighters were needed, and however large the demand, they were always forthcoming. Their very abundance created new uses for them.'[103] The comment stresses a point which has been made here, that mercenaries were ready in organised units *before* a prospective paymaster came forward; but the steady high numbers employed conceal the erratic nature of mercenary employment. The sources, as is natural, have much more to say about recruitment than about disbandment. Nevertheless the experience of Cyrus' men from Anaxibius' promise of pay to their incorporation in Thibron's army,[104] and the wait of about two years in the Peloponnese which Phalaecus and his men underwent before they were hired by the Cnossians,[105] both illustrate that soldiers could be a long time without an employer. The Cyreians, except on a few occasions when supplies were offered,[106] lived by plundering.[107] Phalaecus' men, Diodorus states, lived on the last of the treasure robbed from Delphi until it ran out, at which time Phalaecus made his plan to sail west.[108] Diodorus' source here is thoroughly hostile to the Phocians,[109] so the possibility that the allegation that there was Delphian treasure available to them during their wanderings is a lie ought at least to be considered, but it is not *prima facie* implausible that Philip may have allowed Phalaecus under the terms of the truce[110] to leave with money. At any rate, most unemployed mercenary units can have had no such resource. Plundering must have been the usual practice.

But Parke's table must be used with some care. The numerical inferences he draws from it are certainly well below the minimum figures for the numbers of mercenaries actually employed, because it is certain that the number of mercenaries kept by employers not on the table, including some small employers, was not negligible. Examples are: Iphicrates' Thracian employer (Seuthes or Cotys),[111] who may have enrolled as many as 8,000 soldiers, if Polyaenus' information is correct;[112] Temenus the Rhodian, who nearly seized

Teos;[113] and Python the Clazomenian, who succeeded in seizing Clazomenae.[114] More important, perhaps, than a few examples is the fact that Aeneas Tacticus devotes sections of his work to suggesting how city governments should deal with mercenaries not on campaign but when employed as guards within the walls.[115] The scale of employment by individuals and groups requiring comparatively few soldiers each may well have been substantial, though the scrappy evidence of the sources makes it impossible to reason to a conclusion about how much the lack of employment could have affected the life of the wandering units of mercenaries in the years represented by the few relatively blank parts of Parke's table.

But although the number in absolute terms of soldiers employed cannot have dipped very low, room must be left in the picture for the unemployed-and-wandering mercenary. It would be implausible to suggest that no forces except Xenophon's and Phalaecus' suffered periods without pay; in fact confirmation of Isocrates' image of wanderers 'causing trouble to everyone they meet'[116] can be found in the assumptions behind Polyaenus II.30.1. This stratagem describes a debate between Clearchus of Heraclea and the Heracleots, after mercenaries (secretly organised and paid by Clearchus) had started a nocturnal crime wave in the city ('robbing, mugging, beating people up, wounding ...'). The terms in which Clearchus presents his suggestion for solving the problem acknowledge that the community has to deal with a mercenary gang from outside – 'he said there was no other way to stop their insanity but for someone to lock them up'. Not that there were no rascals in Heraclea for Clearchus to hire (surely there were), but hiring mercenaries created a recognisable social problem (which those with long memories will have remembered from the visit of the Ten Thousand to Heraclea).[117] No suspicion fell on Clearchus as a result of the wave of violence in the night. Surely it is reasonable to infer that harassment of this sort was seen as needing no organiser: a city was all too likely to suffer the attentions of a group of desperate men from outside.

Griffith takes a rather optimistic view of life between periods of employment for a Hellenistic mercenary:[118]

> suppose that the war ends after six months and that the recruit has not been killed – he will be discharged with perhaps 180 drachmae for pay, of which he will not have spent more than the half on food ... our imaginary mercenary can now afford to take his ease for six months, or to travel overseas in search of new employment....

But his scheme depends on the assumption that the soldier has no family to support,[119] and that he will have kept at least half his gross pay until discharge. Griffith uses this example to contend that the pay of mercenaries offered at least as high a standard of living as that of some other wage labourers. His comparisons cannot be examined here, but his fundamental contention that[120] 'if he [*sc.* the mercenary] is content to travel about enlisting for short periods as the opportunity appears, the odds are that he will be able to live either comfortably all the time or riotously in short bursts' is surely rather sanguine. In the Hellenistic Age, and *a fortiori* in the fourth century, a mercenary's wages, if spread out over periods of unemployment (with a care which far from all soldiers would display), were worth so little more than the subsistence minimum that no one can have lived comfortably on them. Lived on barley gruel, perhaps.

Examination of the soldiering life with reference to wanderers, then, leads to two main conclusions: first, that Isocrates was right in saying that the wanderers were banding together, and that units of wandering mercenaries, recruited into large armies, in some cases had an important influence on the course of events; second, that the rate of pay was consistently low (though subject to less fluctuation than has sometimes been thought) and that employment was not always certain. Life without employment (once any saved-up money was gone) was a choice between beggary and banditry – or more likely a mixture of the two, such as the Cyreians adopted. When a significant proportion of the sum of Greek professional soldiers were homeless, it is not surprising that Demosthenes needed his persuasive powers in his first speech to the Athenian assembly when he wished to assure his hearers that the king's wealth would not buy him Hellenes to campaign against Hellas.[121] And when mercenary service, the way out of 'the existing poverty',[122] was itself a very poor way of life, it is not surprising that Isocrates hoped for 'a man of high ambition and a philhellene' to release the people who were serving as mercenaries from 'the troubles which they have and infict on others'.[123]

Notes

1 Fuks, 'Isocrates', p. 29 n. 46.
2 See above, chapter 2.
3 See above, p. 24 and n. 46.
4 Parke, *Greek Mercenary Soldiers*, pp. 43–8.
5 Xenophon, *Anabasis* VII.2.3.
6 A phrase used at *Antidosis* 115.
7 Xenophon, *Anab.* VI.4.8. J. Roy, 'The mercenaries of Cyrus', *Hist.* 16 (1967), pp. 287–323, at p. 245 and n. 39, disputes whether *andras agontes* can mean 'bringing slaves' (as Parke, *Greek Mercenary Soldiers*, p. 29, renders it). Certainly *aner* is an odd word to use of a

slave; but, as Roy concedes, Xenophon is professedly speaking about the soldiers generally in this passage. It does not serve his rhetorical purpose to point out that some members of the army had recruited others. This could not strengthen his suggestion that the soldiers were mostly respectable Greeks. More the reverse. Parke is probably right, despite the difficulty.

8 Isocrates, *Panegyricus* 146.

9 Parke, *Greek Mercenary Soldiers*, p. 29. G. T. Griffith, too, accepts this picture (if cautiously): *Mercenaries*, p. 3.

10 Cf. above, pp. 20–1 and n. 27.

11 Griffith, *Mercenaries*, does not raise the question (the point at which he might have done so is probably the introduction, pp. 1–7), and Parke, *Greek Mercenary Soldiers*, seems to assume that mercenaries owned their equipment (see later in this section, with n. 37). Roy, 'Mercenaries', p. 310, discusses ownership of arms in Cyrus' army (without discussing Xenophon, *Anab.* II.5.38) and concludes, on the ground of a general doubt whether Arcadia could supply 4,000 hoplite mercenaries and Achaea 2,000, that Cyrus had probably supplied equipment. He does not attempt to generalise to other mercenary forces.

12 In my Oxford D.Phil. thesis 'Greeks outside the *polis* in the fourth century BC' the evidence on the cost of armour and weapons is discussed at some length. Here it will be sufficient to quote a few pieces of evidence which point in the direction of the level of cost suggested here. (*a*) J. Pouilloux, *L'Histoire et les cultes de Thasos* I (Paris, 1954), p. 371 (No. 141) (Thasos, dated by Pouilloux at p. 372 to the second half of the fourth century, decrees that orphaned male children of citizens killed in war shall receive a panoply to the value of 300 drachmas.) (*b*) *IG* XII (5) 647 (=F. Sokolowski, *Lois sacrées des cités grecques*, Paris, 1969, No. 98), decreeing the prizes in the context of a religious festival, mentions a shield worth 20 drachmas. (*c*) The Athenian cavalry tablets (K. Braun, 'Der Dipylon-Brunnen B1: Die Funde', *Ath. Mitt.* 85, 1970, pp. 114–269, and J. H. Kroll, 'An archive of the Athenian cavalry', *Hesp.* 46, 1977, pp. 83–140), mostly of third-century date with some fourth-century ones, value cavalry horses between 100 drachmas and 1,200 drachmas (most between 300 drachmas and 700 drachmas). The armour dealt with in (*a*) would probably have been of high quality, while estimation from a 20-drachma shield to a whole panoply might suggest a cost of about 100 drachmas. As cavalrymen had to be quite a bit richer than hoplites, this would be in proportion to the cost of a good horse being at or above 300 drachmas.

13 Xenophon, *Anab.* II.5.31–7.

14 Xenophon, *Anab. II.5.38.*

15 In the context of the uniformity of equipment in Cyrus' army it is worth adding that peltasts were probably not much different from 'gumnetes' at the time of the *Anabasis*. It seems fair to think that I.8.4–5 would be best interpreted as picturing a combined light

division: both Clearchus' peltasts (300: I.1.3. and I.4.7) and Proxenus' (500: I.2.3). If the *gumnetes* were with Proxenus' main body, they would have had to be in the hoplite line. Surely it is easier to understand their being employed together with the thousand Paphlagonian cavalry. If so, the the whole light division is called the *peltastikon*. The objection that the separation of Proxenus from his light troops is not mentioned is worth little: nor is the separation of Clearchus from his light troops made explicit. And, given the standard equipment in I.2.16, the difference between peltasts and *gumnetes* may only have consisted in what sorts of spears and swords they had. *Gumnetes*, in spite of Herodotus IX.63, were not necessarily quite without armour (Xenophon, *Cyrop.* I.2.4.). In later Greek authors the word was flexible enough to be used of Roman light-armed troops (Plutarch, *Titus Flamininus* 4.4; *Aemilius* 16.5); *peltastikon* might perhaps seem more technical. The connection with slingers mentioned by Hesychius (s.v. *gumnetes*; cf. also D.S. V.17, Strabo III.5.1 (=254) and Aristotle, *Mir.* 837a30) is certainly not applicable in the context of Xenophon, *Anabasis*, where the *gumnetes* are definitely Greeks (I.2.3). *Suda*, s.v. *gumnetes*, is a confusing passage: 'a type of foot-soldiers' is as expected and Xenophon's name is mentioned (as an author who uses the word), but later the sentence *'gumnes, gumnetos* is also used of a hoplite' comes in. It is perhaps best ignored. Other references: Tyrtaeus 8.35 (11.35); Thucydides VII.37; *Hell. Oxy.* 6.6; Euripides, *Phoenissae* 147; Xenophon, *Anab.* IV.1.28. There is no suggestion of a definite technical meaning for *gumnes* which would distinguish it from *peltastes*.

16 D. M. Lewis has stressed this difficulty in conversation and *per epistulas*. Cook, *Persian Empire*, p. 132, by contrast, says, 'all men under the King's rule are his slaves, so he had power of life and death. All property was at his disposal', but he offers no references to support the last proposition.

17 Cook, *Persian Empire*, p. 132 n. 3, comments, 'the Greeks used the word "doulos" (slave) frequently in this context ... Darius uses the word "bandaka" (bondsman) of his generals and satraps. The treaty with Evagoras of Salamis about 380 BC turned on the question whether he was to be called the slave of Artaxerxes II or a King vis-à-vis his suzerain ...'

18 Hence the distinction made between two meanings by J. E. Powell in *A Lexicon to Herodotus* (Oxford, 1938), s.v. *doulos*, is misleading.

19 D.S. XIV.10.4; XVI.10.1.

20 D.S. XVI.9.2.

21 Consider also Dionysius' actions during his rise to power at D.S. XIII.96.1 (406).

22 D.S. XIV.41.3–4 and 42.2–3. Cf. Agesilaus' armaments programme at Ephesus in 395 (Xenophon, *Hell.* III.4.17).

23 D.S. XIV.41.4.

24 D.S. XIV.41.5.

25 D.S. XIV.43.2.

26 D.S. XIV.47.7.
27 D.S. XIV.47.4.
28 D.S. XV.13.2.
29 D.S. XIV.41.2.
30 D.S. XX.3.3.
31 D.S. XVI.6.5–10; and Plutarch, *Dion* 25.1–27.3.
32 Plutarch, *Dion* 10.1 and 3.
33 Plutarch, *Dion* 26.2 and 27.3.
34 Lysias XIX(*Aristophanes*).21 and 43; add Xenophon, *Hell.* IV.8.24.
35 Lysias XIX(*Aristophanes*).43. Few enough to be transported in ten ships which they were (probably) not rowing. Perhaps 200 would be a sensible guess. The situation is not perfectly clear from the sources and it might be possible to think of the Athenians giving bare hulls to the envoys and leaving them to fill them. It is not possible to discuss the point closely here, but this alternative appears unlikely.
36 Polyaenus III.9.56 (374 BC).
37 Parke, *Greek Mercenary Soldiers*, pp. 105–6.
38 D.S. XV.41.4.
39 Polyaenus IV.3.13.
40 See earlier in this section, with nn. 31–3.
41 Polyaenus IV.8 (266–263 BC).
42 Aeneas Tacticus 30.1.
43 *IG* II² 1424a, lines 128–9 and 139–40. Cf. J. K. Davies, *Athenian Propertied Families* (Oxford, 1971), p. 435.
44 *IG* II² 1424a, line 133.
45 *IG* II² 1424a, line 134.
46 *IG* II² 1424a, line 384.
47 For example, *IG* II² 1455 (340s) and *IG* II² 1469B (320s).
48 Here cf. W. K. Pritchett *The Greek State at War* III (Berkeley and Los Angeles, 1979), pp. 240–95. The distinction was clear at the time – it was usual to take the handles off dedicated shields to make them useless: Aristophanes, *Knights* 846–59.
49 Thucydides III.114.1.
50 See Davies, *APF*, p. 589.
51 Plutarch, *Mor.* 852C (the whole decree, in response to the claim of Lycophron son of Lycurgus for the right to have meals in the Prytaneum, runs from 851E to 852E). It is worth noting here that M. I. Finley (*The Use and Abuse of History*, London, 1975, pp. 116–67, cf. n. 10) argues (commenting that there is no specific evidence on the point) that arms were probably given to Spartiates as a public provision: *perioeci*, he suggests, made the munitions – and he thinks it more likely that the state procured and distributed these than that the Spartiates obtained them individually for payment in kind.
52 Isocrates, *Ep.* 9(Archidamus).8–9.
53 Xenophon, *Anabasis*, is of course a relevant text, but not typical of later practice. Cyrus began by instructing garrison commanders in the cities he controlled to recruit as many Peloponnesians as possible for him (Xenophon, *Anab.* I.1.6; cf. Roy, 'Mercenaries', pp. 296–9).

However, a feature which will be stressed in this section was present in Cyrus' army, that is, the importance of the separate contingents with their own commanders; on which see Roy, 'Mercenaries', pp. 287–96.
54 Parke, *Greek Mercenary Soldiers*, p. 97.
55 Demosthenes 23(*Aristocrates*).139.
56 Clearchus: Parke, *Greek Mercenary Soldiers*, pp. 97–100; Jason: pp. 100–4. The other nine: p. 100 n. 1. H. Berve, *Die Tyrannis bei den Griechen* (Munich, 1967), pp. 373–9, makes reflective comments on the historical function of fourth-century tyranny, including one (pp. 373–4) on how the tyrants, by fighting wars with their own mercenaries and promoting scientific and technical achievements, increased the size of the area in which the government looked after the material prosperity of a state. He connects this extension of the responsibilities of government with a tendency for private concerns to matter more in Greek society in the fourth century than earlier, and for citizens to be disinclined to do military service.
57 Demosthenes 23(*Aristocrates*).154 shows Charidemus seizing Scepsis, Cebren and Ilium. Cf. Parke, *Greek Mercenary Soldiers*, pp. 128–9.
58 Aeneas Tacticus 28.5 – his seizure of the gates, with mercenaries hidden near the city. He also had confederates in the city.
59 Strabo XIII.1.57.
60 D.S. XVI.52 (cf. also Didymus cols. 4–6). Mentor, Artaxerxes' general, ousted Hermias from control of the many fortresses and cities he was by then controlling. W. Leaf in his presidential address 'On a commercial history of Greece' to the Hellenic Society (*JHS* 35, 1915, pp. 161–72) took the phrase 'Hermias and his comrades' preserved in Tod II.165 to refer to Hermias' business partners ('Hermias and Company, Bankers and Despots', p. 169), though Tod II.165 is more down-to-earth ('probably his chief officers'). A point worth noting is that Hermias had the resource an employer of mercenaries needed most: money.
61 See above, p. 18.
62 Pasinus took Paros before the speaker and the others went to Melos. They, in turn, had left Melos, presumably before Conon arrived there. This makes 394 a likely year for Pasinus' conquest.
63 Aeschines 2(*Embassy*).71–2.
64 Cf. below, pp. 106–15.
65 Pritchett, *The Greek State at War* II, pp. 77–85.
66 Aeschines 2(*Embassy*).73.
67 Pritchett, *The Greek State at War* II, p. 82.
68 Pritchett, *The Greek State at War* II, p. 83, 'drapetas anthropous ek tes Hellados suneilegmenous' means 'wandering men collected together out of Greece'; 'vagabonds of Hellas', as a translation, represents a considerable sacrifice of accuracy for the sake of brevity.
69 J. Cargill, *The Second Athenian League* (Berkeley and Los Angeles, 1981), makes a series of brief comments on Chares (pp. 2, 181, 185 and 194) in which the failure of the Athenians to win the Social war is blamed on him and his exceptionally bad generalship: but Chares'

career is not regarded as an unique phenomenon (p. 185).

70 Polyaenus III.10.10.

71 Parke, *Greek Mercenary Soldiers*, p. 108.

72 The part of the army which followed Xenophon when the army split into three at Xenophon, *Anab*. VI.2.16, did so in spite of the overall command held by Cheirisophus. The solidarity between the Arcadians and Achaeans, by contrast, was ethnic: they chose new generals.

73 Parke, *Greek Mercenary Soldiers*, p. 106.

74 D.S. XVI.62.1–3.

75 D.S. XVI.59.3.

76 I.e. 355–352: D.S. XVI.24.2, 25.1, 28.1, 30.1, 32.4, 36.1.

77 Aeneas Tacticus 22.29 (a difficult passage) shows how a *proxenos* could be involved in dealings concerning a contract to guard city walls. What seems to be envisaged is that guards would have been hired as a unit from a city, whose *proxenos* in the hiring city would take responsibility for them.

78 Isocrates, *Ep*. 9(*Archidamus*).8–9. See the beginning of this section.

79 D.S. XVI.59.3. A few years later in *Ep*. II (*Philip I*).19, Isocrates recommends Philip not to hire 'the armies of the *xeniteuomenoi*' (*xeniteuomenoi* is equivalent to 'wandering mercenaries': cf. Isocrates, *Philippus* 122) but there he suggests that Philip might try to get an alliance with Athens instead (which would save him paying wages): not that he should hire mercenaries in the cities of Greece.

80 Parke, *Greek Mercenary Soldiers*, chapter XXII; pp. 227–38.

81 'Wages' in this section denote money given for pay, as distinct from money given for buying supplies on campaign. W. K. Pritchett's work (*The Greek State at War* I, Berkeley and Los Angeles, 1974, pp. 3–52, especially pp. 40–41) has established that payment of rations in kind was exceptional from the time in the fifth century when *misthos* was introduced (p. 40); though the cases he cites are nearly all of citizen armies, there is no reason to postulate a general difference of practice between citizen and mercenary armies on this point – and he makes the point that a soldier had to receive his *siteresion* in order to live (p. 41). This must be of general application.

82 Parke, *Greek Mercenary Soldiers*, pp. 231–4; Griffith, *Mercenaries*, pp. 294–7.

83 Parke, *Greek Mercenary Soldiers*, p. 232: 'Demosthenes believed he could actually find mercenaries to serve for 2 obols a day' (in 350/349). Griffith, *Mercenaries*, p. 297: 'between 400 and 250 BC the rate has fallen, perhaps as much as from 8 to 4, and certainly as much as from 7 to 5 or 6 obols' is surely more likely to be right.

84 D.S. XVI.25.1 (355/354): 'making the pay half as much again'. D.S. XVI.30.1 (354/353): 'when he had established pay for the mercenaries at one and a half times the standard rate'. D.S. XVI.36.1 (353/352): 'having doubled the pay' on the first of these occasions Philomelus gathered 'no less than five thousand soldiers' – including the Phocians themselves, though. This is not an enormous number, comparatively, though the size of the army had been increased by the time of the

battle of the Crocus Field to 10,000 or more (cf. Parke, *Greek Mercenary Soldiers*, p. 137).

85 Griffith, *Mercenaries*, p. 308.
86 Parke, *Greek Mercenary Soldiers*, p. 233. Menander, *Perikeiromene* 380, and Fragment 297 (Koerte).
87 Griffith, *Mercenaries*, p. 308; Parke, *Greek Mercenary Soldiers*, p. 232.
88 Griffith, *Mercenaries*, p. 308.
89 Griffith, *Mercenaries*, p. 309: 'the man who could ... live on two obols a day in 340 BC would require more money in 300 BC to produce an equal standard of life'. Parke, *Greek Mercenary Soldiers*, p. 233.
90 Griffith, *Mercenaries*, pp. 308–9.
91 Isaeus 2(*Menecles*).6.
92 Xenophon, *Anab.* VI.4.8.
93 Parke, *Greek Mercenary Soldiers*, p. 232.
94 Isaeus 2(*Menecles*).42; and cf. Davies, *APF*, p. xxiii.
95 Isaeus 2(*Menecles*).3 and 5.
96 Some time after the brothers' return from their first period abroad, Menecles offered to adopt one of them. The speaker's brother answered, 'I travel abroad, as you know. But my brother here will look after your affairs and mine, if you like to adopt him'. Isaeus 2(*Menecles*).12.
97 Parke, *Greek Mercenary Soldiers*, p. 233.
98 Isocrates, *Panegyricus* 168.
99 Isocrates, *Philippus* 121.
100 Cf. above, p. 85.
101 W. K. Pritchett, *The Greek State at War* I (Berkeley and Los Angeles, 1974), pp. 53–84, sums up available evidence on booty. The section on distribution of booty (pp. 82–4) does not have much to say on the particular point of distribution of booty among mercenary armies.
102 Bound in at the end of the book.
103 Parke, *Greek Mercenary Soldiers*, p. 227.
104 Xenophon, *Anab.* VI.1.16–VII.8.24.
105 The two-year wait: H. D. Westlake, 'Phalaecus and Timoleon', *CQ* 34 (1940), pp. 44–6. Hired by the Cnossians: D.S. XVI.62.3. Westlake says (p. 44), 'they can scarcely have been transported to Crete later than the autumn of 344'.
106 E.g. Xenophon, *Anab.* VI.2.3–4.
107 E.g. Xenophon, *Anab.* VI.5.7, 6.5, 6.38. Defending his collaboration with Seuthes, Xenophon argues that, though deprived of pay, the soldiers have at least had a winter 'with adequate supplies' (VII.6.30–2). A third-century Samian inscription shows that some soldiers may have sought more respectable occupations while unemployed than plundering. It disqualifies slaves, soldiers, time-expired soldiers and temple suppliants from acting as traders in the market at the temple of Hera (Habicht, 'Hellenistische Inschriften', No. 9, at pp. 210–12).
108 D.S. XVI.61.3–4 and cf. above, p. 88.
109 N. G. L. Hammond argues persuasively that his source is Demophilus'

monograph on the Sacred war ('The sources of Diodorus Siculus XVI. I. The Macedonian, Greek and Persian narrative', *CQ* 31, 1937, pp. 79–91, especially pp. 82–5). It is hard to understand his assertion that the tone of the monograph is 'a blend of piety and impartiality' (p. 83). His own account of it shows its anti-Phocian character. As Parke wrote (*Greek Mercenary Soldiers*, p. 136), 'bias [*sc.* of the authors of the ancient narratives of the Sacred war] is intelligible; but it is strange to find its echo in a modern historian'.

110 D.S. XVI.59.2.

111 Parke, *Greek Mercenary Soldiers*, p. 55, sums up the evidence on this point.

112 Polyaenus III.9.46. Parke, *Greek Mercenary Soldiers*, p. 56 n. 1, gives this reference and comments, 'certainly a high figure if correct'; but, as it is not included in table II, presumably Parke's opinion is that it is probably not correct.

113 Aeneas Tacticus 18.13–19 is the only record of this incident.

114 Aeneas Tacticus 28.5 is the only record of this incident.

115 See Aeneas Tacticus 13, 22.26–9, 24.1–3.

116 Isocrates, *Philippus* 120.

117 Xenophon, *Anab.* VI.2.4–8.

118 Griffith, *Mercenaries*, pp. 310–11.

119 Griffith, *Mercenaries*, p. 311: 'he may have to forgo the pleasures of a legal wife and legitimate children'. (This rather overlooks the fact that a concubine and illegitimate children would cost as much to support.)

120 Ibid.

121 Demosthenes 14(*Navy Boards*).31.

122 Ibid.

123 Isocrates, *Philippus* 122.

5
Leistai

It has been argued above that as the tendency to use mercenary armies gained strength so the numbers of unemployed and wandering mercenaries increased.[1] In this chapter it will be suggested, first, that *leisteia* (which may as well be rendered as 'piracy' until the word's content is discussed) became more common, and so more of a social problem, in the fourth century, and, second, that its growth was concomitant with the rise of mercenary service because the same sorts of people were engaged in both (respectively, or successively).

Establishing these suggestions will involve an overview of fourth-century *leisteia*. To put this view in perspective, the chapter begins by focusing on three key aspects of fifth-century and earlier *leisteia*, then turns to a consideration of what meaning is conveyed by *leistes* and cognates in literature dealing with the Classical period.

Before the fourth century

These key aspects of earlier *leisteia* represent areas of comparison with fourth-century events and trends. They are: first, the importance of raids on land from the sea; second, instances of communities settling in places to raid them; third, the nature of *leistai* as people independent of control by a city-state.

Raids on land from the sea

In Thucydides I.4–7 these are treated as the primary kind of *leisteia*. Communities, under the leadership of 'not the least powerful men',[2] attacked unwalled cities, inhabited them as villages, making most of their living in this way. This was what Minos put a stop to.[3] It was also the reason for founding cities inland:[4] the coast was liable to be attacked.

Herodotus II.152.4, dealing with the revolt of Psammetichus in

Egypt in the seventh century, describes the arrival of the 'bronze men', the Ionian and Carian hoplites, who later fought for Psammetichus. They came from the sea into Egypt 'for plunder'. It is an early example of mercenaries being demonstrably the same people as *leistai*.

Raids from the sea were an important feature of the Peloponnesian war. They were undertaken both by armies and by parties of exiles. At an early stage the Athenians fortified Atalante, an empty island, against the *leistai* from Opus who were attacking Euboea.[5] Conversely, the capture of Cythera by the Athenians was a serious blow to the Spartans. Not only was the opportunity to attack merchant shipping from Egypt and Libya, which the commandant of Cythera and his hoplites had formerly enjoyed, now denied, but also the presence of Spartan forces on the island before the Athenians captured it had limited the extent to which Laconica could be attacked from the sea by *leistai*.[6] It seems right to infer that the Spartans could expect others to follow the example given by Nicias and the Athenian navy.[7] At III.85.2 the oligarchic Corcyreans set up on the mainland opposite Corcyra and 'plundered the people on the island and did them much harm'; soon, though, they were able to come back to the island (III.85.3).

Communities settling in places to raid them

Pylos, as well as Cythera, became a base for Athenian attacks on Spartan territory[8] – which was what the Spartans had expected since the fall of Cythera, and had prepared for by sending squads of hoplites to guard the countryside.[9] Later, too, the Athenians – specifically Demosthenes – took a 'sort of isthmus' in Laconice to use as a base for raiding.[10] Both sides were able to encourage communities of exiles to settle and raid their mother cities. Athens supported the Messenians and Helots at Pylos[11] (and the Megarians at Pegae served Athenian interests by invading Megara twice a year[12]); Sparta supported the Samians at Anaea.[13] But there is evidence in Thucydides' narrative of some more independent settlements. Zancle in Sicily was first founded by *leistai* who arrived there.[14] In the same way later Dionysius of Phocaea settled in Sicily, escaping after the Ionian revolt, and attacked Carthaginians and Tyrseni, but not Greeks.[15] The raiding by land and sea carried out (with barbarian help) by the Epidamnian oligarchs[16] was certainly the same sort of harassment-by-exiles later encouraged by both sides in the Peloponnesian war. This activity was as common as it was because of the prevalence of civil strife, noted by Thucydides at III.82.

Leistai as persons independent of control by a city-state

Thucydides implies that it was not respectable in his day to be a *leistes*.[17] But sometimes *leistai* could expect the authorities in their city-state to allow them to carry on their activities: at Thucydides IV.67.3 the Megarians who were conspiring to betray the city to the Athenians are recorded as having got permission to move a boat in and out on the ground that they were raiders. Similarly Nicias thought (mistakenly) that Gylippus had come west not to help Syracuse but for *leisteia*:[18] 'But Nicias, when he found out about his arrival, overlooked the large numbers of the ships (as the Thurians had done) and thought they had gone to sea as raiders – and he kept no guard.'[19]

The fact that Nicias kept no guard indicates that he did not expect Gylippus to attack his forces. That neither the Megarians nor Gylippus were *leistai* does not affect the conclusion: the expectations of the observers are an adequate gauge of what was normal practice. The Megarians' activities must have been presumed to be against coastal areas: a boat small enough to be carried into the city would hardly be large enough or fast enough to attack a ship.

Nicias presumably expected Gylippus to carry on the raiding which the Spartans had made part of their strategy: the capture of Minoa relieved Athens of Peloponnesian raiding from this island off Megara. He cannot have expected his forces to be the victims of such incursions, at least initially. Earlier the Athenians had taken measures to prevent 'the Peloponnesians' raiding force' from interrupting the transport of cargo ships to Athens.[20]

Themistocles and Cimon had both acted against piracy,[21] taking up the task begun by Minos[22] and undertaken later by the Corinthians.[23] Most of the *leistai* active during the Peloponnesian war were exiles acting against their native lands, and the only independent *leistai* who seem not to have been exiles are those attested at Thucydides II.32. Most of these exiles were encouraged by one side or other in the war (in fact F. M. Cornford seems right to say[24] that the Messenians in the triaconter at Thucydides IV.9.1 were simply acting as allies of Athens), so it must be inferred that the years when Athenian sea power was at its height were the years when the sea was kept clear of *leistai* other than exiles attacking their own lands (and Thucydides III.82 shows that there will have been fewer even of these before the war) and kept clear by Athens alone: the fact that the speaker of [Dem.] 7 (*Halonnesus*) objects to the idea that anyone else need guard the sea (section 14) adds weight to A. B. Bosworth's argument that Plutarch *Pericles* 17 must be based on a fourth-century forgery (see below, n. 196). This is the most striking difference between the *leistai* of the fifth century and those of the fourth: that in the fourth century there was a strong element outside the protection of any of the states. The most striking similarity, on the other hand, is the prevalence in both cases of raids on the land: not that it is possible to quantify, numerically at least, but because throughout Thucydides (and specially in I.4–7, dealing with prehistory) *leistes* is better rendered into English as 'raider' than as 'pirate'.

Leistes: interpretation

'Raider' is indeed almost always a good translation of *leistes*, in fourth-century as well as earlier contexts. It does not always have an outlaw connotation. It can be used of people sent out by armies to ravage the land. This is its almost exclusive meaning in Xenophon, *Hellenica*: (*a*) at II.4.26, where *leistai* are foragers organised by the Peiraeus party in 404/403; (*b*) at III.4.19, although the authors of two modern works on ancient piracy have taken the passage as referring to pirates; Agesilaus (in 395) was prepared to make a point by having barbarians sold naked, but it stretches credulity to suggest that he, a Spartan king, had turned trader and bought from pirates the barbarians his heralds were to sell: much more likely, surely, that the barbarians were taken by Lacedaemonian raiding parties;[25] (*c*) at IV.8.35, where (in 389) 'Anaxibius and Iphicrates made war on each other by sending out *leistai*'; (*d*) at V.1.1, where Eteonicus in Aegina 'allowed anyone who wished to make raids on Attica': this clearly refers principally to Aeginetans (under the protection of his army), but falls into the picture of pillage authorised by armies – it continued for two years until the peace of Antalcidas (V.1.29), and seems to have resumed after the battle of Alyzeia (VI.2.1, cf. V.4.61–6); (*e*) at V.4.42, where (in 378) 'Phoebidas plundered the Thebans by sending out raiding-parties'; and (*f*) at VI.4.35, where Alexander of Pherae is described as '... an unjust *leistes* both by land and by sea', implying that as tagus of Thessaly he organised and led raids. Theopompus the Milesian *leistes*, on the other hand, appears from II.1.30 to have been an independent operator, working for Lysander in a trusted capacity (taking the news of Aegospotami back to Sparta) – unless, indeed, Xenophon misunderstood something, and 'Theopompus the Milesian *leistes*' is Theopompus the Melian admiral, whose statue later stood at Delphi.[26]

Modern books on ancient piracy have used the differing emphases which the flexibility of the term *leistes* allows. H. A. Ormerod makes the sea the centre of his inquiry, subtitling his book *An Essay in Mediterranean History* and arguing at the beginning of the first chapter that 'the earliest literature of Greece shows us the Homeric pirate pursuing a mode of life at sea almost identical with that of the Frankish corsairs':[27] he wishes to show that piracy had a continuous effect on Mediterranean life.[28] E. Ziebarth's purpose is to make deductions about trade from the evidence available about robbery at sea, so that he says, 'wo aber für den Anfang die Geschichte des Handels fehlt, beweist der blühende Seeraub das Bestehen des Seeverkehrs und des Handels', and 'unsere Darstellung will vielmehr für die historisch greifbare Zeit den griechischen Seehandel in seinem Verhältnis zum Seeraub, d.h. in seiner Abhängigkeit vom Seeraub, schildern und gibt mit der Geschichte des Seeraubs zugleich ein Stück der griechischen Handelsgeschichte'.[29] He can therefore regard any activity which made the seas unsafe as legitimate material for his chapters on *Seeraub*, including the hi-jackings of cargoes by states which will be mentioned in the last section of this chapter but are related only indirectly to the activities of the *leistai* mainly under discussion here.

There were pirates in the Aegean throughout the fourth century. In the *Panegyricus*, in a passage arguing that the imperial rule of Athens was preferable to the state of Greece after the peace of Antalcidas, Isocrates asks,[30] 'who could wish for the kind of state of affairs in which pirates [*catapontistai*] control the seas, and peltasts are capturing the cities?' (and adds further comments on the contemporary state of Greece). Lack of evidence to confirm this statement may make it possible to argue that it was an exaggeration in 380 (or thereabouts) when Isocrates wrote, but things were moving in that direction, and the pirates were certainly very strong later in the century.[31]

For brigandage on land there is very little evidence. The outstanding instance is that of the Chian exiles at Atarneus in the early 390s. They were setting out from Atarneus and plundering Ionia. Dercylidas besieged them until they surrendered, then left Dracon of Pellene as garrison commander.[32] At the other end of the fourth century *Syll.*[3] 363, from Ephesus and dated about 297, shows the Ephesians helping with arms and money some Prienians who were living in a fortified place outside Priene after the battle of Ipsus. They offer in the decree (lines 9 and 15–16) to sell Ephesian citizenship to those of these Prienians who are free and born of free parents. It is easy to understand the whole decree as a move to bring the exiled Prienians under more direct Ephesian control.

Other evidence relates to soldiers: the crimes committed at Heraclea by the mercenaries hired secretly by Clearchus did not give rise to the suspicion that anyone was organising them, and so may suggest that mercenaries were likely sometimes to cause a problem of this sort when unemployed;[33] when Antigonus I wintered in Cappadocia in 320–319, 3,000 Macedonian hoplites deserted him, seized strong hills, and were plundering Lycaonia and Phrygia.[34] Polyaenus does not suggest that Antigonus minded their plundering the countryside: but he was worried that they might join the enemy. The brief narrative does not make it explicit why the soldiers turned to brigandage in this way: they were not led by a strong character (when Antigonus sent Leonidas to them they made him general) and there is no suggestion of a shortage of provisions or pay. That Antigonus allowed them to go to Macedonia, when he had cornered them and seized Holcias and two of the ringleaders, may perhaps suggest that their main motive was to escape further army service. In any case the incident is unique.

The explanation, elaborated below,[35] of the prevalence of *leisteia* by sea and its absence on land is (with all possible simplification) that pirates were mercenaries, and mercenaries pirates. As a reviewer of Ormerod's book wrote, 'from the fourth century they [*sc.* ancient governments] relied largely on mercenary soldiers, who between the land campaigns took to the water like a crocodile'.[36] Mercenary armies when without an employer lived by plundering.[37] So must the smaller mercenary units, from which some of the armies were formed, have done.[38]

The conclusion is that the ancient evidence will be best served by rendering *leistes* as 'raider'. It should be borne in mind that that does not by itself imply outlaw status (as the English 'pirate' does), and it is in general the case that most *leistai* mentioned in the literary and epigraphic sources for the fourth century operated at sea. The *Suda* distinguishes between *leistes* (land-based) and *peirates* (seaborne),[39] and it might be the case (given the quantity of fourth-century rhetoric referred to in the *Suda*) that a fourth-century BC distinction is reflected here.[40] But if so the distinction cannot have been a universally recognised one.

How *leistai* lived

Modern authors have tended to assume that ancient pirates lived by raiding ships at sea. Ormerod's statements 'it goes without saying that the seamanship of pirates was of the highest order' and 'when inexperienced landsmen took to piracy, their end was swift' are conditioned by this assumption.[41] But the assumption is to a large extent misled and misleading. Partly, indeed, for the reason set out by Y. Garlan, who comments that 'isoler la piraterie (sur mer) du brigandage (sur terre), c'est ... rompre l'unité d'un seul et même phénomène historique'.[42] But, having gone so far, Garlan turns to another point.

It is necessary to go further; pirates lived by raiding the land more than by raiding ships at sea. This can be confirmed by looking in two directions: first, at the local effect of a well-documented infestation of pirates; second, at what measures people in coastal areas took which can be treated as implying a need to protect themselves against attack from the sea.

The local argument concerns the north Aegean area. Between 346 and 338 Philip of Macedon and the Athenians were in conflict there: the 'peace' in the earlier part of the period was not very different from the war at the end of it,[43] so that similar conditions seem to have prevailed for the whole eight years. It was a period when *leistai* were very active. They attacked both Athenians and Macedonians, but Demosthenes argues, in the Embassy speech and again in the speech on the Crown, that Philip suffered from piratical attacks in these years much more than did the Athenians. At the outset, he contends, Philip was[44] 'desirous of peace – what with his country being overrun by *leistai* and his trading ports closed'. And much later, referring to the war of Chaeronea, Demosthenes comments of Philip that[45] 'although your generals were carrying on the war against him pathetically badly, he was still suffering countless troubles on account of the war itself and the *leistai*', in fact he claims as an advantage of his (unsuccessful) policy that it resulted in peace in Attica throughout the war of Chaeronea, instead of the pirates ravaging from Euboea. Maintaining power at sea kept Athens safe: loss of control of Euboea to Philip would have given Demosthenes' accusers the chance to complain that the sea was unsafe because of the *leistai* based in Euboea.[46] The assumption behind these statements is that the pirates were a separate factor in the calculations of both sides, and not in an obvious sense part of the war. To be more explicit: what Philip suffered in the 340s was the effect of the normal activities of *leistai*: there was (*contra* Ormerod and Ziebarth) no 'privateer-war'.[47] The model implied by the use of the term 'privateer-war' will be examined below.[48]

[Dem.] 7(*Halonnesus*).14–15 illustrates the community of interest between the antagonists in the matter of the *leistai*. Philip's suggestion that the Athenians should join him in guarding against those who commit crimes by sea, the speaker says, is a request that they should set him up at sea and admit that they cannot maintain a maritime patrol without him (section 14). If a privateer war were being carried on at the time, one would have to assume that both Philip's and the speaker's statements were the purest hypocrisy, and also that the Athenians were carrying on the privateering without the knowledge of their assembly. The fact is that both sides were genuinely anxious to avoid aiding the pirates in any direct or observable way,[49] even though they can hardly have been sorry to see the enemy suffer because of them.

The pirates, then, were an element neither government wanted anything to do with. It must be deduced that both states calculated that open dealings with the pirates would be likely to have a negative marginal utility: the possible military advantages would be outweighed by the certainty of attracting unpopularity in Greece in general – that is, among the cities. This calculation shows how pirates lived outside the cities in the sense of being beyond the pale of political legitimacy. To harness their strength seemed (on this occasion at least) counter-productive.

Treating the pirates as an independent element, it is legitimate to ask how they profited from the tension between Athens and Macedon. Demosthenes' comments quoted above from the *Embassy* and the *Crown*[50] imply that their activity was restricted to the northern Aegean, at least for the most part. Sostratus and his followers had taken Halonnesus, and Philip took action against them,[51] so it can be inferred that they had been harassing Macedonian people and property. The Thasians received 'those of the *leistai* who wished' in their harbour, and the fact that this was regarded by Philip as a cause for complaint *against Athens*[52] (although Athens' corn supply had to come through the northern Aegean) shows that Macedon and Macedonian interests suffered much worse from the pirates than did the Athenian trade. The Athenian supplies were carried in convoy under naval protection, but this measure was certainly taken for security against Philip, who in 340 seized 230 or 180 merchant ships while Chares was away at the muster of the king's generals.[53] Philip had a general strategy of cutting off Athens' supplies, furthered by his action against Byzantium and Perinthus.[54]

Therefore the tendency of the evidence is to show that neighbours of the *leistai* had more to lose than more distant states with a larger volume of trade through the area where the *leistai* were.[55] What might be seen as a counter-example, that of Phrynon of Rhamnus, a case involving an attack on merchant shipping, very likely Athenian, is almost certainly not an instance of Athenians suffering harm at the hands of *leistai* who would as soon have attacked Macedonians:[56] it will be argued below that the *leistai* who took Phrynon were Philip's own courtiers, and their retainers.[57] As for the measures taken by coastal people against pirate attacks, the simplest, naturally, was to beat off the attackers. *IG* XII (3) Supp. 1291, a Theran decree honouring a Ptolemaic navarch, describes how a raid by *leistai* was repelled. But it was as well to be prepared beforehand. Guard towers against coastal attack in wartime are attested (for Sicily) in

Thucydides, who tells how the Athenians captured one from the Locrians in 426, how the Syracusans manned them in 415, and how Nicias argued in 413 that they were a drain on the financial resources of the Syracusans who were keeping them up.[58] Similarly, at the end of the third century, guard towers are mentioned in decrees from Halasarna and Carpathus honouring men who had contributed to defence in the Cretan war.[59] And Epichares of Rhamnus, general of the shore district at Athens in the Chremonidean war, punished those who introduced pirates into the country as well as making vigorous use of defensive works and strengthening them: so the routine work of coastal fortification included defence against pirates.[60]

But references to guard towers and other permanent buildings for coastal defence are uncommon, a fact which lent credence to J. H. Young's re-evaluation of the purpose of the many small towers in the Aegean islands and other coastal areas.[61] There are hundreds of these towers, and Young's selective catalogue of those in the islands is useful, as is his discussion of the comparison between diameter and height.[62] Though noting how many authors have held that the towers served as a refuge from pirates, and even conceding that 'the suggestion . . . seems to fit very well the towers lining the coasts of the Cyclades, especially when we contemplate them on a map',[63] Young rejects completely the idea that the towers had any defensive purpose. He sees them as farm buildings, designed as they were because of the nature of the materials available: 'where we build in wood', he writes, presumably with America in mind, 'the Greek built in stone, and if his building spread out very far, he would have trouble finding timbers long enough to roof it. The answer was obvious: to expand not out, but up.'[64]

Young's general hypothesis is amply established by finds of millstones and olive presses,[65] and confirmed by the evidence of the Chersonesus (Crimea) towers illustrated and discussed by J. Pečirka,[66] and by the Egyptian material quoted by Young himself.[67] But his contention that their security against attack was an accidental attribute, the design being determined by a lack of roofing timbers, appears a little far-fetched. It is only necessary to refer to the finds at Olynthus to prove that large houses could be built and roofed.[68] As for the usefulness of having a defensible place on a farm, [Dem.] 47(*Evergus*).56, in which women slaves on an Attic farm locked themselves in the tower when they were attacked, is one illustration (quoted by Young).[69] *P. Tebt.* I.47, a petition to the comarch Menches in 113 (not quoted by Young), goes further towards suggesting why a tower was useful on a farm: Pyrrhichus, a cavalry officer, and some followers had attacked the petitioner's farm while he was out in the fields, and[70] '. . . they stove in the street door, went up to the tower and cut through part of the door. When they got indoors they stove in the rest of the doors and carried off the items listed below . . .' Here it is not only the fact that the attackers made for the tower first, after gaining entry from the street, but also that, while the other doors could be 'stove in' the one to the tower had to be 'cut through', which suggests that the tower was the farm's most important secure space.

The towers were designed for protection, and in Greece many of them were built on or near the coast. A. W. Lawrence analyses how single towers were used:[71] he lists more towers than Young, balancing his list of island towers[72] with a long list of those on the mainland.[73] These towers, many of which form part of larger defensive systems with walls and other features, were intended mainly for defence against attack over land by neighbouring states.[74] But Lawrence argues that the island towers were built in a period of high pirate activity as a defence against attack from the sea.[75]

Young, however, says that island towers were not a defence against pirates. He makes some serious points which Lawrence does not answer in detail. Young's comments on the distance of some towers from landing places, their lack of view and other features which (he alleges) make them unsuitable rest on the assumption that a place which could not be reached in an attack lasting a few hours at most, would be safe. The assumption is questionable on two grounds. First, land had to be protected against settlement by *leistai* as well as against raiding. As [Dem.] 7(*Halonnesus*).3 says, 'all the *leistai* take places which do not belong to them – and they fortify these places, and from them they attack other people'. In a paper dealing with the island of Thasos, where ruins of at least 20 towers survive, A. Bon deduces (without quoting this text) where and how pirates were likely to live:[76]

> leur raid accompli, ils se réfugiaient sur leurs rochers, ou, s'ils étaient poursuivis, sur un point quelconque d'une côte déserte, où ils puissent se cacher; et de petites plages, comme celle de Hag. Ioannis à Thasos, isolées entre des caps rocheux, entourées de montagnes et de forêts, pouvaient offrir un asile sur à cet élément dangereux.

Second, *leistai* might stay in a place and raid it for some time before going away. Epichares punished 'those who brought the pirates into the country',[77] which implies that they had been harboured for a period of time, not merely that they had been shown the way to Attica. And in the first Philippic Demosthenes, proposing to send a force of 2,000 men to harry the Macedonians, and noting that Athens cannot afford a force fit to meet Philip in battle, says (as an alternative), 'but we must act as *leistai*'[78] – and by this he means that the force is to be based on Lemnos, Thasos, Sciathos and the neighbouring islands in the winter, and when the winds permit is to lie off the Macedonian coast and the harbour mouths.[79] Both episodes point to a technique of plundering the same land for as long as was feasible. Between them, they illustrate why even farms well inland could not consider themselves safe from attack.

A further point indicating the connection of the towers with defence against pirates is the date of their construction. Most of those in Thasos, Bon argues (on grounds of the quality of the building work) were built in the late fourth or early third century;[80] and the six towers in Sunium which Young discusses he dates (on the evidence of potsherds found near the tower, and partly on grounds of the building work) between the late fifth and the third centuries.[81] The fact that the building of towers was concentrated in the late Classical and early Hellenistic periods suggests that in those times a need for defences was felt by farmers living on or near the coasts of Greece.[82]

Bon's and Demosthenes' comments on how pirates settled in other people's lands have been quoted above. Further illustration of the point is available, and will afford the opportunity to draw a conclusion about what was implied by the techniques the *leistai* used in settling and raiding. A brief passage in Demosthenes 23 (*Aristocrates*) deals with the Athenian expedition to the Thracian Chersonese in 359. The army went to Alopeconnesus, a promontory extending towards Imbros, and found it full of *leistai* and *catapontistai*.[84] Here, in an area where the government was weak (at least until the army's arrival), was an ideal place for a pirate camp or enclave. It may be that the pirates had an understanding with Charidemus – certainly he came to their assistance against the Athenians,[85] and Demosthenes hints at his complicity (as distinct from his opposition to Athens at that moment, which could account for his fighting for the pirates on the particular occasion) when he says,[86] 'In writing ... that he did not let the envoys in when Alexander of Pherae sent an embassy to him, he shows up as acting just like the *leistai* he has with him.' But whatever the position of Charidemus, Alopeconnesus is clearly the sort of place referred to by the speaker of [Dem.] 7. So, probably, was Myonnesus – but the single passing reference in Aeschines to 'the reputation of Myonnesus and of the pirates' does not really allow much comment.[87]

Occupying land they had seized, and operating independently as plunderers, the *leistai*, though often treated as beyond the pale, were sometimes able to negotiate with states on a basis of (in a sense) equality when they had something to offer. A likely example is the allegation in [Dem.] 12(*Letter of Philip*).2 that the Athenians had kidnapped Philip's herald, Nicias, from Macedonian territory and kept him prisoner for ten months. No other source mentions the incident. If the Athenians were guilty of the kidnapping, in time (officially) of peace, it would of course have been natural to make that part of the accusation; but if it is assumed that *leistai* took the herald in a raid and (realising where he was of value) let the Athenians have him for a fee, then the terms of the charge against the Athenians are well accounted for.

Being settled almost like cities, and sometimes doing business with cities on almost equal terms, the *leistai* (as might be expected) began to claim treatment as legitimate states. Later literature provides specific evidence of this. The first reference is Cicero *Rep.* III.14.24. (Augustine, *Civ. Dei* IV.4, echoes the passage, and makes still more explicit the point that a state without justice is no better than a pirates' enclave.) It is a little story about a pirate captured by Alexander the Great who, 'when he was asked what criminal impulse had driven him to rampage across the sea in his one pirate boat, said, "The same one that drove you to rampage across the world"'. Even without Augustine's clarification, this would amount to a claim that both the pirate and Alexander alike acted at sea by virtue of being ruler of a sovereign state.[88]

The second reference is Lucian, *Dial. mort.* 24.1, from a dialogue in which Sostratus the *leistes*, presumably the one from Halonnesus, persuades Minos not to have him cast into Pyriphlegethon; as well as being described as *leistes* and temple robber[89] he is called a tyrant. This is surely good evidence that he made himself – or, at least, styled himself – tyrant of Halonnesus. The fact that contemporary documents, [Dem.] 12(*Letter of Philip*) and [Dem.] 7(*Halonnesus*), do not refer to such a claim does not show that it was not made. The Athenians recognised no ruler of Halonnesus but themselves; and Philip's justification for making his offer of Halonnesus as a gift rested on his having taken it from *leistai*.[90] Lucian may well have had access to sources not now extant.

These suggestions about claims to statehood arising out of the characteristic methods of Greek pirates in the fourth century give rise to further questions, concerning their relationship with the states (the cities and later the Hellenistic kingdoms) and the states' attitudes to them. As a preliminary to dealing with these questions, the next section considers the *leistai* themselves, in particular their leaders.

Leistai and their leaders

This section begins with Demetrius Poliorcetes. Not that he was a pirate chief, but because of the propaganda Seleucus directed towards Demetrius' troops in 286. Taking off his helmet, Selecus shouted,[91] 'How long will you keep on with this madness? You're staying with a hungry pirate chief when you could be on the payroll of a rich king, sharing in a kingdom which is a reality, not just a hope!' and the men deserted to his side. The interesting point is the implication that the political legitimacy of an employer of soldiers is a function of his ability to pay them. Not that it should be stressed; Seleucus had to appeal with reference to circumstances. But it will be remembered that small mercenary units with their own leaders lived by plunder (that is, not on pay provided by their leader) when they had no employer.[92] It is clear that a close similarity is detectable between what a mercenary leader would do and what a pirate chief did.[93]

The last paragraph of G. T. Griffith's chapter on the provenance and recruiting of mercenaries in the Hellenistic Age mentions as a method of mercenary recruitment the practice of employing 'for one's own ends a section of the community of pirates that abounded in the Greek seas'.[94] Griffith comments that 'piracy and mercenary service were mutually sympathetic trades', but his analysis of the activities of Charidemus and other leaders through whose connivance (Griffith's word) pirates were used as mercenaries is brief and allows some measure of improvement.

The career of Charidemus, the outstanding example of the fourth-century pirate-and-mercenary commander, is well summarised by W. K. Pritchett, who gives dates for his occupations before he was granted Athenian citizenship.[95] Between 376 and 368 (in Demosthenes' words)[96] 'he had a pirate ship and he was raiding your [*sc.* the Athenians'] allies', that is, he was a pirate captain.[97] Later (Demosthenes adds in the same section) he became the leader of a mercenary force; he rose to a position of influence as a citizen and general at Athens, as Pritchett stresses.[98] But during his rise he took the opportunity to seize Scepsis, Cebren and Ilium, three towns in the Troad.[99] Before relating this, Demosthenes has declared that mercenary commanders go round looking for cities to seize,[100] just as pirates took places – or, if as successful as Sostratus, whole islands – as a base for their operations. In fact the feature of Charidemus' career which makes it untypical is the grant of citizenship from Athens: from being outside the city-states (as there is no evidence that he ever returned to Oreos after his first service)[101] he was admitted to the greatest of them. It did not happen to any of the few other fourth-century pirate chiefs whose names are known.[102]

Besides Charidemus there are four, and two from the early years of the third century. Sostratus has been mentioned,[103] but the feature of his notoriety not yet remarked is how long it lasted. Lucian mentions him 500 years after Philip took Halonnesus from him.[104] Lucian's readers were people with a literary education; but it is worth adding that Lucian notes (with amusement) how Epictetus' pupil Arrian descended to writing the life of one Tillorobus, a bandit from Mysia and Mount Ida.[105] It may be that there was a persistent interest in biographies of bandits; certainly pirates were popular enough in fiction.[106]

Glaucetes was another pirate who seems to have managed to make himself master of an island. *Syll.*[3] 409, a decree honouring Phaedrus of Sphettus, notes as one of the achievements of the honorand's father that 'in the archonship of Praxibulus' (315/314), 'when Glaucetes had seized Cythnos and was bringing ships to land there, he took the city, and Glaucetes himself, and his ships with him, and provided safety for those sailing the sea.'[107]

The end of Aristonicus, the piratical tyrant of Methymna, was brought about by deceit rather than courage. Expecting a friendly welcome from Pharnabazus at Chios, he was admitted to the harbour and then captured for Alexander.[108]

Timocles, the arch-pirate captured by the Rhodians during the siege of Rhodes by Demetrius in 305/304,[109] can introduce the interesting subject of Demetrius' relations with the pirates. Timocles and his followers had three ships, the account of his capture notes, and they seemed to be the strongest of those campaigning on the king's side (of the *pirates*, that is). So there were several units of pirates working for Demetrius, not only because the siege of Rhodes involved operations by sea: on land in Thessaly in 302 Demetrius' army included, besides his Macedonians, his mercenaries and his levies from Greek cities,[110] 'units of light infantry and of all kinds of pirates who gather where there is war and plunder – not less than 8,000 of them.'

Here the pirates are in the lightly armed category. Similarly Charidemus was a slinger and a light infantryman after his years as a pirate captain.[111] Evidence to support Griffith's assertion that 'the mercenary's was the steadier, the pirate's the riskier but more rapid way of making a fortune' is lacking,[112] but it may well be right to think that the *leistai* represented the bottom of the mercenary market, so that Demetrius employed pirates simply in order to be able to get the largest possible number of recruits.[113] None the less, pirate chiefs could be in a position of trust: not only so as to be able to introduce an enemy into a city, as Andron did at Ephesus in 287, betraying Demetrius' general Aenetus,[114] but even (under Antigonus) so as to end up being called 'general', as Ameinias is in Plutarch's *Pyrrhus*.[115]

The change since the 340s is striking. Philip abstained from friendship with pirates for the sake of his international credibility; but in the forty years between the 340s and Demetrius' Rhodian and Thessalian campaigns the pirates had been growing stronger (so that their claim to deal with states on terms of mutual respect was likely to be heeded more often), and the successor kingdoms had been set up, in which (as is argued above)[116] the governments often liked to draw the Greek manpower they needed from outside the cities.

Privateers?

Given the intimate connection between piracy and mercenary service, and the similarity of the pirate chiefs (in so far as anything is known about them) to the leaders of the wandering armies, it may seem strange to argue, as this section will, that there was no privateering in the fourth century. The case of Timocles shows that pirates were prepared to serve in generals' maritime campaigns. In this Timocles, at the end of the century, was probably doing no more than Theopompus the Milesian had done for Lysander.[117] But 'privateering' is a word which has been applied by Ormerod to a model a good deal more complicated than that which can be derived from these two cases (Ziebarth appears to assume Ormerod's model,[118] but categories make no great difference to his conclusions): and some considerable importance is attached to a distinction between it and piracy.[119]

Ormerod's case is, briefly, that 'piracy and privateering were intimately connected, and the nomenclature in both cases almost identical' and that privateering can be distinguished mainly because 'closely allied to privateering is the system of reprisals and distraint as recognised in ancient international law'.[120]

The first example which illustrates the 'system of reprisals and distraint' is the episode, related in Demosthenes' speech against Timocrates, of the ship of Naucratis seized at sea by an Athenian naval vessel.[121] The money it was carrying had been kept by three ambassadors who were passengers in the trireme[122] although it had been declared public property by the assembly.[123] As the incident did not involve a private vessel, it is difficult to see what Ormerod means it to indicate about privateering. He seems to show only that in 355 the Athenians were prepared to regard the king's enemies as their enemies.[124] Second, he instances depredations against Attica authorised by the Spartans (and adduces Hellenistic parallels).[125]

This seems to be the nearest approach to privateering as Ormerod defines it: 'hostile action undertaken by privately owned vessels in wartime'.[126] But the third part of Ormerod's case for ancient privateering on the modern model is less easy to follow: it depends on a point of Attic law. If anyone were killed abroad,[127] his relatives might take up to three hostages from those at whose house he died, with a view to their standing trial or the murderer's being given up.[128] Ormerod takes it that the kidnappings mentioned at [Dem.] 51(*Trierarchic Crown*).13 are family reprisals of this kind, and not merely unauthorised kidnappings, with a view to ransom, by the unscrupulous trierarchs whom Demosthenes is describing. But surely there would have been little if any profit for these trierarchs (contractors who had 'hired' a trierarchy from the liturgy-payer responsible for it)[129] in helping relatives of murdered persons to seize hostages? And surely too few Athenians were murdered outside Athens for seizures of hostages to make Athens unpopular?[103] Ormerod's use of [Dem.] 51(*Trierarchic Crown*).13 is in any case thoroughly misleading, since (again) naval vessels, not privately owned ships, are involved.[131]

Further on Ormerod writes, 'the official custodian of the seas [*sc.* Athens] had issued general letters of marque during the Social war, with a view to destroying enemy commerce'.[132] This is based on the scholiast in Demosthenes 21(*Meidias*).173 (=570.15): 'the Athenians in the Social war voted to raid those of the enemy who were sailing the sea even if they were merchants'. The scholiast goes on to explain that it was on this pretext that Meidias had seized more than five talents from the Cyzicenes, who came to Athens and vainly protested friendship towards the city. But this does not amount to an issue of 'letters of marque'. Meidias was a servant of the Athenian state – the treasurer of the state trireme *Paralus* – when the alleged seizure was made.[133] There is no suggestion that the Athenians envisaged their decree being carried out other than by the navy.[134]

The Spartan authorisations of raids on Attica are not by themselves sufficient to support Ormerod's idea of privateering on the modern model. It seems fairer to interpret them as a rather more obviously open encouragement to piracy than the harbour facilities allowed to pirates from time to time at Thasos, Chios and Syracuse (for example).[135] States wishing to help the *leistai* and benefit from their activities had the option of giving passive support in this way, or hiring pirates as mercenaries. Once hired, they were not at liberty to plunder the enemy as they thought fit: they were part of an army.[136]

The pirate chief was in a simpler position than either Griffith or Ormerod allows. Making his followers mercenaries did not involve 'connivance':[137] it was part of his normal function as chief. If they were without an employer, they lived by raiding: some cities allowed them into port, some did not, and others tried to suppress them. In the absence of the relationship expressed by letters of marque, the next section examines the dealings of *leistai* with Greek communities.

Trade and piracy

As Ziebarth remarked, trade and piracy were closely connected. He writes, not perhaps without some obscurity, of seaborne trade '... in seinem Verhältnis mit Seeraub, d. h. in seiner Abhängigkeit vom Seeraub ...'.[138] This cannot refer only to the fact that evidence of piracy is indirect evidence for trading activity (a point he makes elsewhere),[139] nor yet can it be taken as implying that the pirates were strong enough for transport by sea to depend on their goodwill. (Ziebarth notes that trade grew *in spite* of piracy;[140] and that there were times, especially after the end of the fourth century, when the pirates were very strong indeed.)[141] It seems fair to suggest that part at least of what Ziebarth had in mind was the role pirates had in trade: trade involving the Greek cities.

Pirates were involved in the slave trade. Explicit statements are not common in the sources relating to the fourth century, but traffic in slaves must have been an easy extension of the normal piratical activity of seizing people and holding them to ransom. Besides selling free people as slaves, pirates must have had a good chance of taking some slaves along with the ransomable victims in any successful raid. The place attacked by pirates in a third-century attack on Thera was full of women, children and slaves.[142] And, to turn to fiction, in the prologue of Menander's *Sicyonius* a young girl and her maid,[143] both captured by pirates, are bought in the slave market at Mylasa by 'a thoroughly decent and wealthy officer' – the Sicyonian of the title.[144] M. M. Austin comments on the passage, 'though fictitious, this prologue from Menander's most recently discovered play shows how completely piracy and the slave trade were taken for granted as a reality of everyday life in the later fourth and early third centuries'.[145]

Menander's story in the *Sicyonius* has a heterosexual theme. A fourth-century Cyrenean inscription (a difficult text) appears to record the damages recovered, by a Cyrenean embassy to several Peloponnesian (mostly Arcadian) cities, in consideration of (probably) moral offences committed against Cyrenean males on some occasion by men from the cities mentioned.[146] If this interpretation of the text (P. M. Fraser's) is right, then it would seem likely that a group of Peloponnesians from different cities had carried out a homosexual kidnapping raid on Cyrenean territory. The cities seem to have been willing to help the Cyreneans recover damages,[147] so although the circumstances of the events (which may have happened in the 360s[148]) are highly obscure, it would seem that the perpetrators organised themselves privately (without city backing) to carry out the raid.

Granted, though, that some trade in slaves was carried on by some pirates, it is still a question how much of the slave trade was in the hands of *leistai*. W. W. Tarn was not in doubt. 'The pirate,' he writes, 'had a most useful place in the economy of the old world; he was the general slave merchant.'[149] Strabo, though (writing about a later era than that discussed by Tarn), draws a distinction between those who were normally pirates and those who traded in slaves. During the boom in slave trading after the destruction of Carthage and Corinth, pirates found it easy to trade in slaves at Delos, and Strabo comments,[150] 'and at the same time *leistai* pretending to be slave traders could not be stopped from carrying on their evil practices'. Making the same point, M. I. Finley argues that piracy

> ... was not the basic way in which slaves were procured (and especially not during the long periods when one major power or another succeeded in reducing such activity to very small proportions): second, that even when it was most active piracy could not have been a complete explanation.

He adds that pirates, when they did not exact a ransom for their captives, 'turned them over to professional traders'.[151]

This illustrates an aspect of the *Abhängigkeit* of trade on piracy for which Ziebarth argued.[152] The pirates were a source of supply. Two (or perhaps three) Attic decrees may offer a little more information on the fourth-century slave trade. They honour persons who had ransomed Athenians and sent them home, and are most easily understood if it is assumed that the benefactors had found the Athenians for sale in slave markets: *Syll.*³ 263, honouring Cleomis of Methymna (*c.* 336/335) says (lines 10–13), '... and since he ransomed the people captured by the *leistai*, and he does any good he can to the Athenian people ...'. Although this is not explicit enough to *show* that the captives had been offered for sale in Methymna (though the word 'ransomed' cannot, on the contrary, be taken to imply that the captives were *not* in a slave market: it is inconceivable that the Athenians should have used a word meaning 'bought' in the case of free citizens), it is on the whole unlikely that pirates would have contacted Cleomis and asked him to ransom Athenians, or that Cleomis would have heard by chance that Athenians were being held to ransom by the pirates his regime had evidently not eradicated.

The second decree is *IG* II² 399 (320–319?), which reads (lines 17–19), '... and he was responsible for rescuing them from [the enemies] and bringing them to their own country ...'. Here L. Moretti's suggestion that [the pirates] or [the *leistai*] might be restored is clearly a sensible one.[153] Moretti prefers to think that the Athenians were captured in one or other of the naval battles of the Lamian war,[154] but since they are not mentioned 'serving as soldiers' (a description applied to the Athenians saved by one '—phanes' in the contemporary decree *IG* II² 398 – both were proposed by Demades) it seems better to follow Moretti's alternative explanation, that they were seized by pirates and taken to Crete.[155] In which case the honorand in *IG* II² 399, Eurylochus of Cydonia, probably found the Athenians for sale at Cydonia, paid for them and sent them home.

IG II² 283 may be a third decree of this sort. It honours a man who ransomed Athenians from Sicily and sent them home. But caution is necessary, for two reasons: first because *leistai* are not mentioned in the decree, and then because of Sicily. The fourth-century lettering may perhaps disguise a (republished) text from after Athens' Sicilian expedition.[156] If the decree is from the fourth century, then capture by pirates would seem a plausible explanation of Athenians being ransomed from Sicily.

The explanation that the ransomers found the citizens on the market as slaves – a very plausible explanation at least of the situation outlined in the first two of these decrees – bears out the impression gained from the *Sicyonius* that it was far from unheard-of for free people to be sold as slaves in Greek cities after being captured by *leistai*. That there was no generally applied sanction against selling free Greeks as slaves in Greek slave markets is illustrated by the story of Plato's treatment at the hands of the Spartan admiral Pollis, to whom Dionysius I had handed him over. When Pollis put Plato up for sale in Aegina the Aeginetans, far from rescuing him, almost decided to put him to death – and in the end sold him themselves (D.L.III. 18–20). Though not captured by pirates he was bought and freed by a well-wisher. The Strabo passage cited above suggests that in the case of people captured by pirates middlemen would usually be involved.[157] In the fourth century this fundamental commercial contact between the *leistai* on the outside, and the world of the city, was probably, therefore, indirect most of the time.

Other points of contact between piracy and the cities

Trade (direct or indirect) in slaves was not the only form of contact or basis of relationship between the cities and the *leistai*. Things were more complicated. In a country where communications and trade were largely waterborne, the thing which most affected the *leistai* in their relations with the cities was the extent to which either party had control of the sea. Though, as argued above, raids on coastal regions were the pirates' principal means of acquisition,[158] it would be perverse not to recognise that from the end of the Peloponnesian war seafarers had feared the pirates.[159] Twenty or so years before Isocrates wrote the *Panegyricus*, the speaker against Diogeiton had said of his adversary,[160] 'There's no way he can show that he's been ruined by pirates or been fined or given it away to borrowers ...', listing piracy first among three ways of being parted from one's money. The fall of Athenian naval power must have increased the perennial risk of loss to pirates. Sparta, Ormerod points out,[161] had not Athens' reasons for wanting the sea clear (not that there were no pirates before 404: Theopompus the Milesian, for example, was already a *leistes* when Lysander sent him to Sparta with the news of Aegospotami);[162] and there were states which, it must be concluded, at least winked at the activities of *leistai* who were closely connected with the city community. Lycon of Heraclea, leaving Athens by sea, was caught almost at once by pirates, shot down, and later died *in Argos*.[163] Though this happened some time before the death in 370 of the banker Pasion, it is likely that the Second Athenian Confederacy had been founded (the Argives were not in it) before the incident happened.[164]

Concurrent with the growth in piratical activity which seems to have occurred in the course of the century was a growth in piracy by states: not the bringing of ships to land in time of famine (examined below)[165] but the archaic practice as undertaken by Polycrates of Samos, whose 100 penteconters and 1,000 bowmen 'pillaged everyone without exception' (Polycrates expected to get more thanks from a friend for giving back what he had taken than by not taking it in the first place).[166] The third-century blossoming of piracy was in some measure a renascence of politics of this kind: the Aetolians and Cretans made terms with island cities promising not to rob them.[167] And fourth-century precedents for incorporation of *leisteia* into the communal economy are not lacking, even when wartime pillage is excluded. Aristotle mentions it in the *Politics* quite casually as a form of income, in a section on money-making (*chrematistike*)[168] but, more significantly, a few important persons (from non-city-state parts of Hellas) are called *leistai*, or emerge as *leistai*, in the sources. They are not stateless persons (the main subject of this study), but their treatment in the sources makes clear their similarities to the pirate chiefs discussed above.[169]

Alexander of Pherae is the target of a vigorous piece of Xenophontic rhetoric:[170] 'he was a hard *tagus* to the Thessalians, a hard enemy to the Thebans and Athenians, and an unjust *leistes* both on land and sea'. *Tagus*, enemy, robber; of his own people, other peoples, all peoples. Polemic of this quality would be wasted on someone who was merely a nuisance. But Alexander's piratical exploits were notorious. Not the least of them was his raid on the Peiraeus, when his men seized coin from the bankers' tables.[171] Where Jason had schemed to get the family money,[172] Alexander used more direct means: he illustrates the collapse of what Jason had built up before being assassinated – which is the general purpose of this passage of the *Hellenica*.[173] *Leisteia* typifies Thessaly's retreat from good order, as it were.

Some courtiers of Philip II of Macedon were *leistai*. Demosthenes says so in *Olynthiac* II: '. . . and the rest of his followers are *leistai* and flatterers and the sort of men who would get drunk and dance dances of a kind which I forbear to mention to you now.'[174] ('The rest' are all the people at court: anyone decent, Demosthenes has said, is driven away). This blast of rhetoric might be set aside, or put down only as evidence of drunken feasting in Pella, but for the passage in Aeschines' *Embassy* speech dealing with Phrynon of Rhamnus.[175] After Euboean ambassadors had told the Athenians in 348 that Philip wanted to come to terms with them:[176]

> Phrynon of Rhamnus was captured by *leistai* during the Olympic truce (according to the accusation he himself made); and when he was ransomed and got back here, he asked you to choose an envoy to Philip on his behalf, so that, if there was any way he could, he might get the ransom money back.

The Athenians chose Ctesiphon, who was kindly received (the next section says), but the part of his report back which Aeschines recalls concerns the peace and not the ransom. If Philip had exacted the ransom in the first place, he would hardly have relented and paid it back. But Philip found piety in general the best policy,[177] which is presumably why the Athenians could have entertained some hope that he would be persuaded to make himself responsible for reimbursing what a subject of his had taken. As for whether Phrynon's captor was a courtier of Philip,[178] no more can be said than that it is likely: to complain of a crime Philip could not be aware of would be no better than complaining of one he was known to have committed himself. This, in the context of the accusation in Demosthenes, leads to the explanation that Philip was to be persuaded to repay the money to Ctesiphon, and take an equivalent from the impious *leistes*.

In the fourth century Alexander of Pherae and Philip's Macedonians, in the third century the Aetolians and the Cretans treated *leisteia* as a legitimate form of moneymaking. The divide was between south Greece, the Greece of the city-states, and the more backward areas. It was a question of communities not so much

copying the pirates as resuming a way of life which had been interrupted by the power of south Greece, and especially the power of
Athens, in the fifth and earlier fourth centuries. The taboo against
leisteia was affirmed by Philip himself – if his dealings over Phrynon
did not show it, his complaint against the Athenians for not acting
when the Thasians received 'the triremes of the Byzantines, and those
of the *leistai* who wished' would leave no doubt.[179] The Athenians did
fine the Melians for receiving pirates – ten talents[180] – and elsewhere
took energetic measures against piracy, as the next section will show;
but the cities and the rulers who espoused city-state values had more
than the superficial contacts of trade and harbouring to combat.
They were against an older and less humane view of what statehood
was. The Spartans had social concord, conceded Isocrates on an
occasion when he was disinclined to take their part, but no one
would praise them for it, any more than anyone would praise for it[181]
'the wreckers and *leistai* and those who engage in other crimes ...'.
This is a recognition that there were associations possessing some
attributes of statehood (social concord) but not others. With the
story of Alexander and the pirate,[182] it shows up the contact between
community and piracy which still existed in the life of the outlying
areas of Hellas in the fourth century and beyond.

Defence against the raiders

If the growth of piracy in the later fourth century was aided by the
weakness of the cities it also contributed to that weakness. Before the
Athenian navy was devastated at Amorgos in 322, piracy had grown
into a very widespread phenomenon, able to survive Alexander's
attempt to reduce it;[183] which explains the urgency of the moral
obligation assumed by leading maritime states, and referred to by
states which were far from fulfilling it,[184] to act against the pirates.

Action against pirates was part of the *phulake* undertaken by
Athens. Commenting on *IG* I[2] 18, line 4, D. M. Lewis notes of this
word that 'its basic meaning is abstract, something like "watch",
"defence", or frequently "blockade" ... this is the only meaning it has
in inscriptions'.[185] The word is used in a naval context as early as
Herodotus,[186] and at Thucydides VII.17.2–4 it is used in connection
with a squadron of 20 ships put at Naupactus by the Athenians in
414/413 to prevent communication between the Peloponnese and
Sicily – again in the abstract: the squadron is not *called* a *phulake*,
but it is noted (section 4) that it had to direct its *phulake* against the
Corinthian counter-force of 20 ships.

In the fourth century the Athenian founders of Adria made a
detailed and positive statement of what they expected to achieve in

respect of the piracy prevalent at the time:[187]

> that the people may have, for all time, its own trade route and corn supply, and that by the establishment of this naval station there may be *phulake* against the Etruscans, and that Miltiades the founder and the settlers may be able to use their own fleet, and that both Greek and non-Greek seafarers may safely berth at Adria, the Athenians' harbour, enjoying safe possession of their ships and other goods, knowing that . . . [lacuna].

The *phulake* against the Etruscans is naval defence: it needs a secure harbour (lines 220–1), and it is directed towards the security of trade and corn imports (lines 219–20) as well as safe use of Adria by Greek and foreign ships (lines 226–33). In fact, from the viewpoint of the Athenian assembly that made the decree, the colonists seem not to be the main intended beneficiaries. The colony was to maintain (in the mid-320s) the Athenian *phulake* against piracy and so secure safe shipping.

This *phulake* was also defence of the territory of Attica: *phulake* of the land. The same decree, after further provisions about the colony at Adria, adds (lines 270–1), 'these provisions shall all be for the *phulake* of the land' (*sc.* of Attica). The uses of the phrase 'defence of the land' (*phulake tes choras*) have been examined by P. J. Rhodes, who remarks how it and the phrase 'safety of the city' figured in Athenian political deliberation and decisions.[188] Rhodes assumes no important distinction between *phulake* and '*phulake* of the land' when he uses Demosthenes 18(*Crown*).248 to establish the connection between the two phrases in political usage: *phulake* appears without the qualifying phrase in this passage.

The connection between *phulake* of the land and the *phulake* against pirates being established in *IG* II² 1629, two other texts can be interpreted in this context. First, *IG* II² 1623, lines 276–82 (between 335/334 and 331/330), speaks of two ships sent out for *phulake* against the *leistai*, confirming the evidence of *IG* II² 1629 to the effect that pirates were part of the threat against which *phulake* was maintained. Second, even more explicitly, in [Dem.] 7(*Halonnesus*).14 the speaker tells the assembled Athenians that if Philip's cession of Halonnesus as a gift is accepted, it will be an admission that '. . . without Philip you are not even able to maintain the *phulake* on the sea'. This was the *phulake* to which the trader honoured in *IG* II² 283, who ransomed Athenians from Sicily, contributed silver.[189] And with good reason: with trading interests at both ends of the Mediterranean (he had sent the Athenians corn from Egypt as well as ransoming the citizens from Sicily),[190] it was clearly in his interest to encourage anyone who was combating the pirates. Rhodes records other instances of contributions to the *phulake/phulake* of the land.[191]

These phrases and ideas are not confined to Attic sources. The phrase *'phulake* of the land'* appears in a third-century decree from Teos (not available to Rhodes, since it was not published until 1976);[192] in an oath to be taken by the inhabitants of Cyrbissus there occurs the clause (lines 51–2): 'and I will do whatever the garrison commander orders, where the *phulake* of the fort or of the land is concerned'. An earlier oath to be taken by citizens of Teos contains the clause (lines 12–14): 'I will elect as garrison commander for Cyrbissus the person who seems to me likely to take care in the best and fairest way of the *phulake* of the fort and to guard the fort safely for the city.' So that a particular and general element can be identified in the inhabitants' oath – the general element concerning *phulake* of the land. In the first years of the third century the Delians borrowed 5,000 drachmas from Apollo for *phulake* against the Etruscans.[193] Since the battle of Amorgos there had been no Athenian fleet to keep the seas safe: probably this was the Delian substitute for the systematic watch the Athenians had maintained.

But even before Amorgos others besides Athens took on themselves the responsibility of acting against the pirates. In the west, Dionysius I had initiated a movement to settle the Adriatic so as to make the Ionian sea, the route from south Italy to Greece, safe – though, according to Diodorus, his object was to make the sea safe for his own raiding on Epirus and (much worse) Delphi itself.[194] His son, Dionysius II, founded two cities in Apulia at the beginning of the 350s to make that same Ionian sea safe from the barbarians living on the sea coast, who were making the Adriatic impassable with their pirate ships.[195]

In the Aegean Philip II, though probably spurred on by the trouble *leistai* were causing Macedonia, made his policing of the sea a propaganda point. Such is the implication of the dispute 'over syllables', whether or not it is accepted that [Dem.] 12(*Letter of Philip*).12–15 represents Philip's own view of the matter:[196] Philip was drawing attention to himself as the liberator of an island from *leistai*. And his son Alexander made an effort to follow the same path of self-definition. The operations at sea he delegated to Amphoterus, with a grandiose commission 'above all, to rid the sea of piratic fleets'.[197] The style of Alexander's order is as important, for the purpose of understanding his stance on the *leistai*, as how effectively it was carried out. It amounts to a claim (and the incident with the pirate chief bears this out)[198] to a legal, quasi-constitutional guardianship of the sea: to an assertion that Macedon had assumed, as well as hegemony on land, the leading role of Athens at sea.

But his death and Athens' irreparable defeat at Amorgos left that role unfilled. The state which tried to take it up between 322 and 305 was Rhodes – and with some success.[199] 'Rhodes . . . reached such a level of power that she resumed the war against the pirates on her own, on behalf of the Greeks, and made the sea clear of evildoers.' The 'war against the pirates' is treated here as a continuous factor in the life of Greece – the Rhodians 'resumed' it, and 'on her own' suggests that the undertaking afforded the Rhodians some prestige.

In the context of this keenly felt moral obligation for leading states, or states which claimed to be such, to clear the sea of pirates, it is possible to understand the passage in Strabo which notes how Alexander, and later Demetrius Poliorcetes, complained to the Romans about the piratical activities of the men of Antium.[200] Modern writers are divided on whether to believe the story. Tarn doubts, on the ground that[201] 'Rome in 290 could not be said *strategein tes Italias*; and in 337 she had captured Antium, burnt its ships and forbidden its people the sea'. (Note, though, that the Greek phrase he quotes is from Demetrius' polite message to Rome: there may be a case for treating it as flattery.) H. Berve is confident enough to use the story to confirm other alleged dealings between Alexander and Italy.[202] Ormerod says that the story about Alexander 'may be apocryphal' but finds no reason to reject the corresponding story about Demetrius.[203] A *prima facie* reason for scepticism about Strabo's account is his mention (as part of Demetrius' message) of the Romans' 'kinship with the Greeks' – a commonplace of later literature, but surely unimagined in the early third century. But this seems more like a little elaboration than the point of the whole thing; exhortations from one leading state to another to take part in the 'war against the pirates', on the other hand, can easily be believed in, given that the Greeks expected a leading state to work for the safety of the seas.

Discussing the suppression of piracy, Tarn concludes that 'it was only small states like Rhodes, subsisting entirely on sea-borne corn, that felt any real interest in clearing the seas', and one of his main arguments is that 'the governments could have put them down; but all the governments had their hands pretty full, and it suited them better to wink at the evil'.[204] This section has shown that the conclusion requires some amendment, at any rate for the fourth century (and Tarn is not on this occasion considering only the third); it may be that the premise too ought to be modified. All through the fourth century, piracy grew; and all through the fourth century the states with the large navies fought it. It must be inferred that in general the measures they took were ineffective.

This is not to say that some times were not better than others. The

Second Athenian Confederacy may well have made some difference. Referring to the capture and death of Lycon of Heraclea,[205] Ormerod notes that[206] 'this event took place soon after the year 378–377 BC, when there are already signs of an improvement in the Aegean'. 'There is comparative silence as to the existence of piracy on a large scale during the early years of the second Athenian Confederacy.' This has to be qualified in a footnote remarking that Charidemus' early exploits took place in these years,[207] but the very fact that the allies worked together with Athens in guarding the seas should have made a difference.[208] The years from 338 to 322, by contrast, seem to have been difficult: the first of the Attic decrees honouring ransomers of captives taken by *leistai* come from that period,[209] and the foundation of Adria against the Tyrrhenians dates from the mid-320s.[210] It can be doubted whether Alexander's effort against the pirates was as successful as Ziebarth suggests;[211] his undoubtedly 'serious attempt ... to reduce piracy'[212] must have been much diminished in effectiveness by the scale of the phenomenon and the shortness of his reign.[213]

The conclusion is that the reason for the ineffectiveness of action against piracy throughout the century was not lack of eagerness to protect shipping, nor any lack of resources in absolute terms (since the navies of Athens, Alexander and Rhodes were, each in its time, the strongest the Greek world possessed in the fourth century), but simply that the pirates were too strong, or at least too pervasive. The states captured and punished many, but others took their place. The *fact* that the pirate ships were kept filled (though the explanation Aeschines offers for it may be set aside)[214] was what defeated attempts to control the *leistai* outside the city-states.

Related matters

This last section deals with two matters related to Greek *leistai*: the Tyrrhenian *leistai*, and the bringing of ships to land by maritime cities.

When the Etruscans ventured into the eastern Mediterranean they had not the same local ties as the Greek *leistai*. Booty they seized went right out of the Greek world. It was no use attacking their enclaves (as Halonnesus, Alopeconnesus and Cythnos could be attacked), because these were in Italy (and in many cases, as that of Antium, may have been regular communities, using piracy as a form of production in the way which was not extinct in the backward parts of Greece).[215] These considerations explain the foundation of Adria:[216] it was an adaptation of normal naval techniques for dealing with piracy, founded when they proved insufficient. The Tyrrhenians must have seized a large amount of booty over a fair length of time (years at least; not inconceivably decades) before the Athenians determined to found a colony against them in the west.

And yet the decree establishing Adria is the first fourth-century reference to Etruscans as pirates, except D.S. XVI.82.3, which refers only to Sicilian waters.[217] Doubtless, too, Ziebarth is right in noting that conditions in east Greece made contact with the Adriatic increasingly important for Athens at this period. As he and Ormerod say, Deinarchus' lost *Tyrrhenicus* and Hypereides' lost speech 'on the *phulake* against the Tyrrhenians' must fit in here.[218]

Tyrrhenian pirates had been passing the straits of Messina as early as the beginning of the fifth century, until Anaxilaus, tyrant of Rhegium (494–476), equipped a harbour and denied them passage.[219] Dionysius I in the 380s had an Adriatic policy (which, A. G. Woodhead argues, amounted in practice to nothing more than occupying Lissus with a Syracusan naval squadron for a few years in the mid-380s);[220] the existence of pirates in the Adriatic may have been the problem to which it was a response.[221] There were also Greeks raiding Italy – at any rate when Camillus fought them off by denying them the chance of landing in the early 340s.[222] After Dionysius, as D.S. XVI.82.3 shows, Postumius, who had twelve pirate ships, landed at Syracuse expecting to be treated as a friend. Timoleon, more or less fresh from the victory at the river Crimisus, put him to death. *IG* XI (2) 148, from Delos, provides in the very first years of the third century for a *phulake* against the Etruscans; and there are a few scattered items associating the trumpet with raiders, and so with Etruscans, which go back to Menander.[223] If these show anything, they show that *leistes* was an idea which could readily be substituted for 'Tyrrhenian' in the mind of Menander's audience, and this is confirmed by the Rhodian inscription *Syll.*[3] 1225. Three sons of one Timacrates, all Rhodian officers, are commemorated. They were killed in separate engagements, two against *leistai*, the other against Tyrrhenians.[224] As the engagements occurred at or about the same time,[225] it seems clear that for the Rhodian navy the problems of raiders and Tyrrhenians were at least closely related.

Another phenomenon parallel to the activities of the Greek *leistai* was the practice Greek cities had of hijacking each other's food. G. E. M. de Ste Croix argues that 'any city which was itself suffering from a corn shortage had a tacitly recognised right to *katagein* ("bring to land") corn ships passing near by' and that 'such an action would not necessarily be regarded as an act of war against the city to which the ships were sailing'.[226] He has collected the *testimonia* relating to the practice.[227] The case is perhaps overstated where 'right' is mentioned: at the foundation of the League of Corinth it was provided that all the parties should sail the sea, and that no one should prevent them or hijack (*katagein*) a ship belonging to any of them; whoever acted otherwise would be the enemy of all the parties to the peace.[228] If the right to sail the sea unmolested is guaranteed, then any 'right' of maritime cities to relieve their famine by forcing ships to land is implicitly denied. But certainly there is a *de facto* recognition in the sources that communities would (in conditions of necessity) rob persons trading with other communities with which they wished to remain at peace.

To illustrate how close the parallel with piracy is, it is necessary only to consider two instances. In the late 360s the Athenians took action to prevent the Byzantines, Chalcedonians and Cyzicenes from seizing cargoes of corn bound for Athens;[229] and in 315/314, under Thymochares of Sphettus, they attacked Cythnos and took the city[230] because Glaucetes had established himself there and was bringing ships to land.[231] Ormerod speculates that he may have been acting in the interest of Antigonus I.[232] Be that as it may, Glaucetes was certainly (in Athenian eyes) a pirate rather than a garrison commander. Bringing ships to land was not a practice exclusive to legitimate states.

But the fact that foreigners and Greek communities both from time to time acted like the Greek *leistai* does not pose a serious problem of definition. The *Halonnesus* speech pointed out the cardinal characteristic of the *leistai*:[233] 'all the *leistai* take places which do not belong to them – and they fortify those places, and from them they attack other people'. As homeless people they made themselves a place in the Greek world, and provoked opposition, fear[234] and perhaps some admiration (as Tarn says, 'probably "Arch-pirate" was a very honourable appellation'[235]). That is to say, they were viewed in terms analogous to those in which the mercenaries, employed and unemployed, were viewed.[236]

Notes

1 Above, pp. 91–3.
2 Thucydides I.5.1.
3 Thucydides I.4.
4 Thucydides I.7.
5 Thucydides II.32.
6 Thucydides IV.53.2–3.
7 Thucydides IV.54.4.
8 Thucydides V.14.3.
9 Thucydides IV.55.1.
10 Thucydides VII.26.2.
11 Thucydides VI.41.2; V.56.3.

12 Thucydides IV.66.1.
13 Thucydides IV.75.1. B. R. MacDonald, 'ΛΗΙΣΤΕΙΑ and
   ΛΗΙΖΟΜΑΙ in Thucydides and in *IG* I³ 41, 67 and 75', *AJP* 105
   (1984), pp. 77–84, surveys the use in the Peloponnesian war of the
   technique of establishing groups to carry out guerilla warfare against
   enemy communities (pp. 77–9) and shows how the Athenians took
   precautions in some peace settlements to avoid their own interests
   being damaged by guerrilla warfare of this sort (pp. 80–2).
14 Thucydides VI.4.5.
15 Herodotus VI.17.
16 Thucydides I.24.5.
17 Thucydides I.5.2.
18 Thucydides VI.104.3.
19 Thucydides III.51.5.
20 Thucydides II.69.1.
21 Nepos, *Themistocles* 2.3; Plutarch, *Cimon* 8.3.
22 Thucydides I.4.
23 Thucydides I.13.5.
24 *Thucydides Mythistoricus* (London, 1907), p. 93.
25 H. A. Ormerod, *Piracy in the Ancient World* (Liverpool, 1924), p. 114;
   E. Ziebarth, *Beiträge zur Geschichte des Seeraubs und Seehandels im
   alten Griechenland* (Hamburg, 1929), p. 13. Ziebarth deduces that
   Agesilaus had good relations with the pirates. ('Agesilaos lässt sie
   unter Heroldsruf verkaufen, muss also zu den Seeräubern gute
   Beziehungen gehabt haben', 'Agesilaus had them sold at auction, so he
   must have had good relations with the pirates'.)
26. Cf. ML 95 (e) and (f). D. Lotze, *Lysander und der peloponnnesische
   Krieg* (Berlin, 1964), p. 37 n. 6, refers to this suggestion of E.
   Cavaignac, 'Les dékarchies de Lysandre', *REH* 90 (1924), pp. 285–
   316, at p. 293, and comments, 'aber die Namengleichheit kann
   natürlich auch Zufall sein', 'of course, the similarity of the names may
   be accidental'.
27 Ormerod, *Piracy*, p. 13.
28 Ormerod, *Piracy*, p. 14: 'if we remember that piracy was for centuries
   a normal feature of Mediterranean life, it will be realised how great
   has been the influence which it exercised on the ancient world'.
29 Ziebarth, *Beiträge*, p. 1: 'but where the history of trade is unavailable
   for the early period, the fact that piracy was flourishing is evidence for
   sea transport and trade'; 'this essay will principally concern, for the
   period for which there is historical evidence, Greek seaborne trade in
   its connection with piracy – that is, in its dependence on piracy. It will
   offer a part of the history of Greek trade along with the history of
   piracy.'
30 Isocrates, *Panegyricus* 115.
31 Cf. below, pp. 122–6.
32 Xenophon, *Hell.* 2.11. Cf., for the fifth century, the Samians who were
   at Anaea on the Asian coast south of Ephesus and opposite Samos.
   They opposed Athens (Thucydides III.19.2), negotiated with the

Peloponnesians (Thucydides III.32.2) and caused trouble to the
Samians at home (Thucydides IV.75.1).
33 Polyaenus II.30.1.
34 Polyaenus IV.6.6.
35 See below, pp. 112–15.
36 Anonymous review of Ormerod, *Piracy, JHS* 45 (1925), p. 149.
37 E.g. Xenophon, *Anab.* VI.1.16–VII.8.24.
38 See, for example, Demosthenes 23 (*Aristocrates*).139; Isocrates,
    Philippus 120 and 122; Polyaenus II.30.1; D.S. XVII.111.1.
39 *Suda*, s.v. *leistai.*
40 I owe this point to the anonymous judge of the 1982 Oxford
    University Ancient History Prize Competition.
41 Ormerod, *Piracy*, pp. 30–1; his single citation, Josephus, *Bell. Jud.*
    III.9.2, is far from sufficient to establish the general point.
42 Y. Garlan, 'Signification historique de la piraterie grecque', *DHA* 4
    (1978), pp. 1–16; quoted from p. 2: 'to isolate piracy (on the sea) from
    brigandage (on land) is to break up the unity of a single historical
    phenomenon'.
43 [Dem.] 12(*Letter of Philip*).5.
44 Demosthenes 19(*Embassy*).315.
45 Demosthenes 18(*Crown*).145.
46 Demosthenes 18(*Crown*).230 and 241. Tod II 154, directing the
    Athenian council to submit to the assembly a proposal to the effect
    that no Athenian nor any other is to harm any of the allies, 'whether
    setting out from Attica or from any place in the allied cities' (lines 4–
    5), and in particular providing for the punishment of 'those who
    campaigned against the land of the Eretrians' (lines 6–7), seems to
    have the aim of suppressing *leisteia* based in Attica and directed
    against Euboea. Assuming that Dittenberger was right to connect this
    text with Tod II 153 (see Tod II, p. 163), it dealt with 357/356.
47 Ziebarth, *Beiträge*, p. 17 ('Kaperkrieg'); Ormerod, *Piracy*, p. 117 ('both
    sides resorted to energetic forms of privateering').
48 See below, pp. 115–17.
49 See below, pp. 122–6.
50 See earlier in this section, with nn. 43–5.
51 [Dem.] 12(*Letter of Philip*).13.
52 [Dem.] 12(*Letter of Philip*).2. It is necessary to say something about
    the value of the *Letter of Philip* as evidence. P. Wendland argues on
    the ground of Didymus, *In Dem.* 11.7, that it, together with [Dem.] 11
    Reply to the Letter of Philip, is excerpted from Anaximenes: and
    shows by referring to Demosthenes 11.1, 17 and 20, sections which
    refer to the message from Philip (e.g. section 17: Philip 'dared to send
    the sort of letters you heard a little while ago'), that the two pieces as
    they now stand in the Demosthenic corpus belong together. (P.
    Wendland, *Anaximenes von Lampsakos*, Berlin, 1905, p. 13.) It may
    none the less be right to suggest, with A. W. Pickard-Cambridge, that
    the *Letter* 'accurately represents Philip's view' when it deals with 'the
    acts of hostility which the Athenians had committed against him since

346' (*Demosthenes and the Last Days of Greek Freedom*, New York and London, 1914, p. 356 n. 6 and p. 350); it is certainly plausibly phrased, in view of the public commitment made by Athens to suppress piracy (cf. below, pp. 122–4) since it represents Philip as saying about Halonnesus (section 13), 'in fact I didn't take the island from them [*sc.* the Peparathians] or from you, but from Sostratus the *leistes*. If you admit that you gave it to Sostratus, you're admitting sending out *leistai*. If he got control of it against your will, then what damage have you suffered as a result of taking the place and making it safe for seafarers?' This is exactly the sort of thing an aggrieved Philip would have said after Athens had administered the snub advised in [Dem.] 7(*Halonnesus*). It would be surprising if he had not communicated something on these lines to the Athenians. So, though the *Letter* almost certainly did not come as it stands from the pen of Philip II, it can be treated as evidence for events and Macedonian interpretations of events after 346.

53 Philochorus, *FGrHist* 328 F 162 (=Didymus, *In Dem.* 11.1, col. 10.45–col. 11.5).

54 Didymus, *In Dem.* 11.1, col. 10.35–40.

55 The argument of this section should not be thought to imply that raiding shipping was unimportant to *leistai*: the point is to put it in perspective.

56 Aeschines 2(*Embassy*).12–13.

57 Cf. below, pp. 122–6.

58 426: Thucydides III.99; 415: Thucydides VI.45; 413: Thucydides VII.48.5. For an example earlier in the fifth century, cf. ML 30 B, lines 11–23: in this part of a list of public imprecations from Teos, betrayal of the city and land of the Teians (12–14), or of the men (14–15), or of 'the Peripolion in Aroia' (16–17) is mentioned, and being or receiving brigands (*kixallai*) or pirates (*leistai*) is the next item on the list of prohibitions. In the circumstances, it seems more natural to treat the *peripolion* as a coastal guard-post than as a suburb (contrast ML, p. 65), especially since it is mentioned separately from the city and land. W. Dittenberger argues for the derivation of *peripolion* from *peripolos* (a guard) and not from *peri* plus *polis* (whereas *proasteion* is from *pro* plus *astu*) at *Syll.*³ 570 n. 2.

59 Halasarna: *Syll.*³ 568 and 569; Carpathus: *Syll.*³ 570.

60 The inscription: B. Ch. Petrakos, 'Νέαι πηγαὶ περὶ τοῦ Χρεμωνιδείου πολέμου', *Arch. Delt.* 22 (1967), pp. 38–52; later in H. Heinen, *Untersuchung zur hellenistischen Geschichte des 3. Jahrhunderts v. Chr.* (Wiesbaden, 1972), pp. 152–9. English translation in C. Austin, *Comicorum Graecorum fragmenta in papyris reperta* (Berlin and New York, 1973), pp. 97–8 (=section 50). See lines 5–23. Routine preparations against pirates appear to be attested in *SEG* XXVI.1306, where detailed provisions are made for a permanent guard at Cyrbissus (near Teos) to be commanded by an elected magistrate (lines 8–11) who is to have at least 20 citizens as guards and three dogs (lines 18–20). Consciousness of danger that a commander might not hand

over the fort to his successor is attested by the penalties laid down at lines 21–7. Cf. below, p. 124 and n. 192.

61 In his work on south Attica, 'Studies in south Attica: country estates at Sounion', *Hesp.* 25 (1956), pp. 122–46.

62 The catalogue: J. H. Young, 'Country estates', pp. 144–6; diameter and height: J. H. Young, 'Country estates', p. 135.

63 J. H. Young, 'Country estates', pp. 132–3.

64 J. H. Young, 'Country estates', p. 143.

65 J. H. Young, 'Country estates', p. 140.

66 J. Pečirka, 'Homestead farms in Classical and Hellenistic Hellas', in M. I. Finley (ed.), *Problèmes de la terre en Grèce ancienne* (Paris, 1973), pp. 113–47, and in particular pp. 123–9.

67 J. H. Young, 'Country estates', p. 133 n. 22.

68 D. M. Robinson, *Excavations at Olynthus* II (Baltimore, 1930), pp. 35–98 and especially fig. 116, which gives the ground plans of some large houses.

69 J. H. Young, 'Country estates', pp. 133–4. And a (non-Greek) farm with a tower occurs at Xenophon, *Anab.* VII.8.8–15.

70 Lines 13–20.

71 A. W. Lawrence, *Greek Aims in Fortification* (Oxford, 1979), pp. 187–97.

72 Lawrence, *Greek Aims*, p. 187 n. 12.

73 Lawrence, *Greek Aims*, p. 187 n. 11.

74 See, for example, W. J. Woodhouse, *Aetolia* (London, 1897), pp. 159–61, where three towers in the region of Stamna in south-west Aetolia (up the river Acheloos from Oiniadae) are identified as the 'towers ... in the countryside' destroyed in Philip V's invasion of Lower Aetolia in 219 (Polyaenus IV.64.11).

75 Lawrence, *Greek Aims*, pp. 187–8.

76 'Les ruines antiques dans l'île de Thasos et en particulier les tours helléniques', *BCH* 54 (1930), pp. 174–94, at p. 186: 'after a successful raid they took refuge on their cliffs – or, if they were pursued, on some point on a deserted coast where they could hide. Little beaches, like St John's beach at Thasos, isolated between rocky headlands and surrounded by mountains and forests, could offer a safe haven to this dangerous element.' Pages 184–6 argue specifically and persuasively for the connection of the towers with the prevalence of piracy. For the bay of Hag. Ioannis, cf. p. 162.

77 The Epichares inscription (cf. above, n. 60), lines 21–2.

78 Demosthenes 4(*Philippic* I).23.

79 Demosthenes 4(*Philippic* I).32.

80 Bon, 'Les ruines antiques', p. 179.

81 1 (J. H. Young, 'Country estates', p. 124): fifth to fourth centuries; 2 (p. 126): fourth; 3 (p. 126): fourth to third; 4 (p. 128): not definitely stated; 5 (p. 128): third, perhaps; 6 (pp. 130–1): fifth to fourth, partly on the evidence of the masonry.

82 Lawrence, *Greek Aims*, pp. 187–8, argues that the main period of construction of island towers was the second to the first centuries BC

in the period of Cretan and Cilician piracy. As for mainland towers, he considers that historical considerations make it unlikely (p. 188) that many were built as late as the third century BC. The writers of the published accounts of towers are often too shrewd to commit themselves to mentioning a date for the building of the structures, so that Lawrence's idea cannot be refuted by reference to them, but it is clear what has happened: the periods of construction have been fixed by Lawrence from outside considerations. 'The seaborne danger ... would have reached its maximum with the slave-raiding by Cretan and Cilician pirates, ... from the middle of the second century well into the first. ... That was surely the islanders' main period of construction' (p. 187). Observation is a better guide: the bulk of towers are of Classical date (see above, nn. 80 and 81). Lawrence was perhaps not aware of the evidence for great pirate activity in the fourth century, though single towers were built at a wide variety of periods. L. E. Lord, 'Watchtowers and fortresses in Argolis', *AJA* 43 (1939), pp. 78–84, suggests a Mycenaean date for some in the Ligurio/Nemea areas.

83 See earlier in this section, with nn. 76 and 78–9.
84 Demosthenes 23(*Aristocrates*).166.
85 Ibid.
86 Demosthenes 23(*Aristocrates*).162.
87 Aeschines 2(*Embassy*).72; cf. Ormerod, *Piracy*, p. 116.
88 De Ste Croix, *Class Struggle*, p. 477, notes that 'one is irresistibly reminded' of this incident by the conversation of Bulla Felix with the Praetorian prefect Papinianus (Dio Cassius LXXVII.10.7). A statement in such terms is incapable of refutation, but the two conversations are very different. Bulla's 'Why are you the prefect?' stresses that his position in the world is *different* from the prefect's (and implies that the prefect's question was a foolish one: as if, for example, he had asked a horse why it was a horse), but this pirate's claim is that his position is *analogous* to Alexander's.
89 On temple-robbing by third-century pirates cf. M.I. Rostovtzeff, *Social and Economic History of the Hellenistic World* (Oxford, 1941), pp. 201–2.
90 [Dem.] 7(*Halonnesus*).2.
91 Polyaeanus IV.9.3. Cf. Plutarch, *Demetrius* 49.2. The anonymous judge of the Oxford University Ancient History Prize competition draws my attention to Plutarch, *Dem.* 25.4 – the story of how Demetrius was pleased (*c.* 303) when his courtiers at parties characterised the other new kings as if they were Demetrius' subordinates: e.g. Seleucus, the elephantarch. He suggests that this may have been Seleucus' rejoinder. Griffith notes (*Mercenaries*, p. 60) that Demetrius' men had already had a great deal to endure in following Demetrius before they finally chose to desert: 'they had shown that mercenaries can be heroes, and had endured far more than

any commander has a right to demand of his men for pay alone'.
92 Cf. above, p. 106 and n. 38.
93 It was of course a commonplace of invective to call one's enemy a pirate. Augustus at *Res gestae* 25 says 'mare pacavi a praedonibus', meaning Sextus Pompeius. But Seleucus' comment, at least, was not wholly unfounded: cf. later in this section.
94 Griffiths, *Mercenaries*, pp. 262–3 (the quotation from p. 262).
95 Pritchett, *The Greek State at War* II, p. 85.
96 Demosthenes 23(*Aristocrates*).148.
97 Pritchett, *The Greek State at War* II, p. 85, calls Charidemus a 'naval privateer' in this period: but Demosthenes does not even suggest that he was working on behalf of a state, still less that he was part of a navy. And cf. below, pp. 115–17.
98 Pritchett, *The Greek State at War* II, pp. 86–9.
99 Demosthenes 23(*Aristocrates*).154. The date was 360: cf. Pritchett, *The State at War* II, p. 85, and J. M. Cook, *The Troad* (Oxford, 1973), p. 338.
100 Demosthenes 23(*Aristocrates*).139.
101 Cf. Pritchett, *The Greek State at War* II, p. 85.
102 Callias, the tyrant of Chalcis (on whom see Aeschines 3(*Ctesiphon*). 85–105), received Athenian citizenship (section 85). This need only be mentioned because of [Dem.] 12(*Letter of Philip*).5, where the writer, referring to Callias' capture of the cities on the Pagasaean Gulf, uses the phrase 'you sent out *leistai*'. But this passage does not show that Callias was a *leistes* from outside the cities: it is analogous to (e.g.) Xenophon, *Hell.* IV.8.35, on which cf. p. 104 above.
103 See above, p. 108.
104 But probably in one work only (*Dial. mort.* 24). Ziebarth, *Beiträge*, p. 17, treats the Sostratus in Lucian, *Alexander, or, The False Prophet* 4 (the reference in Ziebarth to this passage is extravagantly wrong) as the same man; but there are alternatives (which do not present themselves in the Dialogue because Sostratus is called 'the *leistes*'), for example the Syracusan Sostratus recorded at D.S. XIX.3.3 as having spent most of his life 'in plotting and murder and great sacrileges'.
105 Lucian, *Alexander, or, The False Prophet* 2.
106 Cf. Ormerod, *Piracy*, pp. 260–70. R.A. MacKay, 'Klephtika: the tradition of the tales of banditry in Apuleius', *G&R*, 2nd Ser. 10 (1963), pp. 147–52, suggests reasons. Cf. also F. Millar, 'The world of the Golden Ass', *JRS* 71 (1981), pp. 63–75, at pp. 66–7 on Apuleius, *Met.* VII.6.
107 *Syll.*³ 409, lines 9–13.
108 C.R. IV.5.19 and Arrian, *Anab.* III.2.7; cf. Ormerod, *Piracy*, p. 121.
109 D.S. XX.97.5.
110 D.S. XX.110.4.
111 Demosthenes 23(*Aristocrates*).149.
112 Griffith, *Mercenaries*, p. 262. Aeschines 1(*Timarchus*).191 might be mentioned in support of Griffith, but the point of the passage is simply that *aselgeia* (section 190) gives rise to ruinous consequences. It does

not say or imply that the pirate recruits are likely to make their fortunes.

113 But note Thucydides IV.9.1, where 40 Messenians out of the combined crews of a triaconter and a *keles* were hoplites. Herodotus VII.184.3 mentions 80 as the complement of a penteconter, but there is no evidence bearing specifically on how large a crew a triaconter or a *keles* would have had, so there is no telling what the proportions were.

114 Polyaenus V.19.

115 Plutarch, *Pyrrhus* 29; cf. Polyaenus IV.6.18.

116 Above, p. 9.

117 Xenophon, *Hell.* II.1.30. If Theopompus' ship was the quickest vehicle for the news to Sparta, it was probably a trireme. If a trireme, it was probably in the battle.

118 For instance, Ziebarth, *Beiträge*, p. 15, speaks of *Kaperkrieg* (privateer war) between Iphicrates and Anaxibius (Xenophon, *Hell.* IV.8.35, cf. above, p. 1), and notes (p. 17) how, between the Halonnesus affair and Chaeronea, 'beide Parteien, sowohl Philipp wie die Athener, im Kaperkrieg Erhebliches leisteten', 'both sides, Philip and the Athenians, had considerable successes in the privateer war'.

119 Ormerod, *Piracy*, p. 60: 'throughout our discussion it will be necessary to make a careful distinction between piracy and such measures of war as would in modern times be classed as privateering'. The whole second chapter (pp. 59–79) is directed towards establishing this distinction.

120 Ormerod, *Piracy*, p. 61.

121 Demosthenes 24(*Timocrates*).11–12. In section 11 Archebius and Lysitheides are said by one Euctemon to 'have [as a result of] having been trierarchs some Naucratite money', and in section 12 a trireme conveys the three ambassadors. It would be perverse, in the circumstances, to think that it was not an Athenian naval trireme.

122 Demosthenes 24(*Timocrates*).13.

123 Demosthenes 24(*Timocrates*).12.

124 Ormerod, *Piracy*, p. 62.

125 Ormerod, *Piracy*, p. 63 with nn. 1 and 2; to Xenophon, *Hell.* V.1.1. (cf. above, section 2) he adds Thucydides V.115.2. Thucydides III.51.1 could also be added.

126 Ormerod, *Piracy*, p. 61.

127 *Abroad*, not that Demosthenes makes this explicit (cf. below, n. 128) but because the lexica say so: there are two notices on *Androlepsia*, one in the *Etymologicum Magnum* and the *Suda*, the other in Harpocration (all of it) and Hesychius (part of it). Both notices stress that seizure outside Athens is in question. Pollux (VIII.41.40) says little.

128 Demosthenes 23(*Aristocrates*).83–5. The formula 'for so I shall suppose. . .' in section 85 shows that Demosthenes' instance of how the law works, dealing with someone who has gone into exile after committing a homicide, is given *exempli gratia*; so it must be assumed (*contra P–W* s.v. *Androlepsie*), or at least hoped, that the notices in

the lexicographers (cf. above, n. 127) had some source other than just this passage.

129 [Dem.] 51(*Trierarchic Crown*).7.
130 Cf. [Dem.] 51(*Trierarchic Crown*).13–14.
131 B. Bravo, 'Sulân. Représailles et justice privée contre des étrangers dans les cités grecques', *ASNP*, Ser. III, 10 (1980), pp. 675–97, is a semantically based study of the practice of the remedy of self-help. Bravo includes a translation and elaborate exegesis of [Dem.] 51(*Trierarchic Crown*).13: διὰ τὰς ὑπὸ τούτων ἀνδροληψίας καὶ σύλας κατασκευασμένας he renders (p. 739) as 'à cause de l'etat de saisies portant sur les personnes et sur les biens qui a été fabriqué par ces gens' ('on account of the state of seizures applicable to persons and property which was brought about by these people') and notes (p. 740), 'remarquons que le verbe κατασκευάζειν designe souvent l'action d'établir, d'instaurer, de mettre sur pied, de construire, de fabriquer. C'est manifestement de cette manière qu'il est employé ici' ('note that the verb *kataskeuazein* often denotes the action of establishing, starting, setting up, building or making. This is obviously how it is being used here'). But it can be argued that κατασκευασμένας is better translated, on the analogy of Demosthenes 27(*Aphobus* I).61, [πρόσοδον] οὐ μικρὰν κατεσκευάσαντο, 'they made themselves a pretty good [income]' (and cf. *LSJ* s.v., especially sections 3 and 4), so that the translation should be 'because of the kidnappings and seizures carried out [*sc.* on their own behalf] by these men'. Bravo strains the evidence available from this passage when he infers (p. 848) that 'à la piraterie non autorisée qu'exercent les triérarques athéniens, les cités lésées répondent en autorisant la piraterie contre Athènes'.
132 Ormerod, *Piracy*, p. 117.
133 Demosthenes 21(*Meidias*).173.
134 Nor was the navy expected to act in its own interest, despite the activities of a few unscrupulous trierarchs (cf. above, n. 129).
135 Thasos: [Dem.] 12(*Letter of Philip*).2. Chios: (Aristonicus), cf. above, p. 114 and n. 108. Syracuse: (Postumius) D.S. XVI.82.3.
136 See, for example, D.S. XX.83.3.
137 The word used at Griffith, *Mercenaries*, p. 262.
138 Ziebarth, *Beiträge*, p. 1: 'in its connection with piracy, i.e. in its dependence on piracy'.
139 Ziebarth, *Beiträge*, p. 5: 'Indirekt bieten die Nachrichten über Seeraub uns aber auch Zeugnisse für die Bedeutung des griechischen Seehandels der damaligen Zeit.' And cf. above, p. 105.
140 Ziebarth, *Beiträge*, p. 1: 'weiter aber will sie verfolgen, wie und in welcher Form sich der Seehandel trotz des Seeraubs weiter hat entwickeln konnen'.
141 Rostovtzeff, *History*, pp. 198–9, shows how maritime cities (especially islands) made treaties with the Aetolians and Cretans rather than be raided. Page 202 says of piracy, 'the frequency of the Hellenistic inscriptions that refer to it, though inscriptions of this period are comparatively rare, indicates that this ancient practice had now

become very common and was carried on with cynical ruthlessness'.
142 *IG* XII (3) (Supp.) 1291, lines 11–13 (cf. above, p. 108).
143 Menander, *Sicyonius* 5. A third captive, an old woman, the pirates in the story found it unprofitable to bring to market (lines 3–5).
144 Menander, *Sicyonius* 9–10.
145 Austin, *Hellenistic World*, p. 156 (=section 86).
146 *SEG* XX.716 (=*SECir*, No. 103; *Supplemento epigrafico cirenaico = Annuario della Scuola archeologica di Atene* 39–40, n.s. 23–4, 1961–2, Rome, 1963, pp. 219–375). The arguments leading to these conclusions are complex. I have had access to them from notes kindly made available to me by S. Hornblower and taken by him at classes given by P. M. Fraser on 8 and 15 May 1979. The following points are crucial: that σύλα λύω πρός + personal name in accusative + amount of money in accusative = settle for damages against [someone] in [a certain sum] (so that λύω [again!] here does not mean 'pay'); that ἀπολομένων (line 16) means 'corrupted'; that φιλόπαιδας (line 25, which Fraser suggests amending to φιλόπαιδες) does, *contra* G. Pugliese Carratelli and D. Morelli at *SECir*, p. 279, mean 'pederasts'; and that the placing of the inscription in several important shrines, and particularly its going to the Θεσμοθέται in Athens, who dealt with moral offences, shows how highly the Cyreneans rated the importance of publicising their success in getting compensation for what their community had suffered.
147 See in particular lines 15–20.
148 S. Hornblower's notes suggest that Fraser argues for a date *c.* 365.
149 W. W. Tarn, *Antigonos Gonatas* (Oxford, 1913), p. 88.
150 Strabo XIV.5.2 (668–9).
151 M. I. Finley, 'The Black Sea and Danubian regions and the slave trade in antiquity', *Klio* 40 (1962), pp. 51–60. Quotes from pp. 57–8.
152 Cf. above, p. 105.
153 L. Moretti, *Iscrizioni storiche ellenistiche* (Florence, 1967), p. 2.
154 Moretti, *Iscrizioni*, p. 3.
155 Moretti, *Iscrizioni*, p. 3, quotes as a parallel the Athenians captured a century later by Bucris of Naupactus and taken to Crete (*Syll.*³ 535).
156 D. M. Lewis points out 'the similarity of situation to *IG* I³ 125' (there is no close *verbal* similarity between the texts).
157 Strabo XIV.5.2 (668–9); cf. above, p. 118.
158 See above, pp. 106–12.
159 Cf. above, p. 105.
160 Lysias XXXII(*Diogeiton*).29.
161 Ormerod, *Piracy*, pp. 113–14; cf. Ziebarth, *Beiträge*, pp. 12–13. Incidentally, Isocrates, *Trapeziticus* 35–6, which Ormerod and Ziebarth both take as showing that the general risk of sea travel was greater because the Spartans controlled the sea, very likely means that Stratocles was afraid of being robbed *by Spartans*. The point of 'specially since the Spartans were in control of the sea at the time' is diffuse otherwise: and the Spartans were interfering with traffic across the Aegean before the battle of Cnidus (*Hell. Oxy.* 7.1).

162 Xenophon, *Hell.* II.1.20; cf. above, p. 104.
163 Demosthenes 52(*Callippus*).5.
164 Cf. below, pp. 125–6.
165 Cf. below, pp. 127–8.
166 Herodotus III.39.3–4.
167 Rostovtzeff, *History*, pp. 198–9 (cf. above, n. 141), gives an account of these events. Ziebarth, *Beiträge*, p. 108, notes the formulaic similarity between the decrees, citing by way of example *Syll.*³ 554. J. K. Davies (*CAH* VII.1² (Cambridge, 1984), pp. 285–90), gives a general discussion of the place of piracy in third-century political developments.
168 Aristotle, *Pol.* 1256a 19–21 and 35.
169 See above, pp. 112–15.
170 Xenophon, *Hell.* VI.4.35; cf. above, p. 104.
171 His raid on the Peiraeus: Polyaenus VI.2.2; in the Cyclades and Peparethus: D.S. XV.95.1; in Tenos: Demosthenes 50(*Polycles*).4.
172 Polyaenus VI.1.2–7.
173 Xenophon *Hell.* VI.33–7, gives a brief account of Thessaly from Jason's death until the time when that part of the *Hellenica* was finished (section 37).
174 Demosthenes 2(*Olynthiac II*).19.
175 Cf. above, p. 108 and n. 56.
176 Aeschines 2(*Embassy*).12.
177 As his Amphictyonic dealings show: D.S. XVI.1.4.
178 Cawkwell, *Philip of Macedon*, pp. 38–9, shows how Philip made the Macedonian nobility his courtiers; but G. L. Cawkwell points out to me that not all Philip's courtiers were Macedonians: Theopompus *FGrHist* 115 F 225a. F 225b amplifies this by noting that Philip's non-Macedonian courtiers 'preferred to plunder and murder rather than live a disciplined life'.
179 [Dem.] 12(*Letter of Philip*).2. On the *Letter* see above, n. 52.
180 [Dem.] 58(*Theocrines*).56.
181 Isocrates, *Panathenaicus* 226.
182 Cf. above, p. 112.
183 Discussed later in this section.
184 Demetrius' kingdom, for instance: cf. above, pp. 114–15.
185 D. M. Lewis, 'Notes on Attic inscriptions', *BSA* 49 (1954), pp. 17–50. Quoted from p. 24.
186 Herodotus VII.203.1.
187 *IG* II² 1629 (=Tod II 200) lines 217–33 (with Dittenberger's restorations: *Syll.*³ 305, lines 52–68).
188 P. J. Rhodes, *The Athenian Boule* (Oxford, 1972), pp. 231–5.
189 Cf. above, p. 119.
190 Lines 8–10; 2–3.
191 Rhodes, *Athenian Boule*, p. 233.
192 *SEG* XXVI.1306. The *editio princeps*, with detailed notes, is L. and J. Robert, 'Une inscription grecque de Téos en Ionie: l'union de Téos et Kyrbissos', *JS* (1976), pp. 153–235.

193 *IG* XI (2) 148, line 73.
194 D.S. XV.13.1.
195 D.S. XVI.5.3.
196 Cf. above, n. 52. A. B. Bosworth, 'The Congress Decree: another hypothesis', *Hist.* 20 (1971), pp. 600–16, arguing that the Congress Decree in Plutarch, *Pericles* 17, is a post-338 forgery, notes (p. 607) that there is no earlier agreement comparable to the provision in the common peace at Corinth that all the parties to the peace should sail the seas without hindrance (Tod II 177 and [Dem.] 17(*Treaty with Alexander*).19) and that 'Philip was undoubtedly the first to present the freedom of the seas as a clause in a common peace agreement'. This, if correct, would illustrate further Philip's commitment to being seen to be against the *leistai*. B. R. MacDonald, 'The authenticity of the Congress Decree', *Hist.* 31 (1982), pp. 120–3, suggests that the decree may be a genuine Periclean document (p. 123); in doing so he argues that suppression of piracy was no part of its purpose and that the Persian threat was being presented by Pericles as the sole necessary and sufficient reason for the maintenance of the Athenian fleet. This is a difficult problem. I note only that, given the very brief and general nature of the decree, the fact that pirates are not mentioned specifically is not a very strong point in MacDonald's favour.
197 Q. Curtius Rufus IV.8.15. Read 'in bellum utroque rege converso' (edition of K. Müller, Munich, 1954, following some or all of the twelfth to fifteenth-century *deteriores*, see pp. 734 and 739). The state of chaos in Crete was evidently giving rise to opportunities for pirates; Amphoterus was to gain control of the whole island from the Persians and Spartans and so enable himself to suppress the pirates. Here perhaps piracy was only an *indirect* result of Persian influence; but there was more direct support for piracy, too: see C.R. IV.5.18–19 and Arrian, *Anab.* VI.1.2 and III.2.4, with A. B. Bosworth, *A Historical Commentary on Arrian's History of Alexander* (Oxford, 1980), *ad locc.*
198 Cf. above, p. 112.
199 D.S. XX.81.3.
200 Strabo V.3.5. (=232).
201 Tarn, *Greeks*, p. 48 and n. 22 (quotation from n. 22).
202 H. Berve, *Das Alexanderreich auf prosopographischer Grundlage* I (Munich, 1926), p. 326 n. 3.
203 Ormerod, *Piracy*, p. 129. He argues against Tarn's view, p. 129 n. 4 and p. 161.
204 Both quotations from Tarn, *Antigonos Gonatas*, p. 88.
205 See above, p. 120.
206 Ormerod, *Piracy*, p. 114.
207 Cf. above, p. 113.
208 See S. Accame, *La lega ateniese del sec. IV. a. C.* (Rome, 1941), p. 137; and cf. pp. 124–35, which cites [Dem.] 58(*Theocrines*).53 but comments, 'lo psefisma di Merocle [from [Dem.] 58(*Theocrines*).53] non si sa con precisione a quando risalga, ma certo a prima dell' anno

342/1 in cui si può datare al più presto il discorso pseudodemostenico *contro Teocrine*' ('it is impossible to assign a precise date to the Moerocles decree – but it was certainly before 342/341, the earliest possible date for the pseudo-Demosthenes speech *Against Theocrines*'). So it is not known when this co-operation began. On Moerocles cf. below, chapter 7 n. 62.

209 *Syll.*³ 263 and *IG* II² 283.

210 See the beginning of this section, with n. 187.

211 Ziebarth, *Beiträge*, p. 20: 'wenn wir vom Seeraub, so lange Alexander regierte, abgesehen von den angeführten Fällen nichts weiter hören, so wird das seinen Grund darin haben, dass der grosse König es verstanden hat, auch auf dem Meere Ordnung zu halten' ('since, as long as Alexander was king, we hear no more of piracy – except for the cases already mentioned – we have grounds for thinking that the Great King undertook to keep order at sea as well').

212 Ormerod, *Piracy*, pp. 121–2.

213 Ormerod, *Piracy*, p. 122, suggests that 'we may suppose also that the famous rescript of 324 B.C. to the Greek cities, ordering the restoration of the exiles, was occasioned not least by the necessity of ridding the Greek world of the homeless outlaws who now formed a large element in the pirate bands'. Ziebarth follows him (*Beiträge*, p. 20).

214 Aeschines 1(*Timarchus*).191.

215 Cf. above, pp. 121–2.

216 See the beginning of this section, with n. 187.

217 The fact that the site of Adria is unknown should induce some caution in the reader of Ziebarth, *Beiträge*, p. 18: 'wir treffen damit zum ersten Male auf die tyrrhenischen Seeräuber in Westmeer Griechenlands' ('this is the first context in which we come across Etruscan pirates in the west Greek sea'). Adria was certainly on the *west* coast of the Adriatic – that is, in Italy – but the attempts of G. Vallet, 'Athènes et l'Adriatique', *Mélanges de l'Ecole française de Rome* 62 (1950), pp. 33–52, and A. Gitti, 'La colonia ateniese in Adriatico del 325/4 a. C.', *PP* 9 (1954), pp. 16–24, to be more precise are not conclusive. It does not seem quite right to include the Adriatic in the 'Westmeer Griechenlands' and exclude Sicilian waters.

218 Ziebarth, *Beiträge*, p. 19, and Ormerod, *Piracy*, pp. 128–9.

219 D.S. XV.13.1; A. G. Woodhead, 'The "Adriatic empire" of Dionysius of Syracuse', *Klio* 52 (1970), at pp. 503–12, p. 507.

220 D.S. XV.13.1; Woodhead, '"Adriatic empire"', at p. 507.

221 Woodhead, '"Adriatic empire"', p. 508.

222 Livy VII.25.4 and 26.13.15.

223 Conveniently collected at Ziebarth, *Beiträge*, p. 106, they are: Aristides XLIII, p. 540 K; Pollux IV.87 (=Men. Fr. 869 Koerte); Photius s.v. *Leistosalpinctas*; Hesychius s.v. *Leistosalpinges*. The trumpet is associated with the Etruscans in Greek literature as early as Aeschylus, *Eumenides* 567–8.

224 *Syll.*³ 1225, lines 4–5, 8 and 10. Cf. M. Segre, 'Due novi texti storici', *Riv. Fil.* 60 (1933), pp. 446–61, at pp. 461, where an honorific

inscription shows that the sons of Timacrates were not 'semplici soldati di fanteria marina' (p. 455). Cf. also C. Blinkenberg, 'Triemiolia: étude sur un type de navire rhodien', *Archaeologisk-Kunsthistoriske Meddelelser* II, 3 (1938), pp. 1–59, at p. 14.

225 The brothers were buried under the same mound (*Syll.*³ 1225, lines 1–2) as well as being mentioned in the same epitaph. And cf. Ziebarth, *Beiträge*, p. 22.

226 De Ste Croix, *Class Struggle*, p. 47.

227 De Ste Croix, *Class Struggle*, appendix VIII.

228 [Dem.] 17(*Treaty with Alexander*).19.

229 [Dem.] 50(*Polycles*).6.

230 Cf. above, p. 114.

231 *Syll.*³ 409, lines 10–11.

232 Ormerod, *Piracy*, p. 124 n. 3.

233 [Dem.] 7(Halonnesus).3; cf. above, p. 110.

234 Opposition, see above, pp. 122–6; fear, Theophrastus, *Char.* 25.1.

235 Tarn, *Greeks*, p. 88.

236 Compare Isocrates, *Peace* 44, with Aeschines 1(*Timarchus*).191 – differently worded but essentially similar accusations of greed.

6

Mobile skilled workers

So far this study has concentrated on people who lost the settled places in Greek society which they would have been glad to keep. It has been suggested that the nature and growth of mercenary service and of *leisteia* indicate that many stateless people turned to them.[1] But it would be incomplete and misleading not to mention the people whose occupations caused them (irrespective of political events) to move from city to city.

Some comments on the matter of definition are perhaps necessary. The subject matter of this chapter is wide, but it does not extend to fully settled metics. There is a fine line to be drawn here, though: many – indeed, most – of the skilled workers under consideration were people who could expect to stay in one city for several months, or even for years. Yet they would find it normal to move when the time came.[2] They were not the people whom Xenophon in the late 350s wanted to attract to Athens (to become long-term taxpayers).[3] This subjective criterion, the criterion of what people in the occupations dealt with below would have found normal, is the criterion on which their definition as outsiders in the Greek cities will be based. It would be nice to be able to be more obviously rigorous – nice, for instance, if it were possible to make Isocrates' teacher Gorgias of Leontini, who did not establish a permanent home in any city and so avoided spending money on community interests or paying taxes,[4] a paradigmatic case, and compare with his way of life the pattern observed for other philosophers and similar people. But though a great quantity of evidence relevant to this inquiry is available (mostly in literary sources), it is not usually informative about the skilled workers' tax position or their juridical status in the communities they visited.

Any of the sorts of people covered in this inquiry could justify separate study. Most have already received it. So the intention here is not to deal in any detail with the technical aspects of the callings under consideration, nor to compete against any of the specialised works referred to below. But it is very much the aim to provide a general picture of the role of travelling skilled workers in Greek society in the fourth century; and, where possible, to say in what respect things were changing, and how the changes were related to the other events concerning Greeks outside the cities. In view of the importance of seeing the picture whole, the final section will make some general observations on the activities of skilled workers, who will be referred to as *technitai* (without prejudice to the claim the Dionysiac artists later had on the word), over the fourth century. First, come sections on building, on medicine, and on education and entertainment.

It will be as well, at the outset, to answer the objection that people whose occupation caused them (irrespective of political events) to move from city to city are unlikely to have been influenced in their choice of occupation by the state of the Greek world as a whole. Certainly many followed their parents' occupations, but some had to find means of livelihood when the need arose: a story told to illustrate the unorthodox wit of Diogenes the Dog says that he praised a fat cithara player whom everyone else was railing at, and explained, when asked why, that it was because he was a cithara player when a man of his size could have been a bandit.[5] Clearly a cithara player (and a bad one, at that) had a shorter and less highly technical training than a sculptor, a doctor or a philosopher – but there is an extent to which external circumstances counted, even in those cases. Greek philosophy would have developed differently (perhaps less richly) had circumstances not driven Diogenes of Sinope (the Dog) and Zeno of Citium to follow a philosophical career. Zeno, shipwrecked on a voyage to Athens, is recorded by Diogenes Laertius as commenting,[6] 'Fortune has done me a good turn by driving me to philosophy...' Diogenes the Dog made a sharper comment to someone who reproached his exile:[7] 'but that's why I became a philosopher, you fool!' And he is recorded as quoting (on another occasion) two iambic trimeters against himself:[8] 'Cityless, homeless, deprived of a fatherland – a beggar, a wanderer, living from day to day'.

Building and related skills

This section draws in many places on the work of A. Burford,[9] who writes,[10] 'craftsmen who worked in expensive materials and unusual techniques – not, of course, the shoemakers, blacksmiths, weavers, house builders, harness makers and so on – had to face the problem at one time or another of finding adequate employment for their special skills'. These specialist craftsmen moved to find work.

Detailed evidence is to be found in *The Greek Temple Builders at Epidaurus*, where Burford analyses the levels at which craftsmen of different nationalities could work on the Epidaurian temple: Epidaurians on the foundations and invisible fittings, Corinthians and Argives on the main structure, Athenians and Parians on the pediment sculptures, the decorative stonework and the statue of the god.[11] For the chryselephantine statue itself the ivory-workers were from Corinth, Paros, Sicyon, Aegina and Ephesus; the painter was from Corinth; the stonemasons were from Corinth and Athens, and the joiners from Corinth.[12]

But the mobility in evidence at Epidaurus was not, in general, mobility over a very long distance. The craftsmen working there were mostly from Athens, Argos and Corinth[13] – places not particularly distant (on the scale of the Greek world) from Epidaurus. This may in some measure have been due to the fact that Epidaurus happened to be near some of the largest cities in Greece, with the best resources,[14] but it will be worth noting (for comparison with material below)[15] that the only workers at Epidaurus who had come a really long distance fell (like the Ephesian ivory-worker) into the top grade of skill – virtually the internationally reputed artist category.[16] It may be possible to infer that in most circumstances an 'ordinary' skilled man might find it normal to maintain a workshop in one city and travel (for months at a time) to sites not far away, expecting to go home again at the end of a run of work.[17]

This expectation will have ceased to apply when economic conditions became particularly strained for one reason or another. Burford explains the lack of activity in temple-building in mainland and island Greece between 400 and 375 as a consequence of the damage done to each other by both sides in the Peloponnesian war. Dionysius I made a great success of his building and armament work in Sicily soon after the fall of Athens because he had so many workers, and many of those who went to Sicily must have been from Athens. Agesilaus made Ephesus a centre for the manufacture of armaments from 396, and so must have attracted workers because of the relative economic weakness of Athens in the 390s.[18] The damage done to Sparta's allies is less easily documented. G. T. Griffith argues from Corinthian hoplite numbers in 479 and 394 for a decline in manpower at Corinth and severe economic harm caused by the Archidamian and Decelean wars,[19] but J. B. Salmon doubts the legitimacy of inferring significant population decline from the hoplite figures and suggests that classical Corinth suffered no serious economic setback due to war until the Corinthian war in the 390s.[20]

Until the workers returned from the periphery of the Greek world to its centre, Burford argues, the Epidaurians could not begin work on their temple.[21] The tholos at Epidaurus, started later than the temple, took much longer to complete: Burford connects this with a new shortage of available labour.[22] The case for her suggestion that 'the presence in the community of skilled men, whether doctors, sculptors, engineers, or temple builders, was a matter for congratulation; if they were absent, they must be encouraged to come and reside in the city'[23] is well made out, and it is clear that there was usually a seller's market for highly skilled labour in the building trade, so that 'the city-governors could not compel constant loyalty from the craftsmen'.[24] But since in the fourth century there were more and more Greeks living outside the cities, it is necessary to ask why there is no obvious evidence to suggest that there was any great expansion in the number of people following the building trades.[25]

Since building workers, once their skills were acquired, were indispensable to the patrons of great works,[26] the reason for the lack of expansion must be sought in the system under which skills were acquired. First, they were acquired in cities:[27] temple-builders and sculptors are likely to have taken apprentices from their own cities, if they took any at all apart from sons and slaves. It is known that certain fourth-century sculptors were succeeded by their sons, as Praxiteles was by Cephisodotus, Lysippus by Laippus, Boedas and Euthycrates, and Timarchides by Polycles and Dionysius.[28] It seems likely that the pattern was general (the sons of Praxiteles and Lysippus had more reason than most artists to dwell on their fathers' reputations, which may explain why the relationship came to be mentioned in Pliny's source), and that it applied also to the crafts which attracted less literary attention than the sculptor's. It is likely, then, that the highly specialised skills connected with temple-building and sculpture were guarded by their possessors in a way in which (it will be shown below) certain other skills were not.[29]

After 375 a wide range of work was available to those with the skills needed in monumental projects. The Mausoleum at Halicarnassus, on the edge of the Greek world, was worked on by six[30] Greek sculptors, and it may be presumed that other skilled workers went from Greece to Halicarnassus.[31] S. Hornblower dates the construction of the Mausoleum by considering what is known of the careers of the six sculptors, and arrives at 'a date in the 350s or thereabouts'.[32] He makes the point strongly that no craftsman could afford to work except when he was being paid,[33] and this was certainly in general the case, but it should be noted that exceptional artists may sometimes have made more than they needed to live on. Lysippus, the most famous sculptor of the late fourth century (when there was more money in circulation than there had been before Alexander's conquests), is recorded as having saved up a gold piece from the price of each of his 1,500 works. The number seems too great, but the principle that the very best artists could accumulate savings is not implausible.[34]

Work on the temples at Ephesus, Delphi and Tegea was done by sculptors,[35] and by others as well. Sculptors had commissions for work not connected with building, and so in some cases travelled where other skilled workers were not required. The sons of Praxiteles made an altar in Cos, for example, and both Bryaxis and Aristodemus made portrait statues of Seleucus Nicator.[36] In other cases commissions recorded for sculptors imply the employment of others on the less spectacular work connected with the commissions. Cephisodotus made a statue of Zeus at Megalopolis,[37] but it is certain that many were employed on public buildings at Megalopolis throughout the 360s. Leochares worked on statues of Philip II and his family for the Philippeium at Olympia,[38] which others must have helped to build. In the later years of the century there must have been work available in the reconstruction of Priene,[39] and as for the period of the city foundations of Alexander and the Successors, it is certain that work will have been available for skilled workers in many places. Indeed, a shortage of them may have been the partial cause of some delays.[40] Proximity to the centre of the Greek world had continued to be a help to cities wanting to carry out building projects: when Thebes was re-established in 316 the Athenians built most of the wall, and some of the other Greeks helped in the building work.[41] Their resources enabled the work to be done quickly, as was the case with the refortification of Phocian cities before Chaeronea.[42]

The building project begun at Delos in the last years of the fourth century continued well into the third. M. Lacroix, noting that Delos produced little and supported few native people, finds nothing surprising in the fact that the inscriptions of the hieropoioi and the other contemporary inscriptions show that a high proportion of those involved in the work were not Delians.[43] As the third century progressed, Delians took on more of the contracts, but earlier 'pendant toute la fin du IVe [siècle les métèques] semblent avoir nettement la prédominance'.[44] Some of the suppliers of materials seem to have lived in Delos, others not, but in general the suppliers of stones were, at least originally, from the areas from which they imported stone.[45] Lacroix attempts to gauge what rank the foreigners concerned with the temple occupied in the population of Delos: he finds that some large-scale entrepreneurs would also take small jobs, and that some served as choregi.[46] A few foreigners were in trades not necessarily connected with the temple (metalworkers, sculptors, traders),[47] but it is interesting that participation by non-Delians in the economic life of the city declined sharply after 250, except in agriculture.[48] Though builders and similar craftsmen might stay put for some time, they eventually moved on.

Medicine

Whatever the difficulties involved in deciding the authorship of particular works in the corpus which bears his name, Hippocrates was certainly at the centre of an important change in the practice and transmission of the Greek medical craft. S. M. Sherwin-White, reviewing the development of the Coan school of medicine, mentions the key element:[49] Hippocrates (*c.* 460–*c.* 370)[50] 'is the earliest Greek physician whose practice of teaching pupils for a fee is attested'. Previously the Asclepiads had reserved their knowledge for transmission to relatives; by the beginning of the fourth century the effects of a widening of access of medical knowledge were beginning to be felt.

Not that doctors first began to travel as a result of the Hippocratic revolution. In the sixth century Democedes had made a large amount of money by being retained (at progressively larger fees) by the Aeginetans, the Athenians and Polycrates of Samos,[51] and it seems that it was normal for a physician to travel at all periods, as far back as Homeric times.[52] But a scientific interest in the possibilities afforded by travel accompanied the expansion of the medical profession which will have occurred once the principle of instruction for payment was established. *Airs Waters Places* is the outstanding early example of this: H. Diller argues convincingly (against the theory that the ethnographic chapters 12–24 were written by someone other than the author of the more obviously medical chapters 1–11) that the second part of the work forms the basis of the author's claim that climatic conditions affect people's constitutions, and so is integral to the whole.[53] *Epidemics* I.1–20, a study of conditions in Thasos, caters for readers with the same scientific interest, and *Medicus* 14 notes that a military expedition is the only context in which a physician will learn the techniques concerned with extraction of missiles.[54]

Another kind of scientific travel involved collecting ingredients for drugs. Theophrastus records how Thrasyas of Mantinea, who compounded a deadly drug of hemlock and other ingredients, gathered his hemlock 'not from just anywhere but from Susa (?) and any other place which was cold and shady'.[55]

The possibilities offered by travel were not only scientific. The career of Ctesias of Cnidos illustrates this. Artaxerxes II's personal physician, he dressed his wound at the battle of Cunaxa and afterwards participated in the negotiations as a result of which Conon became the admiral of the Persian fleet.[56] He became a man of influence – though this may have imposed certain restrictions as well as offering enviable opportunities.[57] T. S. Brown suggests that his scientific interest in travel may have been connected with a wish to escape from restrictions on medical innovation in the Cnidian school.[58] Perhaps this was so: but Ctesias also used his experience with the king in the composition of his *Persica* – not a work in the tradition of *Airs Waters Places* (still less in that of *Epidemics* I), but none the less a literary enterprise grown out of the opportunity afforded by mobility as a physician.[59]

Few physicians' careers were as brilliant as Ctesias'.[60] But doctors, though their normal expectation was to travel, were in a very prestigious craft.[61] There must have been some people who treated the sick without having been apprenticed to a skilled doctor, but two points should be given some weight before any strong distinction is made between 'mere leeches' and 'physicians'.[62] First, although modern writers often point out that study and examination were not formal conditions of entry to the profession,[63] several treatises in the Hippocratic corpus stress the need to acquire the attributes which make the real physician a distinctive and recognisable character'.[64] L. Edelstein discusses medical style,[65] but it should be stressed rather more than it is in his paper that an authoritative demeanour and impressive bandaging are the result of practice. The importance attached to them in Hippocratic writings indicates a progressive strengthening of the trained physicians' hold on medical practice, not a weakening of it. Second, it is only in modern times that there has been a 'single, socially chartered therapeutic system with final authority':[66] in ancient Greece there was perhaps less to be gained from pretending to be a Hippocratic physician than from offering another style of healing.

The Hippocratic treatises have a good deal to say about the doctors' travelling way of life.[67] The *Law*, apparently a kind of manifesto to new or prospective medical students, sets out the things which those bent on the medical craft need in order to be thought physicians, not just in word but in deed, when they go 'to the cities'.[68] The *Law* treats training as a preparation for a mobile way of life – it would have been possible (had it been the usual pattern) to say, 'to a practice in some city' instead of 'to the cities'. And one of the things which (the *Law* says) a student needs is 'to become a young pupil in a place such as is suitable for learning'.[69] The implication is not that no one should think of becoming a physician unless a medical school is near by, but that action may be required if the intending physician is to comply with this one of the author's six conditions for gaining understanding.[70] Travelling to study is a possibility at least.[71] It would be odd were this not so, as it would otherwise be impossible (on the author's terms) for a travelling physician's son to acquire his father's craft. *Decorum* adds detail: the physician is to have a second set of equipment for journeys; it is to be a simpler one, and portable.[72] A description of the doctor's travelling kit introduces a short section on how to prepare himself[73] and his medicines,[74] and it seems natural to apply the hints on these subjects to the context of travel. He is to commit information on drugs and diseases to memory, and he is to have a range of preparations ready for instant use – 'gathered from the appropriate places', says the author, bringing out again the scientific value of travel, which will afford opportunities to obtain a range of items not all available in a single locality.[75]

A doctor coming to settle in a town for a while could (if he felt the need) use a Hippocratic treatise as a source of instruction on how to set up a surgery. These pieces of the *de Medico* advise on position, light, furniture and water supply before turning to the quality and suitability of medical supplies and instruments.[76] The treatise is too short to give much technical information, and is perhaps best seen as a kind of check-list for students at an advanced stage:[77] those about to begin practising on their own account. Naturally they would need suggestions written down for reference when they arrived at a new place. *In the Surgery*, a treatise which gives more technical information than the *de Medico*, also provides a laconic list of requirements 'for operation in the surgery'.[78] These snippets of advice are an attestation in the medical literature to the way of life of doctors who settled for years in a single place (possibly making tours from it: the portable set of equipment in the *Decorum* implies a more comprehensive set at home).[79]

Some of these (so to speak) semi-settled doctors were public physicians, receiving payment or a retainer from the state in which they lived. They almost certainly did not provide free treatment[80] (except in so far as they obeyed the writers' exhortations to do so in special cases),[81] but their presence in the community was sometimes recognised by the passing of honorific decrees (in the fourth century, and more often as the Hellenistic Age progressed).[82] It is reasonable to assume that a state paying a retainer would expect its doctor to devote all his attention to patients in the city and not go on tour: the purpose of the retainer was probably not only to attract him in the first place, but also to free patients of the anxiety described in [Hp.] *Precepts* 4, that the doctor who begins by talking about his fee may be about to leave the patient with no bargain made.[83]

Education and entertainment

It may seem odd to couple education and entertainment, and capricious to deal in the same section with philosophers and their students, with *hetaerae* and with actors (mentioning also orators, musicians, soothsayers and cooks). But when the *hetaera* Glycera said to the Megarian philosopher Stilpo,[84] 'We're guilty of the same thing, Stilpo. They say you corrupt the men who associate with you by teaching them useless eristic tricks – and I corrupt the men who associate with me by teaching them useless erotic tricks,' the pun took added bite from the resemblance between the life styles of philosophers and *hetaerae*. (Nor, in all likelihood, was she entirely unfair in her reporting of what 'they say': in some quarters philosophy attracted opposition.)[85] This account is intended to bring out the similarities, and in general to examine the place of mobility between cities in the cultural life of Greece.

Plato and Aristotle, the Academy and the Lyceum, represent the heart of Greek philosophy in the fourth century. Just because this is so, it is dangerous to concentrate on them in an examination of how philosophers lived. But their great importance in this inquiry lies in the fact that their achievements ensured that nearly all the philosophers of the fourth century had to come to Athens to study before they could make a living as travelling philosophers. In this respect fourth-century Athenian philosophy represents a partial victory for Socrates' reaction against the methods of the sophists and in favour of 'being together' (*sunousia*).[86] After 399 there was a sort of diaspora of Socrates' followers, connected with a withdrawal to the house of Euclides at Megara after his death.[87] Phaedo went back to Elis.[88] Aeschines the Socratic went to the court of Dionysius I in Sicily,[89] introduced to the tyrant's patronage by Aristippus, who had entered upon the life of a travelling philosopher before the death of Socrates.[90] Aristippus' career shows traits which come out also in the careers of later alumni of the Athenian schools. He was a success, made money and sent it to Socrates (who refused a gift of 20 minas but presumably accepted more modest offerings),[91] and enjoyed a flamboyant level of consumption.[92] Diogenes Laertius tells two stories about Aristippus on sea voyages,[93] which suggest the role of travel in the life of the philosopher; and he spent time in Athens with Socrates, in Sicily, in Corinth, in Asia and almost certainly a good deal of time in his native Cyrene.[94] Clearly he attained star status, and clearly it was important to do so: Diogenes of Sinope, on an occasion when no one would listen to his serious lecture, changed the style of the address.[95] Self-publicity was central to philosophical success. Not that Diogenes had the same attitude to earning and spending as Aristippus,[96] but he travelled widely – at least to Megara, Myndus, Samothrace, Lacedaemon and Delphi, besides Athens[97] – and, like Aristippus,[98] encountered pirates on one of his voyages.[99] A third self-publicist who attained star rating in the philosophical business was Bion the Borysthenite.[100] The slave and protégé of a rhetor in Olbia from childhood to the age of about 20, he sold his master's books when he inherited them and went to Athens to learn philosophy.[101] He, too, became a travelling philosopher (another who met with pirates),[102] and the story of his arrival in Rhodes indicates the kind of scene which might have been expected when a philosopher came to town (an extremely successful philosopher: the point of the story is that Bion was trying to create an exaggerated impression of his own standing in the philosophical world). He persuaded the sailors from his ship to wear academic dress and made an entrance into the gymnasium with them in tow.[103] Diogenes Laertius gives the fact that Bion was a big spender as explanation of the fact that he moved from city to city:[104] probably frequent moves helped maximise a philosopher's revenue from lectures.

Lectures were meat and drink. They represent an area where education and entertainment shaded into each other. Diogenes of Sinope's adaptation of his material in order to gain a bigger audience has been noted, and the writer of the Hippocratic *Precepts* makes disparaging reference to the wish to give a lecture for the sake of attracting a crowd. (He pleads with doctors at least not to quote poetry as evidence.)[106] Aeschines the Socratic, returning to Athens from Sicily, found that the circles of Plato and Aristippus were so well established that he dared not teach philosophy (to private pupils, the context implies) and he therefore gave lectures with an admission fee[107] and composed law-court speeches.[108] The distinction between education and intellectual entertainment is rather a fine one, and it should be said that the criticism in Diogenes Laertius of Menedemus for not keeping order at his lectures ('it was impossible to see any order at his place, and the benches were not in a circle, but each would listen wherever he happened to be walking about or sitting, and he himself followed the same pattern')[109] suggests that it was usual for a rather disciplined atmosphere to prevail.[110] But the content of lectures had to appeal to paying customers: an audience came to hear Plato lecture on the Good – an understandably popular theme – and was not prepared for the mathematical content.[111] By contrast Bion's Diatribes may well have contained a good deal of entertaining material.[112]

To achieve success in Athens was the pinnacle of a philosophoical career, at least for an ambitious practitioner. Some, like Aristippus, were content to return to their original home and become, as it were, a big fish in a small pond (though even Aristippus recognised the importance in his own case of having left Libya for Greece).[113] Alexinus, the pupil of Eubulides, went to Olympia in the hope of founding an Olympian *haeresis*. This may have been an attempt to create a new philosophical centre (the grandeur of the name would suggest a rival to Athens), but it came to nothing – the money ran out and Alexinus went into inglorious retirement.[114] Talented philosophers – for example, Aristotle[115] and Epicurus[116] – became experienced, established practitioners by working outside Athens, then came to the big city. J. P. Lynch speaks of Athens attracting sophists who had 'given up their itinerant practice',[117] and N. W. de Witt, commenting on Epicurus' career, says that 'from the very first it had possibly been his plan, after trying out his teaching in the provinces, as it were, to establish himself in Athens, where a new philosophy, if bidding for general recognition, was bound to locate itself'.[118]

Pupils, as well as masters, would travel. This fact is certainly referred to by Aeneas Tacticus, when he advises his readers that a register should be kept of people from neighbouring cities who are in town 'for the sake of education or for any other purpose'.[119] And it is amply illustrated by the wide range of ethnics in (for example) the list of Plato's disciples.[120] These were people who came to Athens because they had heard of Plato or, as Bion did at the end of the century, because it was the only possible destination for a young man who wanted to be a philosopher.[121] Disciples would, when necessary, follow their master when he moved from one place to another – like the disciples who asked Alexinus why he had moved from Elis to Olympia,[122] or the 'very many disciples' who followed Eudoxus of Cnidos from the court of Mausolus to Athens.[123]

Considering the worry about security (attested in Aeneas) which could arise from the presence of a man with a group of dedicated followers, it is perhaps surprising that there is not more evidence of philosophers' being banned from cities, as Epicurus was from Mytilene in 310.[124] Aristotle fled from Athens in 323, and had found it prudent to leave in 348.[125] Even on the later occasion his pupils seem not to have followed him, but this is accounted for by the established nature of the school in the Lyceum by 323. Philosophers were travelling persons, whether they were masters of their profession or students, but, particularly in the case of serious students of philosophy, the roads they travelled tended to lead to Athens.

Philosophy was usually regarded as unimpeachably respectable. *Hetaerae*, by contrast, are treated by the ancient authors as having existed in a *demi-monde*. The writers, and their readers, knew what the facts were (and felt no strong disapproval of the society in which *hetaerae* had a not unimportant place), but it was possible for anyone with a claim to unworldliness to pretend ignorance of them: hence Socrates' 'feigned innocence' in Xenophon, *Memorabilia* III.11, and its literary effectiveness.[126] The speech against Neaera, probably written by Apollodorus, gives a unique view of the fourth-century *demi-monde*, and expresses a wide variety of moral views on the *hetaerae*, their occupation and their clients. There is an implicit distinction between merely consorting with *hetaerae* and living a dissolute life:[127] little or no blame seems to attach to a man for the former.[128] It was apparently regarded as normal that the *demi-monde* should exist, and moral debate tended to concern its proper *Sitz im Leben*, so that censorious comments about *hetaerae* and their life style in Greek literature tend to come in the form of objections to lapses in the usually rigid separation of the (so to speak) wifely mode of existence and the *hetaera*'s.[129] That is, it seemed reprehensible to marry a *hetaera* (and correspondingly some fun is made of *hetaerae* who marry);[130] but it seemed normal for a *hetaera* to be almost everything a wifely woman was not allowed to be[131] – seen in public, present at dinners, property-owning[132] and mobile. Neaera lived in Corinth, and later in Megara, as well as in Athens, and travelled to the Peloponnese, to Thessaly and Ionia in connection with her work.[133] Her moves seem to have been occasional, brought about by circumstances at particular moments; and this gives a definite point of comparison with the physicians and philosophers.[134] Other *hetaerae*, too, found that fourth-century conditions made it desirable or necessary for them to adopt a mobile life style.

Athenaeus XIII provides a fund of insights, mostly in the form of anecdotes, or quotations from comedy, into the *demi-monde*. Many periods are represented, but there is a particularly impressive fund of stories dealing with the later part of the fourth century and the first century or so of the Hellenistic Age. It was perhaps a sort of Golden Age for the *hetaerae* – at least for the most successful of them. Alexander the Great and several of the Successors and Epigoni are named as lovers of *hetaerae*: Alexander of Thaïs (whom Ptolemy Soter later married),[135] Antigonus of Demo,[136] Demetrius Poliorcetes of Lamia, Leaena and 'many others',[137] Ptolemy Philadelphus of a whole list of women.[138] It would be foolish to forget that colourful stories easily attach to colourful characters, but the way in which *hetaerae* seem to have entered the milieu of the Macedonian courts is not only paralleled by the involvement of artists, physicians and philosophers[139] but also comparable with the way in which slightly earlier dynasts on the fringes of the Greek world brought Greek girls into their courts. Many sources refer to Cyrus' two Greek concubines, one of whom (the more famous) was captured by the

Persians at Cunaxa while the other escaped.[140] Athenaeus quotes Theopompus on Strato, king of Sidon:[141] 'Strato arranged for flute girls and dancing girls and cithara girls at his dinner parties – and he sent for many *hetaerae* from the Peloponnese, and many women musicans from Ionia, and other girls from throughout Greece' and goes on to note Strato's rivalry with the court of Nicocles, the dynast of Cyprus.[142] The princely practice of keeping *hetaerae* was copied by others, from Harpalus[143] downwards in the scale of wealth and influence, through Demetrius of Phalerum to the philosophical and literary figures: Menander, Stilpo, Epicurus.[144]

Of those *hetaerae* not travelling to the courts of kings and dynasts, probably many stayed in the same city for long periods.[145] Athens was as much a centre for *hetaerae* as for philosophers (Aristophanes of Byzantium compiled from literary sources a list of 135 Attic *hetaerae*),[146] and probably the people ensuring Athenian cultural predominance in this area[147] were drawn largely from outside,[148] just as the philosophers were. As early as the Periclean period 'crowds of beautiful women' had been imported by Aspasia (who was from Miletus),[149] and there are several examples afterwards of a style of 'apprenticeship' (so to speak) which involved a working *hetaera* buying girls as slaves (hence from abroad) and bringing them up to the hetaeric way of life. Neaera, the speaker alleges, became a *hetaera* in this way.[150] Sinope, who moved her business from Aegina to Athens, was succeeded by Bacchis, and Bacchis by Harpalus' mistress, Pythionice.[151] Gnathaenium was the granddaughter (whether by blood or by convention)[152] of Gnathaena.[153] The maintenance of these dynasties is likely to have required an inflow of young girls and to have created a situation in which some *hetaerae* left to seek work elsewhere (as philosophers left Athens and physicians left Cos): the passage which says that Aspasia imported women says also that Greece was filled with her *hetaerae*.[154]

The philosophic and hetaeric occupations were arguably paradigmatic callings in education and entertainment respectively. Something can be said about the other specialists in these areas, particularly about comic and tragic actors, though perhaps less than one would like. Orators may not have been very mobile:[155] only one speech in the extant corpora of fourth-century rhetoric was for delivery in a law court outside Athens (Isocrates, *Aegineticus*).[156] It may well be the case that, though the Syracusan Lysias made a name for himself as a metic in Athens, and the Corinthian Dinarchus became the city's top orator roughly from the death of Alexander to the restoration of democracy in 307,[157] the connection between political and forensic oratory was so close that usually only teachers, not practitioners, of rhetoric could come in from outside and establish themselves in business in a city.[158]

It was always the business of actors to go on tour,[159] and by about 290 the guilds of Dionysiac artists were beginning to be formed.[160] An Amphictyonic decree of 278 granting extensive privileges 'to the *technitai* in Athens' shows something of their importance.[161] A. Pickard-Cambridge argues that organisation on these lines had been rendered almost inevitable by the growing importance of dramatic and musical performances in the fourth century.[162]

P. Ghiron-Bistagne draws attention to the central importance of the fourth century in the development of the Greek theatrical tradition.[163] In this period some of the works of the great playwrights of the Classical Age gained through continued performance the canonical character which ensured their survival into modern times and put them at the heart of the repertoire which the Dionysiac artists of later centuries drew on. It would be a mistake to underestimate the importance of the fourth-century antecedents of the Dionysiac artists.

Throughout the century there were famous actors.[164] When Macedon came to prominence the court of Philip[165] and the court of Alexander could attract the top performers.[166] The anecdotal sources which tell stories of these actors do not in general have anything informative to say about their life style, but the Samian decree honouring Polus the Aeginetan, passed in 306,[167] is an exceptionally interesting text relating to one of the most attractive of fourth-century actors from the anecdotal sources' point of view.[168] The Samians, wanting to celebrate a festival to Antigonus and Demetrius on the news of Demetrius' naval victory at Cyprian Salamis, sent ambassadors to Polus to ask him to perform, and agree to an arrangement which would involve a lower fee than he would normally have expected.[169] The grant of citizenship and other privileges recognises his acceptance.

Naturally Polus' earning power at the height of his career had put him in a position where he could take note of the things which in the highest social circles were more important than money. But there is a third-century Euboean inscription which provides evidence on actors' pay.[170] In this text a living allowance of nine obols per day is laid down for actors during festivals; performance fees are in hundreds of drachmas.[171] These fees, as Ghiron-Bistagne notes, would be only to the protagonist, who would maintain his troupe out of them.[172] The division is clear: the star performers would become rich and famous, and need not spend on their assistants any more than necessary to assure themselves of capable support in their performances.[173] Organisation among travelling actors should be envisaged on the lines of a star performer gathering a retinue of assistants

and personal servants and maintaining them out of his earnings.
These star performers were welcomed in cities at festival times.
The popular appeal of their product is easily understood in the
modern mind;[174] but it is as well to remember that in acting plays
they carried out religious ceremonies which audiences and city
governments regarded as having an importance beyond entertainment.[175] Hence the apparent unanimity between city governments
(who paid) and the public (who made the star actors famous) in
valuing actors highly.

But Ghiron-Bistagne makes the point that whereas people putting
on festivals were carrying out a civic and religious duty, actors were
paid workers.[176] They were people who had chosen a specialised
career. Some achieved stardom, more did not: and this posed a
certain ideological difficulty. Aristotle observes (in a section on
complimentary and uncomplimentary words denoting identical
referents) that some call actors 'Dionysus flatterers' but that they call
themselves *technitai*.[177] As time went on the literary tradition
continued (at points where it was very representative of the aristocratic tradition in serious mood) to show hostility to actors. The
Aristotelian *Problems* ask why Dionysiac artists are wicked,[178] and,
in another place, why some people choose inferior occupations
(wizard, actor, piper) rather than more serious ones (astronomer,
orator).[179] This second passage is interesting because it recognises
that they develop a different value-system from that to which the
reader is presumed to subscribe.[180]

While actors' work was in entertainment and religious worship, the
work of soothsayers was to do with religion, and was perhaps only
incidentally a sort of showmanship. But analogies can be drawn with
the medical and dramatic professions. Costume and demeanour had
a definitive and authenticating function. Family, as with the
Asclepiads in the medical sphere, could be of importance: ten or
eleven of the 69 soothsayers listed in the prosopography in P. Kett's
study[181] were members of the Iamid family from Elis. But no
monopoly was maintained, as the case of Thrasyllus in the
Aegineticus shows, and soothsayers from a wide variety of cities lived
the life of wanderers in the practice of their craft.[182]

All armies required soothsayers,[183] and being on campaign with an
army was the mobile life *per excellence*, but even employment in
cities might involve fairly frequent travel. Soothsayers could be
called on during epidemics or other critical periods and would
presumably move on once a situation had returned to normal.[184] At
least at the most successful end of the profession, soothsayers would
be imposing figures,[185] regarded as being at a comparable level of
prestige to great generals and Olympic victors; but there must have

been ordinary soothsayers besides those who achieved the reputation of being star performers – Xenophon in the *Anabasis* refers to 'all the soothsayers' in the army of the Ten Thousand.[186] Clothing, books, family, friends, personal reputation and results achieved would be the factors which could influence the level of success.

Another area which produced specialists was that of cookery. If one can judge from the growth in the incidence of references to cooks in comedy, their profession came to be distinctive and of recognisable character (such as to be parodied and made a joke of) in the century after Aristophanes' career ended.[187] The evidence of comedy should be treated with great care, all the more so when access to it can be had only via Athenaeus, but it can establish some points. First, that it was usual for cooks to be free men and not slaves.[188] Second, that two masks were in use on the comic stage, one representing a native cook, the other a foreign cook.[189] Third, that specialist cooks were hired for particular occasions.[190] All these points favour the supposition that cooks were free to travel between cities when they thought business might be better elsewhere. And the flow of technical knowledge into Greece from outlying areas of the Hellenic world would suggest that cooks, like doctors, were prepared to travel partly in order to gain experience;[191] this is corroborated by evidence (again from Athenaeus) for the existence of technical treatises, that is, cookery books.[192] There was money to be made from cooking – more, probably, after the beginning of the Hellenistic Age than before it (though the cook had become a stock character in the days of Middle Attic comedy)[193] – and the best-informed, most skilful and most plausible cooks were best placed to make it.

The general picture

The list of travelling specialists could be extended almost indefinitely. Laches in Plato, *Laches* 183A–B, says how travelling professional drill sergeants seem to regard Sparta (the home of military training) as a place too holy to enter, and go anywhere but there to practise. Tissaphernes employed a Greek military expert,[194] and an Attic decree honours a Methonaean who was a drill master to Athenian ephebes.[195]

It can be said with some confidence that in the fourth century BC more Greeks than ever before were receiving the technical training that would enable them to live from skills whose exercise normally involved enough travelling to make their practitioners effectively persons whose lives were lived outside the cities. A piece of evidence for this statement, to add to the observations above on the flourishing state of particular specialisations, is the 'protreptic' literature of the fourth century: the texts written to encourage young men to undertake training. [Hp.] *The Art* is a specially interesting example of the genre,[196] because in the introduction to its defence of medicine as a definable technique of demonstrable utility it shows an awareness of *technai* (almost 'the professions') as a group of occupations of the same kind.[197] The author undertakes to oppose the detractors of the medical craft and leaves it to suitably qualified persons to put forward appropriate defences of other *technai*.[198] Some other Hippocratic treatises appear to be directed at audiences similar to the intended audience of *The Art* (though no other is so obviously cast as an apologia): *Ancient Medicine* aims to publicise and defend the author's scientific technique;[199] *Law* challenges the reader to undertake medical study;[200] *Decorum* urges the young towards wisdom 'leading to mastery of a craft' and away from wisdom . . . 'with greed for gain and indiscipline'.[201] Philosophers, too, wrote works to attract young men to philosophy.[202] The obvious example is Isocrates I (*To Demonicus*), most likely written not only to gain favour with the wealthy prospective pupil to whom the work is addressed, but also for public consumption: section 3 almost invites any young man with intellectual interests to substitute his own name for Demonicus' and read Isocrates' pages of good advice as a sample of what philosophy has to offer.[203] A protreptic element came into cookery books too, to judge from Athenaeus' report of the opinions of cookery-book authors Heraclides and Glaucus the Locrian on who was a suitable entrant to the profession.[204]

There was counter-propaganda by the proponents of conventional styles of life: Plato in the *Gorgias* (463A–C) divides 'flattery' into 'cookery, rhetoric, beautician work and being a sophist' and these, except perhaps the beauticians', were skills typically exercised by travelling Greeks. Passages in Plato seeking to limit the application of the term *techne* (*Gorgias* 464B) or to incorporate features of the life of mobile skilled workers into regular city life (*Rep.* I 345E–347A) can be seen as responses to the ideological challenges to conservative thought implicit in the recruitment of young men with means to pay for training into skilled travelling occupations.

The *Etymologicum Gudianum* distinguishes between *technitai* and *banausoi*.[205] This entry would seem likely to be derived from a source which came into existence at a period when there was debate about the prestige and position of 'professional' workers as compared with others and as compared with those who did not need to work. Deprecation of banausic trades in fourth-century sources suggests that the growing numbers of educated and articulate persons in technical occupations will probably have been keen to dissociate themselves from the people whose work seemed menial to most writers.

So the distinction in the *Etymologicum Gudianum* should probably be ascribed to this period. Together with the outpouring of protreptic, it is a pointer to an ideology; a minority ideology, indeed, but one not without importance: an ideology of people whose primary identification was with their job,[206] and whose job would determine where they lived at a given time. People with means to afford training would be the most likely to take the path which would lead to itinerant practice in medicine or education (though there are examples of men from humble origins who took to philosophy):[207] *hetaerae* and cooks would not be recruited from the ranks of the well-to-do. But high income was available for some practitioners in all these occupations. The world outside the cities was not a world of uniform destitution.

G. E. M. de Ste Croix's comments on the sorts of people discussed in this inquiry are limited in their usefulness by the way he classifies them under the miscellaneous category 'other independent producers'.[208] He attempts (as observed above)[209] to treat the physician Democedes as an anomalous case: this treatment, given some plausibility by Democedes' exceptional success and his early date, is inadequate as an analysis of the position of skilled people who loosened, or entirely broke, their city ties in the fourth century. By being outside the cities – on the move, periodically, from one city to another – they put themselves outside the established political order. By being identified primarily with their job, they put themselves outside the established social order: so that de Ste Croix must fail to define their class position,[210] and they must stand as an exception to M. I. Finley's generalisations on orders and status.[211]

They shook away the constraints of the usual kind of life in society. They lived an international life. Their increasing numbers and importance were one of the factors which made the Greek world, as the fourth century progressed, an ideal world for Hellenistic kings to live in: the Macedonian courts fitted in to an already developing system which took people away from home to learn *technai* and into a mobile mode of life to practise them. Athens, the centre of the international scene, became the 'pinnacle of the known world', so that Antigonus and Demetrius, even at the moment of hoping to conquer it,[212] planned not to keep the city for themselves, since it could flash their deeds to all men.[213] They were not intending to restrict their conquests – or, at least, it is not necessary to ascribe to them a motive which would seem uncharacteristic. The point was, as it were, to conquer the intellectual world. Kings needed support from philosophers and people of similar influence;[214] though it might sometimes come unasked, it could not be gained by mere coercion.[215] So their moves towards gaining the allegiance of the practitioners of

159

Mobile skilled workers

technai at the highest level (including the restrained behaviour of several of them, from Philip II onwards, towards Athens)[216] were as much part of their drive to dominate the world of the Greek cities by control of the Greeks outside the cities as were their moves to recruit mercenaries, to drive the *leistai* off the seas, and to found cities to their own glory.

Notes

1 Cf. above, chapters 4 and 5.
2 Whereas it was not usual to assume that a metic would leave a city one day: Plato, *Laws* 850 A–D, which provides that metics are to stay only twenty years in the hypothetical city, is a proposal for an amendment to the standard (Athenian) practice – the amendment being intended to help regulate outside influences on the hypothetical community. The expectation that metics would be settled residents is brought out by Whitehead, *Ideology*, pp. 6–7, who insists that 'immigrant' is a better translation of *metoikos* than 'resident alien' (but cf. pp. 18–19, where Whitehead notes the differentiated nature of the metic community at Athens). Cf. above, p. 4.
3 Xenophon, *Poroi* 2.1–7; cf. Whitehead, *Ideology*, pp. 125–9. This is perhaps an appropriate place in which to add that this chapter will not be concerned with traders (but cf. below, chapter 7). Travel is not by itself the definitive element: the temporary or permanent relaxation of links of citizenship is more important.
4 Isocrates 4(*Antidosis*).155–6.
5 D.L. VI.47.
6 D.L. VII.2.
7 D.L. VI.49.
8 D.L. VI.38 (=Nauck *TGF*² Adesp. 284).
9 A. Burford, 'The economics of Greek temple-building', *PCPh*, n.s. 11 (1965) pp. 21–34; *The Greek Temple Builders at Epidaurus* (Liverpool, 1969); *Craftsmen in Greek and Roman Society* (London, 1972).
10 Burford, *Craftsmen*, p. 65.
11 Burford, *Temple Builders*, pp. 200–1.
12 Burford, *Temple Builders*, p. 201.
13 Burford, *Temple Builders*, p. 199.
14 Burford, *Temple Builders*, p. 200, outlines the resources available: 'the following assumptions may be made, that something more than a dozen stone-masons' workshops existed in Athens and Corinth, and more than half-a-dozen in Argos; that there were several professional timber men in Corinth; (etc.)'. (J. K. Davies, *Wealth and the Power of Wealth in Classical Athens*, New York, 1981, pp. 41–3, gives a list of known slave-worked industrial enterprises at Athens.) On stonemasons' workshops at Athens Burford refers to R. S. Young, 'An industrial district of ancient Athens', *Hesp.* 20 (1951), pp. 135–288, with plates 55–85: pp. 160–7 of this detailed study deal with the 'street

of the marble workers'. See also R. H. Randall, 'The Erechtheum workmen', *AJA* 57 (1953), pp. 37–55.
15 Below, pp. 147–57.
16 See later in this section.
17 Cf. above, n. 14.
18 Burford, 'Economics', p. 32; Burford, *Temple Builders*, p. 204; D.S. XIV.18.3 and 41.3; Xenophon, *Ages.* 1. And two Athenian potters, sons of a very famous craftsman (*IG* II² 6320), were honoured by the Ephesians for settling and working in Ephesus at this period (H. Engelmann, D. Knibbe and R. Merkelbach, *Die Inschriften von Ephesos* IV, Bonn, 1980, No. 1420). This was part of a fairly general trend of emigration of potters from Athens to areas on the fringes of the Greek world from the late fifth century onwards: see MacDonald, 'The emigration of potters'. Among the destinations were Lucania and Apulia (p. 159), Etruria (p. 160), Sicily and Lipari (p. 161), Olympia (p. 101), Corinth (p. 162), Smyrna (p. 163) and Olynthus (p. 163).
19 G. T. Griffith, 'The union of Corinth and Argos', *Hist.* 1 (1950), pp. 236–56, at p. 240 (cf. n. 1). In *Archaeological Reports* 1978–9 at pp. 9–10 C. Williams' excavation of building in the Corinthian forum, the 'Punic Amphora Building', is reported: this building, which began to be used partly in the fish trade in the second quarter of the fifth century and was later apparently used exclusively for this purpose, seems to have been abandoned late in the third quarter of the fifth century. Williams suggests that events at the beginning of the Peloponnesian war may have put the fish importer who used the building out of business. Cf. also D. M. Lewis, *Sparta and Persia* (Leiden, 1977), p. 88.
20 J. B. Salmon, *Wealthy Corinth* (Oxford, 1984), pp. 165–7 and 175–85. On the 'Punic Amphora Building' (cf. above, n. 19) see p. 128.
21 Burford, *Temple Builders*, p. 201: and cf. Burford, 'Economics', p. 31, on how the Epidaurians recruited their temple builders. Burford, 'Economics', p. 33, suggests that the revival of building activity in mainland Greece was connected with the revival of Athenian influence in the 370s.
22 Burford, *Temple Builders*, p. 203.
23 Burford, *Temple Builders*, p. 205. This comment could not be extended without reservation to all the people mentioned on pp. 150–7 below.
24 Burford, *Temple Builders*, p. 205. Burford adds, '... they followed the calling of their craft, and earned their living when and where they could'.
25 Cf. Burford, *Temple Builders*, p. 205: 'skilled labour was always scarce'.
26 Cf. Burford, 'Economics', p. 34: 'the patrons of temple building supplied money and motive for the work. The craftsmen alone could ensure the achievement of the patrons' aims.'
27 Cf. above, n. 14. Randall, 'Erechtheum workmen', p. 204, notes from the Erechtheum accounts that slaves were owned only by carpenters,

masons and the architect on this project (cf. table on p. 202). On this reckoning prosperous trades might pass from master to slave, but trades less in demand would go only from father to son.

28 Praxiteles and Cephisodotus: Pliny, *NH* XXXVI.4.24; Lysippus' sons: Pliny, *NH* XXXIV.19.66 (Lysippus, on the other hand, started out as a coppersmith, according to Duris of Samos (quoted at Pliny, *NH* XXXIV.19.61), and seems not to have been anyone's pupil; his brother Lysistratus was a sculptor too: Pliny, *NH* XXXIV.19.51); Timarchides' sons: Pliny, *NH* XXXVI.4.35; Polycles *floruit* Ol. 102 (372–369): Pliny, *NH* XXXIV.19.51.

29 See below, pp. 147–60. Especially, there was no 'Hippocratic revolution'; contrast the development of medical education as discussed at the beginning of section 2.

30 S. Hornblower, *Mausolus*, p. 240: Scopas, Bryaxis, Timotheus, Leochares, Pytheus, Satyrus.

31 S. Hornblower, *Mausolus*, p. 263, notes that 'local labour must have been available on a fairly humble level', and adds that the sculptors must have brought teams of co-workers from home. In n. 321 he suggests Philistides of Athens as one such, and names a few other minor figures.

32 S. Hornblower, *Mausolus*, p. 244.

33 S. Hornblower, *Mausolus*, pp. 239–40. It would be possible to offer alternative exegeses of Pliny, *NH* XXXIV.4.30, '... regina obiit. non tamen recesserunt nisi absoluto, iam id gloriae ipsorum artisque monumentum iudicantes ...' to Hornblower's 'Pliny says that after the death of Artemisia the four artists continued the work unpaid ...'. Pliny does not say 'unpaid'. He implies it, but he was working from a written source and probably understood no more about the likely terms of employment of sculptors by satraps than the modern student. The use of *absolvo* suggests that there was little left to do when Artemisia died (cf. *OLD* s.v. *absolvo* (7)). It is even possible that the sculptors and their assistants were receiving rations in kind as well as money payments, and that Artemisia's death may have affected only the money payments. What lies behind Pliny's comment is irrecoverably lost: but the general point that no one could work for no pay is certainly sound.

34 Pliny, *NH* XXXIV.17.37. S. Hornblower, *Mausolus*, pp. 239–40, shows that the conventional drachma-per-day wage was applicable to the most outstanding craftsmen, as well as the rest. At p. 263 he speculates that the rate for work on the Mausoleum may have been a little above a drachma per day, to take account of the fall in the value of money since the Erechtheum and Epidaurus. This is a sensible suggestion; but it might be worth adding that extra payments may have been made as lump sums, possibly on completion: the drachma-per-day rate became so thoroughly conventional in the Hellenistic period (by the first century AD a denarius per day was the direct successor: Matthew 20.1–13) that it appears in Tobit 5.14–15 – a reflection of the Hellenistic context in which the author or redactor

lived. And in this passage the employer promises the employee a bonus on completion of the job. This may have been a fairly common condition of employment of temporary workers (it would explain Lysippus' savings): cf. (*a*) Antigonus' paying off his athletes and *technitai* (hurriedly) in 302 at D.S. XX.108.1, and (*b*) below, p. 155 and nn. 170–1.

35 G. M. A. Richter, *Sculptors and Sculpture of the Greeks* (fourth edition, New Haven and London, 1970), pp. 199, 207 and 224.
36 Richter, *Sculptors*, pp. 206, 217 and 224.
37 Richter, *Sculptors*, p. 206.
38 Richter, *Sculptors*, p. 220.
39 Pytheus worked on the temple of Athena Polias at Priene: cf. S. Hornblower, *Mausolus*, pp. 323–30, which also puts the case for dating Priene late, rather than in the 350s.
40 Delays like the building of the walls of Alexandria-by-Egypt in the time of Ptolemy Soter: Tacitus, *Hist.* IV.83.1; Fraser, *Ptolemaic Alexandria*, p. 12 and n. 55.
41 D.S. XIX.54.2. Earlier the Athenians had received help in a building project (the stadium and the Panathenaic theatre) from Eudemus of Plataea (329: Tod II 198). *IG* II² 345 (332/331) honours a Plataean whose patronymic ends in -emou and who may be a relative of this Eudemus.
42 Pausanius X.36.3–4 and X.3.3. Cf. above, pp. 50–1.
43 M. Lacroix, 'Les Etrangers à Délos pendant la période de l'indépendence', *Mélanges Gustav Glotz* II (Paris, 1932), pp. 501–2.
44 Lacroix, 'Les Etrangers', p. 506: 'right through the last part of the fourth [century the metics] seem to be in an entirely dominant position'.
45 Lacroix, 'Les Etrangers', p. 508.
46 Lacroix, 'Les Etrangers', pp. 508–9. D. M. Lewis comments (*per epistulam*), 'the choregia seems to have institutionalized foreigners, four citizens and two metics (so described) for each tragedy and comedy ... contrast the Athenian position; metic choregoi only at the Lenaia and perhaps not regularly'.
47 Lacroix, 'Les Etrangers', pp. 511–16. Lacroix distinguishes people who passed from city to city from 'vrais métèques', but his distinction is different from that proposed at the opening of this chapter. He distinguishes those who came to make occasional transactions in high-value goods (pp. 515–16) from the others ('vrais métèques'), but notes that even these were less in evidence after 250.
48 Lacroix, 'Les Etrangers' *passim* and especially pp. 518–20.
49 Sherwin-White, *Ancient Cos*, p. 261.
50 Cf. Sherwin-White, *Ancient Cos*, p. 257.
51 Herodotus III.131.1–3. Cf. L. Cohn-Haft, *The Public Physicians of Ancient Greece* (Northampton, Mass., 1956), p. 10.
52 Cf. Cohn-Haft, *Public Physicians*, p. 21.
53 H. Diller, *Wanderarzt und Aitiologe* (Leipzig, 1934), especially at pp. 3–5 and 28. The other view is put by L. Edelstein, at *Peri aeron und*

die Sammlung der hippokratischen Schriften (Berlin, 1931), p. 59.
54 Again the scientific motive for travel is to the fore. In this section the author of [Hp.] *de Medico* notes on the extraction of missiles that there is little call for it in practices in the city. But the suggestion is not that the doctor should not bother with things which may never happen: it is that anyone who is going to be a surgeon should go on expedition and follow mercenary forces (the date and context of *de Medico* are dealt with below, n. 67). On the scientific importance of travel, cf. Sherwin-White, *Ancient Cos*, p. 264.
55 Theophrastus, *HP* IX.16.8. Manuscripts have Susa; Lousoi, the scholiast conjectures (similarly at IX.15.8). A. Hort in the Loeb edition, vol. II (1926), p. 303, says, 'the mention of Mantinea makes it likely that a place in Arcadia is intended' (Lousoi - otherwise Lousa - is a place in Arcadia). But Pliny, *NH* XXV.95.154, has *Susa*. On this passage cf. above, p. 5 and n. 16.
56 T. S. Brown, 'Suggestions for a *vita* of Ctesius of Cnidus', *Hist.* 27 (1928), pp. 1–9, at pp. 3–4.
57 Brown, 'Suggestions', p. 12.
58 Brown, 'Suggestions', p. 11. Citing his opinions on hellebore (Ctesias, *FGrHist* 688 F 68), Brown puts Ctesias 'in the same class as the better Hippocratic writers'.
59 And Brown 'Suggestions', p. 19, points out that Ctesias' experience as the Persian king's physician probably ensured him a busy practice on his return.
60 Though there were other court physicians: cf. Sherwin-White, *Ancient Cos*, pp. 279–80. The letter of Diocles to Antigonus Monophthalmus (W. Jaeger, *Diokles von Karystos*, Berlin, 1938, pp. 75–8) is not a request for a court appointment but does illustrate the use a physician could make of royalty: E. D. Phillips, *Greek Medicine* (London, 1973), p. 135, notes that 'the letter is an advertisement for the activities of Diocles, and a request for royal support and approval in the age of Hellenistic kings'.
61 [Hp.] *Law* 1: 'medicine is the most outstanding of all *technai*'. This is not an impartial source, but prestige depends on subjective judgements. De Ste Croix, *Class Struggle*, p. 198, doubts the prestige of doctors ('mainly disqualified from the high degree of respect which nowadays is accorded to their profession'), though his mistaken plea (p. 271) that Democedes (cf. above, n. 51) was not giving a form of hired labour because he would collect fees from patients as well as payments from governments (which only shows that he was extravagantly well paid for his medical services, which presumably Polycrates and the rest considered the best available) may perhaps suggest some degree of reservation. De Ste Croix's comments on *technitai* (he does not categorise mobile *technitai* separately) will be considered below, p. 159. D. M. Lewis, 'Dedications of Phialai at Athens', *Hesp.* 37 (1968), pp. 368–80, comments on a text which records a manumitted slave as being a physician (No. 50, line 11) that this is 'a surprisingly complimentary designation for a slave. In the

only medical manumission at Delphi the slave does not have this title' (p. 372). Plato, *Laws* IV 720A, is pertinent here: 'there are people who are doctors – that's what we call them – and people who are doctors' assistants: and we call them "doctors" too'. In B–E the Athenian stranger goes on and says (B) that these assistants may be free or slaves but that they get a different type of training from what a doctor gives to his own children. In C–E the point is made that slaves usually attend slaves. Clearly less prestige would attach to some individuals than to others.

62 Cohn-Haft, *Public Physicians*, p. 16. And [Hp.] *Law* 1 goes on (after its optimistic start: cf. above, n. 61) to say that some practitioners bring the craft into disrepute.

63 Cohn-Haft, *Public Physicians*, p. 16; Edelstein, *Peri aeron*, p. 351; W. H. S. Jones in his Loeb edition of Hippocrates, vol. II (London and New York, 1923), pp. xxxvii–xl.

64 For instance, [Hp.] *Decorum* 8; [Hp.] *In the Surgery* 2 and 4; [Hp.] *de Medico* 1 and 4; [Hp.] *Precepts* 10; and the medical Ionic dialect made the physician *sound* distinctive.

65 Edelstein, *Peri aeron*, pp. 87–110. Craftsmanship, style of life and style of work are discussed at pp. 87–90. A discussion of [Hp.] *In the Surgery* begins at p. 91. At p. 100 Edelstein stresses the need in daily activity for a physician to have oratorical skill.

66 The quotation is from V. Crapanzano, *The Hamadsha: A Study in Moroccan Ethnopsychiatry* (Berkeley and Los Angeles, 1973), p. 133; cited at P. Brown, *The Cult of the Saints* (London, 1981), p. 114. Brown's discussion (at pp. 114–16), though it deals with another period of antiquity, makes a useful point about how therapeutic systems coexisted, and in certain places still coexist.

67 The argument of this chapter will proceed on the assumption that it is at least probable that [Hp.] *Precepts, Decorum* and *de Medico* are products of the same period, and that the period is the later part of the fourth century. J. F. Bensel, 'Hippocratis qui fertur De Medico libellus ed codicum fidem recensitus', *Philologus* 78 (1923), pp. 88–130, comments on the three treatises (p. 101), 'libros iisdem fere temporibus et viris, qui idem de medicorum officiis senserunt, ascribendos esse putem, ut eos altera saeculi quarti parte (350–300) ortos esse crediderim' ('I should think the books should be ascribed to roughly the same period and to authors who took the same view of the duties of doctors – so I tend to believe that they are from the second half of the fourth century'). This suggestion that a broadly similar outlook indicates contemporaneity is reasonable, and is certainly not overturned by W. H. S. Jones's lists of odd words and expressions in his introductions to the *Precepts* and the *Decorum* (Loeb, vol. I, London and New York, 1923, pp. 308–9, and vol. II, London and New York, 1923, pp. 269–70). Bensel, at p. 101, takes *Decorum* 2 as a reference to the banishment of the philosophers from Athens by Sophocles' Law in 306 (on which cf. below, n. 122): there is no objection to acceptance of this as a possibility.

68 [Hp.] *Law* 4. On protreptic, see below, pp. 157–9. A number of texts show how cities (at a slightly later date) would send in quite a formal way to get a doctor. See, e.g., D. M. Pippidi, *Inscripţiile din Scythia Minor greceşti şi latine* I (Bucharest, 1983), No. 26; No. 27 shows the same sort of search for an architect.

69 [Hp.] *Law* 2. This word does not give any information about what exact age, below military age, the author envisaged as the right age to begin study. And it should not be forgotten that *paidomathes*, 'young pupil', is the logical antonym of *opsimathes*, 'late learner', and that *opsimathia* is treated by Theophrastus as the cast of mind which leads people to study things inappropriate to their age rather than as the intellectual result of receiving education late (*Characters* 27; and cf. [Hp.] *Precepts* 13); therefore *paidomathes* may have a connotation concerning the (proper) cast of mind for learning as well as the (proper) age for learning. And cf. below, n. 70.

70 Ibid. A student is in need of 'natural ability – teaching – a suitable place – *paidomathia* – love of hard work – time'. Natural ability is the only one treated as a *pre*requisite: 'it's all useless if natural ability isn't on your side'. The fact that *paidomathia* and time are required may bear out the suggestion (cf. above, n. 69) that *paidomathia* connotes an intellectual quality and so may not necessarily in all cases imply that the 'young pupil' began his study at an exact and prescribed age.

71 Cf. below, p. 152.

72 [Hp.] *Decorum* 8.

73 [Hp.] *Decorum* 9.

74 [Hp.] *Decorum* 10.

75 Cf. above p. 147 and n. 55.

76 [Hp.] *de Medico* 2.

77 [Hp.] *de Medico* 14 (on which cf. above, n. 54) suggests a way for a practising doctor to perfect his craft. Sections 1–13 give brief comments on a very wide range of topics and techniques.

78 [Hp.] *In the Surgery* 2.

79 Cf. comments above, p. 144 and n. 17, on temple builders.

80 Cohn-Haft, *Public Physicians*, pp. 32–45, argues this point.

81 E.g. [Hp.] *Precepts* 6.

82 Cohn-Haft, *Public Physicians*, pp. 76–84, gives an index of epigraphical documents: Nos. 2–6 are dated to the fourth century.

83 This passage requires careful examination. The patient may suspect one of two things: (*a*) that you the doctor will leave him and go away without making a bargain; or (*b*) that you will neglect him and not give him some immediate treatment. (*a*) involves the supposition that when the doctor has gone, he will be beyond recall. (*b*) involves the supposition that treatment may be delayed. Therefore it seems natural to think that the patient's first worry, (*a*), is that the doctor may be about to leave the district (and not just the patient's bedside). Doctors who decided to move cannot always have been able to find a time to do so when no one was ill in the district they were leaving.

84 Athenaeus XIII.584A.

85 See later in this section, with nn. 124–5.
86 On this cf. J. P. Lynch, *Aristotle's School* (Berkeley and Los Angeles, 1972), p. 42.
87 D.L. II.106 (with, for instance, D.L. II.62); and cf. Lynch, *Aristotle's School*, p. 49.
88 D.L. II.105. It is not explicit that Phaedo went back to Elis immediately after the death of Socrates.
89 D.L. II.61–2.
90 D.L. II.65.
91 Ibid.
92 E.g. D.L. II.66 and 68–9.
93 D.L. II.71 and 77. Sea voyages form the background to several anecdotes in Diogenes Laertius. The differences between the stories show that they are not forms of the same account: and naturally the hazards of travel by sea provoked clever comments from philosophers particularly well.
94 D.L. II.65–6, 71, 79. Cf. also the list of his pupils: D.L. II.86.
95 D.L. VI.27.
96 D.L. II.66 and 68.
97 D.L. VI.41, 57 and 59–60.
98 Cf. above, n. 93 and below, n. 102.
99 D.L. VI.74.
100 D.L. IV.46–61.
101 D.L. IV.46–7. Here cf. D.L. II.81, when Aristippus receives money from Dionysius II, and Plato receives a book. Aristippus does not mind the implied slight to his intellectual prestige, saying, 'I need money, Plato needs books.' The implication is that Aristippus (a high-earning practitioner) regarded the possible benefits of reading as marginal to the philosopher's livelihood: his training came by personal contact with a teacher or teachers (Bion attended several schools: D.L. IV.52, and cf. J. F. Kindstrand, *Bion of Borysthenes*, Uppsala, 1976, pp. 10–11) and he subsequently earned money by talking, not by writing. Aristippus' comment can also be read as a rejection of the evaluation of Dionysius' different gifts as implying that Plato was the weightier intellectual figure.
102 D.L. IV.50, and cf. above, nn. 93 and 98.
103 D.L. IV.53.
104 Ibid.
105 See earlier in this section, with n. 95.
106 [Hp.] *Precepts* 12.
107 And cf. above, n. 90.
108 D.L. II.62. It was probably usual for philosophers to turn to speech-writing (Isocrates' adoptive son Aphareus tried to pretend that Isocrates had not done this, but could not convince Aristotle: D.H., *Isocrates* 18, cf. K. J. Dover, *Lysias and the Corpus Lysiacum*, Berkeley and Los Angeles, 1968, p. 25.): certainly it appeared unusual to someone that Aristippus should hire a rhetor. Aristippus, as usual, had a plausible reply: D.L. II.72.

109 D.L. II.130.
110 Cf. D.L. VII.22 (an incident at a lecture); cf. also Athenaeus II.59D-F with Lynch, *Aristotle's School*, p. 57.
111 Aristoxenus, *Principles of Harmony* II.30-1. Aristoxenus quotes Aristotle, apparently as heard rather than as read ('Aristotle always used to say ...'). The picture appears to be of a public lecture; the word *akroasis* is used, and when W. K. C. Guthrie, *A History of Greek Philosophy* IV (Cambridge, 1975), p. 22, comments that 'one would not expect Plato to thrust some of his most difficult doctrine on a completely untrained audience' he appears in some measure to have lost sight of the fact that Aristotle (and Aristoxenus) used the story as a warning against Plato's mistake in producing obscure material on such an occasion (if mistake it was: Plato, the great master, could afford, like Immanuel Kant, not 'to give free rein to that loquacious shallowness, which assumes for itself the name of popularity' (I. Kant, *Critique of Pure Reason*, trans. N. Kemp Smith, second edition, London, 1929, p. 32) – being unintelligible only added to his mystique).
112 A witty comment from the Diatribes is preserved at D.L. II.77. Cf. also Kindstrand, *Bion*, pp. 21-39 (especially pp. 29-30 on Bion's lively style) and pp. 87-99, where Kindstrand denies that the Diatribe was a novel form of literature but classes it as 'popular philosophical dialexis' (p. 97).
113 D.L. II.103. Cf. Phaedo and Elis: D.L. II.105.
114 D.L. II.109.
115 D.L. V.9-10 gives a chronology of his career. D.L. V.2-3 is by contrast a confused passage, putting Aristotle's sojourn with Hermias of Atarneus after Xenocrates' assumption of the headship of the Academy. Lynch, *Aristotle's School*, pp. 94-5, sets out the chronology of Aristotle's time in and outside Athens, making some suggestions.
116 D.L. X.15. Cf. N. W. de Witt, *Epicurus and his Philosophy* (Minneapolis, 1954), pp. 36-7 (also pp. 70-1). He taught at Mytilene and Lampsacus before coming to Athens.
117 Lynch, *Aristotle's School*, p. 52. It is perhaps worth mentioning Timon of Phlius here, though his career fell mainly in the third century. Having started as a dancer, he studied with Stilpo in Megara and Pyrrho in Elis. Being unable to get an income in Elis, he went to the Hellespont and the Propontis. In Chalcedon he set up as a philosopher and had a much better reception than before. Then (having made himself financially secure) he went to Athens and lectured for the rest of his life (D.L. IX.109-10).
118 De Witt, *Epicurus*, p. 37.
119 Aeneas Tacticus 10.10.
120 D.L. III.46.
121 D.L. IV.47.
122 D.L. II.109. And cf. the comments on Bion earlier in this section, with n. 103.
123 D.L. VII.86-91 tells the story of Eudoxus, who went to Athens, Egypt, Cyzicus, the Propontis, the court of Mausolus and Athens again; cf. S.

Hornblower, *Mausolus*, pp. 115–16 and 337.

124 De Witt, *Epicurus*, pp. 70–1: cf. the banishment of philosophers from Athens in 306: Athenaeus XIII.610B–D; D.L. V.38; Pollux IX.42 (cf. D.S. XX.45.2–5 and Plutarch, *Demetrius* 9); Lynch, *Aristotle's School*, p. 103.

125 Lynch, *Aristotle's School*, pp. 94–5.

126 G. E. M. de Ste Croix, *The Origins of the Peloponnesian War* (London, 1972), pp. 179–80.

127 Contrast [Dem.] 59(*Neaera*).122 and 33. K. J. Dover, *Greek Popular Morality in the Time of Plato and Aristotle* (Oxford, 1974), p. 14, notes the speaker's use of the sentiments in section 122 as an important premise in his law-court argument. Similarly in section 33 he is trying to provoke outrage at shocking behaviour. If he had expected his audience to be strongly of the opinion either that respectable men should never have anything to do with *hetaerae* or that no sexual activity with a *hetaera* ought ever to be thought to reflect badly on a man's moral character, it would not have been open to him to make both the suggestion in section 122 and that in section 33. Cf. also Dover, *Greek Popular Morality*, pp. 205–7.

128 See, for instance, [Dem.] 59(*Neaera*).36. Dover, *Greek Popular Morality*, pp. 178–9 calls this passage 'most unusual', but on the ground that it contains an implied compliment to extravagance (this is disputable: a reproach on niggardliness is not the same thing as a compliment to extravagance, nor is it unusual in Greek popular thought: see Theophrastus, *Characters* 22).

129 Though there are some comments in Greek literature of this period against sex outside marriage (e.g. at Isocrates 3(*Nicocles*).40), and some attacks on *hetaerae* as such (e.g. in Anaxilas, *Neottis* (Athenaeus XIII.558A = Kock II, p. 270)). Note that Neaera could charge more when she could claim to be a wife living with her husband ([Dem.] 59(*Neaera*).41): this because she had put herself in the more highly regarded category of women (cf. below, n. 131, and see *IG* II² 9057 with n. 133 below).

130 See, for example, Isaeus 3(*Pyrrhus*).17; [Dem.] 59(*Neaera*).113–14; D.L. IV.46; and Athenaeus XIII.577A, 'when women like that turn to respectability they are better than women who pride themselves on their moral characters'. S. B. Pomeroy, *Goddesses, Whores, Wives and Slaves* (London, 1976), p. 92, observes that there is evidence for *hetaerae* attempting to live as respectable wives, but not for the opposite state of affairs.

131 The word 'wifely' is used here to refer to the respectable citizen women of good family who derived status and commanded respect as members of households (cf. Dover, *Greek Popular Morality*, pp. 95–8) and whose activities were so closely restricted to home life that it had become usual at Athens, in court, not to refer to women by name unless they were disreputable, or connected with one's opponent, or deceased (see D. Schaps, 'The woman least mentioned: etiquette and women's names', *CQ*, n.s. 27 (1977), pp. 323–30). The word

'respectable' could possibly be used (and without implying anything defamatory of the citizen women who were not in a social position in which a fully secluded life could be maintained: cf. Dover, *Greek Popular Morality*, p. 98), but it is less than ideal, for two reasons: first, that the *hetaerae* and their *demi-monde* had a definite and (usually) recognised role and were not social outcasts except in an ambiguous way; and second, that the feeling that there were two kinds of women (suitable wives for well-to-do men and others) was very deep and lasting in antiquity, and was not directly analogous to a modern distinction between respectability and its opposite: Augustine of Hippo in the 380s AD encountered no moral censure for sending his concubine back to Africa from Milan when he was considering marriage – he was as yet still a Manichee, but as P. Brown comments (*Augustine of Hippo*, Berkeley and Los Angeles, 1967, pp. 88–9), 'in Milan ... well-to-do people gave little thought to such things. To abandon one's concubine, in order to take a wife in legitimate matrimony, was "not bigamy, but a sign of moral improvement"' (Brown quotes Pope Leo).

132 De Ste Croix, *Peloponnesian War*, p. 101, notes that a *hetaera*'s economic position 'might be virtually identical with that of a male prostitute or any other non-citizen provider of services in the city'. De Ste Croix mentions *hetaerae* before doctors and after traders in a survey on p. 271, but his comment, 'talented *hetairai* (courtesans) and other providers of essential services sometimes did very well for themselves' appears to be intended as a joke.

133 [Dem.] 59(*Neaera*).26, 35 and 108. The evidence of gravestones about mobility of Corinthian women to Athens is quite striking. D. M. Lewis observes from a survey of fourth-century gravestones from Athens that the only foreigners for whom women outnumber men are Corinthians (*IG* II² 9056, 9061, 9069, 9080 and 9081). Salmon, *Wealthy Corinth*, pp. 398–400, deals with cult prostitution in the temple of Aphrodite and comments on the higher classes of prostitute also afforded by Corinth.

134 Cf. above, pp. 147–52.

135 Athenaeus XIII.576E.

136 Athenaeus XIII.578A.

137 Athenaeus XIII.577C–D; cf. VI.253B, where it is noted that the Thebans founded a temple of Aphrodite Lamia, as a piece of flattery to Demetrius. This was not altogether a new idea: Harpalus had founded a temple of Aphrodite Pythionice (Theopompus, *FGrHist* 115 F 253).

138 Athenaeus XIII.576E–F.

139 Involvement of this sort goes back to Archelaus; in the period more immediately preceding the Hellenistic courts, Philip II had a doctor (Critobulus: Pliny, *NH* VII.37.124, cf. Sherwin-White, *Ancient Cos*, p. 279) as well as a philosopher (Aristotle: D.L. V.4).

140 Xenophon, *Anab.* I.10.2–3. Cf. also Plutarch, *Per.* 24.12 and *Artax.* 26–9, Justin X.2.1–7, Aelian, *VH* 12.1 (a worked-up account) and

Athenaeus XIII.576D (where it is discussed whether Aspasia/Milto was a *hetaera* or a concubine).
141 Athenaeus XII.531B (=Theopompus, *FGrHist* 115 F 114).
142 It is worth noticing that Strato imported musicians as well as *hetaerae*. There appears not to have been a strong practical distinction between the life styles of women musicians and of *hetaerae*: e.g. Athenaeus XIII.576F–577D.
143 D.S. XVII.108.4–6; cf. Athenaeus XIII.584D–595E.
144 Demetrius of Phalerum: Athenaeus XIII.593E–F; Menander: Athanaeus XIII.585C and 593D; Stilpo: Athenaeus XIII.596E; Epicurus: Athenaeus XIII.588B. In earlier days, Plato and Aristotle too: Athanaeus XIII.589C–D.
145 At Plautus, *Asinaria* 230, Cleaereta asks Argyrippus 20 minas for her services for a year (and claims that there may be other bidders (1. 231). It was perhaps usual to hire *hetaerae* for a matter of months or years – this seems to be the situation envisaged at Theophrastus, *Characters* 17.3. There was probably sometimes reason to move on the expiry of the period: cf. [Dem.] 59(*Neaera*).32.
146 Athenaeus XIII.583D.
147 The distinction between *hetaerae* and common prostitutes was not perhaps a strong one, but it was there: cf. Athenaeus XIII.569A–D, quoting Xenarchus, *Pentathlum* (=Kock II, p. 468). Pomeroy, *Goddesses*, p. 89, makes the distinction.
148 Cf. above, n. 133.
149 Athenaeus XIII.569F.
150 [Dem.] 59(*Neaera*).18–19.
151 Athenaeus XIII.595A.
152 Nicarete, Neaera's mistress, called six girls daughters, though she had bought them as slaves ([Dem.] 59(*Neaera*).18–19). On the other hand, in the absence of effective contraception, *hetaerae* must have had daughters.
153 Athenaeus XIII.581A.
154 Athenaeus XIII.569F.
155 The matter of epideictic oratory presents a slightly special case here. A historian or a tragedian, as well as professional speakers, might seize the chance of going and speaking a panegyric at Olympia (Theopompus, *FGrHist* 115 T 6).
156 Isocrates 19(*Aegineticus*) was written in the late 390s. It is perhaps significant that in the last section (51) Isocrates mentions the exceptional degree of unanimity in the diverse legal systems of Greek states about the point of law at issue in the case.
157 It is not clear whether Isaeus was a metic. F. Wehrli, *Die Schule des Aristoteles* IV. *Demetrios von Phaleron* F 206 (from Photius s.v. *Isaeus*), comments on Isaeus: 'An Athenian by race – but Demetrius says he was a Chalcidian.' Wehrli (p. 89) comments on the relatively high probability that the Demetrius in question may not be Demetrius of Phalerum, but no conclusion is possible. The first known Athenian Isaeus, leaving aside the orator, is the archon of 284/283.

158 One Alcimus, whom Stilpo is represented as having trapped into philosophy, is described by Diogenes Laertius as 'the leading orator in the whole of Greece' (D.L. II.114). The 'in ... Greece' suggests that he was a professional, and that the comparison is with professionals. G. B. Kerferd points out (*The Sophistic Movement*, Cambridge, 1981, pp. 15–17) that the fifth-century sophists supplied a *social need* by teaching young men in Athens (and similar cities) to speak in public. The social need was for young men from well-to-do backgrounds to become effective politicians by being able to persuade citizens to follow their advice. With this purpose in mind, they will have found a rhetorical education a better investment than a few prepared speeches, since the ability to prepare speeches for others would give them a valuable asset from the patronage point of view.

159 See also Tod II 140, lines 67–9, for Theodorus, an Athenian actor, who in 363 was in Delphi (quite possibly on tour) to give 70 drachmas (100 Attic drachmas) to the temple restoration.

160 *Syll.*³ 460 (cf. A. W. Pickard-Cambridge, *The Dramatic Festivals of Athens*, second edition, Oxford, 1968, p. 282).

161 *IG* II² lines 1–39, *FD* III (2) 68, lines 61–94. Cf. Pickard-Cambridge, *Dramatic Festivals*, p. 308.

162 Cf. Pickard-Cambridge, *Dramatic Festivals*, p. 279.

163 F. Ghiron-Bistagne, *Recherches sur les acteurs dans la Grèce antique* (Paris, 1976), p. 206.

164 Ghiron-Bistagne, *Recherches*, pp. 154–71, discusses the most famous and gives references to the (usually anecdotal) sources dealing with them.

165 After the fall of Olynthus in 348 Philip held an Olympian festival and called the *technitai* to it (Demosthenes 19(*Embassy*).192–3): this, as Pickard-Cambridge notes, implies that there was a large number of such professionals available (*Dramatic Festivals*, pp. 279–80). And Neoptolemus the tragedian was at Philip's banquet shortly before the assassination, and gave an appropriate performance (of unintentional ominousness): D.S. XVI.92.3.

166 At the beginning of his reign, after the capture of Thebes, Alexander held a nine-day festival in Macedonia (D.S. XVII.16.3–4 and Arrian, *Anab.* I.11.1). The parallel with Philip's celebration of the fall of Olynthus is clear. Thenceforth, as Pickard-Cambridge shows, Alexander showed an even greater passion for musicians and actors than his father (*Dramatic Festivals*, p. 280).

167 *SEG* I.362.

168 Mentioned by Plutarch, Lucian, Stobaeus and Aulus Gellius (see Ghiron-Bistagne, *Recherches*, pp. 167–8).

169 M. Schede, 'Aus dem Heraion von Samos', *Ath. Mitt.* 44 (1919), pp. 1–46, at pp. 18–19, explains the financial arrangement and establishes the date of the inscription.

170 *IG* XII (9) 207 (cf. Pickard-Cambridge, *Dramatic Festivals*, pp. 306–8 and Ghiron-Bistagne, *Recherches*, pp. 181–5), especially lines 21–5.

171 Lines 21–2: for a piper, 600 drachmas; for a tragic actor, 100

drachmas; for a comic actor, 400 drachmas; for a costumier, 300 drachmas.

172 Ghiron-Bistagne, *Recherches*, p. 185.

173 Ghiron-Bistagne, *Recherches*, p. 185, suggests that deuteragonists would be better off than tritagonists. Doubtless it was the next step up, but the idea that the deuteragonist became an *associé* rather than a *simple assistant*, if it is intended to imply that deuteragonists could expect some fair-sized shared of the profits, does not seem satisfactory in view of the degree of concentration on individuals in the sources. After all, Polus (see earlier in section, with nn. 167-9) presumably took his colleagues to Samos.

174 Cf. Pickard-Cambridge, *Dramatic Festivals*, p. 305 (on the imperial age), where a parallel with film stars is caustically drawn.

175 This was the motive for the making of the Amphictyonic decree referred to above (see earlier in this section, with n. 161).

176 Ghiron-Bistagne, *Recherches*, p. 174.

177 Aristotle, *Rh.* III.2 1405a 23-5; at lines 25-8 he notes that *leistai* call themselves *poristai* ('providers').

178 [Arist.] *Problems* XXX.10 956b 11-15.

179 [Arist.] *Problems* XVIII.6 917a 6-16. In connection with these occupations characterized by Aristotle as inferior, this is an appropriate place to mention the work of H. Blümner, 'Fahrendes Volk im Alterthum', *SBA* (1918), Abh. 6, pp. 1-53, who attempts a diachronic overview of what circus-type arts were practised in antiquity (for example, sword dancing, pp. 10-11; tightrope walking, pp. 13-16, and fire-eating, pp. 19-20). Some useful points are made, for example on the life of rhapsodes in Xenophon's time (p. 4), but the study does not consistently encompass close examination of the question whether the people referred to were actually travelling folk: it appears to claim its title more from Blümner's interest in locating classical antecedents of the skills of medieval and modern travelling entertainers.

180 This recognition, not surprisingly, is hostilely expressed: 'their character has been corrupted by ignoble preferences'. However, cf. below, pp. 157-9, on protreptic literature.

181 P. Kett, 'Prosopographie der historischen griechischen Manteis bis auf die Zeit Alexanders des Grossen' (diss., Erlangen-Nürnberg, 1966): prosopography at pp. 18-78.

182 Kett, 'Prosopographie', p. 102.

183 Kett, 'Prosopographie', p. 10.

184 Kett, 'Prosopographie', p. 103, gives a selection of soothsayers who were always taking their services to different cities, generals, or politicians.

185 Kett, 'Prosopographie', p. 103, quotes Quintus Curtius (IV.15.27) on Aristander's clothing at Gaugamela (white), and Plutarch (*Alexander* 33.2), who adds a gold crown. Page 104 expresses the opinion that soothsayers counted as *cheirotechnai* (craftsmen).

186 Xenophon, *Hell.* V.5.3: cf. Kett, 'Prosopographie', p. 104.

187 E. M. Rankin, *The Role of the Mageiroi in the Life of the Ancient Greeks* (Chicago, 1907), pp. 4–5, summarises the few references in Aristophanes.

188 See, e.g., Athenaeus XIV.661D–E (incorporating Alexis, *Lebetion,* Kock II, p. 343, and an anonymous comic fragment, Kock II, p. 442). Cf. Rankin, *Mageiroi,* pp. 17–23.

189 Rankin, *Mageiroi,* pp. 12–17, cf. Pickard-Cambridge, *Dramatic Festivals,* p. 178 n. 6. Pollux classifies each of these types (Maeson, Tettix) as slave characters.

190 A good example of this is Athenaeus VII.291F–292D (=Diphilus, *Zographos,* Kock II, p. 553), where a cook outlines what sorts of party he is prepared to work on, and what sorts he prefers to avoid (those where the host is likely to be parsimonious).

191 Cf. Rankin, *Mageiroi,* p. 4. Rankin stresses the importance of 'foreign' cooks coming into Greece, meaning, by 'foreign', Greek-speaking cooks from remote regions whose appearance on the comic stage would have a suitable effect.

192 See, e.g., Athenaeus XIV.661E (before 300: cf. Rankin, *Mageiroi,* pp. 23–5); Athanaeus VII.282A; Athenaeus I.5B on Artemidorus the Pseudaristophanean (pretended pupil of Aristophanes of Byzantium), who collected cookery books. Even on the comic stage, cooks were not always merely boastful: one, a schoolmasterish character, says, 'but the business makes some intellectual demands' (Athenaeus VII.291D–F = Philemon the younger, Kock II, p. 540). And in a fragment of Straton, *Phoenicides* (D. L. Page, *Greek Literary Papyri* I, Loeb edition, pp. 260–9), an old man talks at length about a cook who affects a haughty Homeric vocabulary – a symbol of intellectual prowess which he will not relinquish merely to please an employer (lines 32–3). A technical, even a philosophical, business.

193 Athenaeus VII.293A quotes Sotades 'the poet ... of the Middle Comedy'. Rankin, *Mageiroi,* pp. 12–17, argues for the cook as a standard character in Old Comedy; but there is certainly a great development between the little material in Aristophanes (cf. above, n. 187) and the kind of comic monologue Sotades wrote (293A–E, =Sotades, *Encleiomenai,* Kock II, p. 447).

194 Xenophon, *Anab.* II.1.7 (cf. Lewis, *Sparta and Persia,* p. 14 and n. 69).

195 B. D. Meritt, 'Greek inscriptions', *Hesp.* 9 (1940), pp. 53–96, No. 8, col. I, lines 33–6. Cf. Aristotle, *Ath. Pol.* 42.3, and P. J. Rhodes, *A Commentary on the Aristotelian Athenaion Politeia* (Oxford, 1981), *ad loc.* On the possible implications of being a Methonaean at Athens in the 330s consider above, p. 49 and Harp, s.v. *isoteles.* Another travelling trainer, this one not military but a chorus trainer, is attested in a choregic dedication: *SEG* XXVII.19, line 5. A third-century Thespian text honours an Athenian for his service in training boys in military skills (P. Roesch, 'Une loi fédérale béotienne sur la préparation militaire', *Acta of the Fifth International Congress of Greek and Latin Epigraphy, Cambridge, 1967,* Oxford, 1971, pp. 81–8).

196 A genre which had become possible in the medical area as a result of

the end of the Asclepiad monopoly in Coan medicine, and of the 'Hippocratic revolution' in general: cf. above, p. 147 and nn. 49 and 50. The sophistic movement 'opened up' philosophy is a similar way.

197 [Hp.] *The Art*, like most Hippocratic treatises, contains no definite dating points. T. Gomperz argues that the author was Protagoras of Abdera (*Greek Thinkers* I, London, 1901, pp. 466–9): the argument rests on Plato, *Sophist* 232D5–E1, where the Eleatic Stranger alludes to some texts which are circulating 'about the *technai* – all of them, and each one of them'. Theaetetus says (D9–E1), 'it seems to me you're talking about Protagoras' books on wrestling and on the other *technai*'. Gomperz, *Greek Thinkers* I, p. 468, takes *The Art* 9 as meaning that the author of *The Art* promises to write other treatises. In fact he merely hopes and presumes that such treatises will be written (and cf. below, n. 198). A difficulty with Gomperz's view is that the Hippocratic treatise is called *Peri technes* and not *Peri ietrikes*: the writer of a series of treatises on *technai* would probably avoid the (medical) usage '*techne* = the *medical* craft'. The argument from likelihood in section 7 is perhaps suggestive of the last quarter of the fifth century, since argument from likelihood is a favourite line in Antiphon: see, for instance, 2(*Tetralogy I*).1–11 and 5(*Herodes*).37.

198 [Hp.] *The Art* 1. Nothing said by the author of *The Art* implies that he is not a physician. Section 14, in particular, does not (*contra* Gomperz, *Greek Thinkers* I, p. 423) say that the author is not one of 'those who know the *techne*'. In section 1 he makes a straightforward claim to be regarded as competent to speak about the medical art, but not about the other arts. The inference that he was a doctor seems easy to draw, particularly in view of the usefulness to doctors in everyday life of rhetorical skill (cf. above, n. 65: this shows that Gomperz, *Greek Thinkers* I, p. 423, draws a faulty conclusion when he says, '*The Art* is a treatise designed for oral delivery, carefully constructed for that purpose, and polished with consummate mastery. These facts alone would go far to exclude the theory of its composition by a physician') and in view of the fact that some Greek philosophers were also doctors, e.g. Eudoxus of Cnidos (D.L. VII.89) and later Timon of Phlius (D.L. IX.109).

199 This is the purpose of Hippocrates, *Ancient Medicine*, throughout, and most obviously so at sections 1–5, 13, 15–16 and 20.

200 [Hp.] *Law* 2–5. This text puts a very high value on disciplined study – an attitude suitable for a piece of publicity material. Section 5 is an enticing offer of initiation into the mysteries of knowledge.

201 [Hp.] *Decorum* 1–2.

202 Authors known to have written protreptics include Aristippus (D.L. II.85), Aristotle (D.L. V.22), Theophrastus (D.L. V.50) and Demetrius of Phalerum (D.L. V.81).

203 Isocrates 1(*To Demonicus*).51–2 graciously adds that Demonicus might also read the other sophists, 'in case they've said anything useful'. It is not suggested that he should go to anyone's lectures except Isocrates'.

204 Athenaeus XIV.661E. Cf. Rankin, *Mageiroi*, pp. 23–5, and above, n. 192.
205 *Etymologicum Gudianum* s.v. *technites*. De Ste Croix, *Class Struggle*, pp. 182–5, following a selection of texts from Aristotle, makes *banausos* and *technites* virtual synonyms. That this is a fair exegesis of Aristotle is not in dispute.
206 The phrase is from J. K. Galbraith, *The Affluent Society* (second edition, Harmondsworth, 1970), p. 276. It is used here to suggest a parallel between the *technitai* and what Galbraith calls the 'New Class'. The ancient and modern contexts are not very similar except in that in both cases observation shows how an increasing number of people were taking up a new sort of labour ('the identity of all classes of labour is one thing on which capitalist and communist doctrine wholly agree ... in fact the differences in what labour means to different people could not be greater' p. 273) for which they were qualified by education (p. 275).
207 For instance, the Cleanthes who supported himself as a gardener while learning philosophy (D.L. VII.168). Menedemus of Eretria, whose father, Cleisthenes, was 'a nobleman, but a building foreman and poor' (D.L. II.125) took to philosophy as a result of meeting Plato during a visit to Athens while he was serving as a guard at Megara (he was probably of ephebic age, as Epicurus was when he had his first encounter with Athenian philosophy (see de Witt, *Epicurus*, pp. 36–7): a man of 20, or a little less, was probably regarded as being at the right sort of age to start serious philosophical study). He abandoned his military service and studied in Megara and Elis (D.L. II.125–6). He would otherwise have followed his father's craft: his becoming a professional philosopher illustrates the possibility of choice in some cases.
208 De Ste Croix, *Class Struggle*, pp. 269–75.
209 Above, n. 61.
210 De Ste Croix, *Class Struggle*, pp. 269–71, treats the question with some diffuseness. His 'other independent producers', he says, 'of course must not be treated as belonging to a single class' (p. 269), but (p. 271) they are 'all, by definition, not members of the "propertied class"'. He promises (p. 269) to 'indicate broadly' how he thinks their class position should be determined, but in the following pages can only suggest that stopping working for one's living was the criterion for membership of the propertied class and that acquiring slaves was the usual way of becoming able to fulfil that criterion (pp. 270–1). These comments have almost no application to the people under discussion here. A famous sculptor or doctor would not hand over his practice to a slave. Still less would a philosopher.
211 At M. I. Finley, *The Ancient Economy* (London, 1973), pp. 35–61. See especially p. 45: 'for the *plousioi* of antiquity – and they alone are at present under consideration – categories of social division other than occupation have priority in any analysis'. But in these cases occupation is crucial.

212 307: cf. D.S. XX.45.1–46.1.
213 Plutarch, *Demetrius* 8.2.
214 Earlier Mausolus' funeral had been graced by the presence of what S. Hornblower calls 'an impressive (and expensive) shipload of Greek intellectuals' (*Mausolus*, p. 334; see pp. 333–9 for the general picture of patronage of Greek intellectuals by the Hecatomnids) brought in by Artemisia. Smaller Asiatic courts also employed Greeks: Arbinas of Xanthus had a tutor for children and a soothsayer (*SEG* XXVIII.1245, lines 7–8 and 18–19). The soothsayer was from Pallene, and the tutor was surely a travelling worker too. What the Hellenistic kings had to gain from employing travelling Greek intellectuals was substantially similar to what the Hecatomnids had hoped for. Their stability depended in part on people's being convinced that their rule was legitimate. Here cf. above, p. 8. Since the days of Plato's support of Dionysius II and Isocrates' support of Evagoras, philosophers had been able and, in certain circumstances, willing to speak (and there were those who found them convincing) in favour of monarchy. And Plato at *Rep.* VIII 568A–D comments on how the tragic poets give support to tyranny and democracy (this point being intended to support his suggestion that the two are closely related, cf. 564A). *Suda* s.v. *basileia* (2), defining what gives monarchies to men, uses the Successors to exemplify the assertion that personal ability, especially in the military sphere, is the decisive thing. This would seem to derive from the work of some theoretical writer sympathetic towards early Hellenistic kingship.
215 It came unasked to Philip II from Isocrates (cf. 5(*Philippus*)), but Ptolemy Soter failed to draw Stilpo into his court circle (D.L. II.115).
216 D.S. XVI.871–3 (Philip); D.S. XVII.15.1–5 (Alexander); D.S. XVIII.74.2–75.2 (Cassander: 75.1–2 outlines the propaganda value of Cassander's installation of Demetrius of Phalerum to rule Athens).

7

Traders

The large volume of modern writing on Greek trade in the fourth century is based on a relatively small corpus of ancient evidence. Much less has been written about traders, though it is a sign of their importance for the study of trade that J. Hasebroek makes them the subject of the first chapter of his book *Trade and Politics in Ancient Greece*.[1] C. M. Reed takes Hasebroek's system further,[2] focusing on them and producing a catalogue of 71 traders as an exhaustive prosography of known traders and ship captains of the Archaic and Classical Ages.[3] The small number of names known is a severe limitation, in that it prevents the accumulation of a 'basis of factual knowledge' similar to that available about, for instance, the Athenian liturgical class;[4] therefore the study of traders is best approached through evaluation of the usefulness and implications of each of the miscellaneous items of evidence available.

In concentrating on the extent to which traders were outside the cities, and the ways in which the world of trade interacted with the world of the cities, this inquiry will have an aim different from that of Reed's study. Reed adds detail to Hasebroek's disproof of the theory that a commercial aristocracy arose in the Archaic age and displaced the landed gentry:[5] it is proof of Reed's sensitivity to the nature of the evidence that he places his treatment of the Archaic period after his chapters building up the fourth-century picture.[6] But a shorter treatment of traders, in the context of the world of Greeks without cities, can be expected to contribute to an understanding of the people who undertook the buying, selling and transport which comprised long-distance Greek trade in the fourth century and to the wider picture of the Greeks who lived by moving about beyond the cities.

Traders, who formed at best a transient element in city populations, stood low in the scale of respectability and integration in the community. It is easy enough to ascertain that the world of traders (*le monde de l'emporion*,[7] 'the "world of the emporium"')[8] had close connections, recognised as such by contemporaries, with what has been described elsewhere in this study as the *demi-monde*.[9] J. Vélis-saropoulos stresses that emporia were parts of towns, and quotes Pollux's comment that shops and brothels are parts of an emporium.[10] Traders were men and travelled without their wives. Other sources connect seafarers with the *demi-monde*. Timarchus, Aeschines alleges, had settled as an adolescent in the surgery of Euthydicus the physician in the Peiraeus and, while pretending to be a student of medicine, was practising homosexual prostitution with some of '... the traders, or other foreigners, or our citizens' as clients.[11] Lucian in one of his *Dialogi Meretricii* illustrates how a naval oarsman would be unable to compete with a successful trader for the attention of a *hetaera*.[12] As short-term visitors the traders came into contact typically, and perhaps chiefly, with elements which were themselves not fixed, and not, or not fully, part of the cities.[13] This is a preliminary indication that the trader, even if he would spend the winters at home as a full citizen of his city, in summer lived outside the city-states for the time being.

G. E. M. de Ste Croix raises the possibility that members of 'what we might almost call an "international merchant class"' may often have had to spend the winter wherever they happened to be when the sailing season ended.[14] It is a sound point, supported by evidence for groups of people from non-Athenian Greek cities having existed in the Peiraeus. There were Citians, who asked the Athenians if they might buy land to build a sanctuary,[15] and, to judge from the 277 gravestones of Heracleots at Athens in *IG* II², a Heracleot presence must have been sustained over a number of centuries.[16] This too suggests that the connections of traders with their home cities could become distant.

The tendency of this inquiry will be to confirm this impression. A text which might be regarded as offering a counter-example is Plautus, *Mercator*.[17] Charinus, having arrived in Rhodes and sold his cargo at a big profit,[18] meets a family friend (*hospes*) at whose house he has an evening meal and stays overnight.[19] While it is not possible to infer from a Roman comedy things about the civil status of the *hospes* in Rhodes which were probably not explicit even in the lost Greek source,[20] it is clear that the *hospes* is meant to be understood as having a settled household.[21] If it were the case that traders could usually have expected hospitality from guest-friends in ports of call, then they could be treated as having had a positive connection with the life of the cities they visited. But it would be unfair to regard the *Mercator* as implying this: Charinus meets the *hospes* by accident (while he is walking round the city enjoying the sensation of having money to spend),[22] and there is no suggestion that traders fitted into a network of friends' houses in every port.

This by way of introduction. The points raised here will be considered further below: section 1 deals with background and the position early in the fourth century; section 2 considers the contribution of the philosophical and theoretical writers; section 3 deals with rhetorical evidence; section 4 comments on Athens and other locations as centres of the trading world; section 5 considers tourism and aristocratic traders; section 6 pays attention to the issues raised by the portrayal of traders in New Comedy and Roman comedy.

The fifth and early fourth centuries

The institution of maritime loans, Reed suggests, originated between 475 and 450.[23] But much less is known about traders in the fifth century than in the fourth, and what little is known has in the past caused almost as much confusion as enlightenment to interpreters of the evidence.[24] But there is a sprinkling of sources dealing with the first decades of the fourth century. Aristophanes groups traders with followers of other modest pursuits,[25] showing that their occupation did not give them high status in the eyes of Athenian citizens. But it was possible to suggest to a jury (with what effect is not known) that the traders were important to the city – that it would be worth the Athenians' while to ingratiate them by putting to death the dealers who had illegally bought up large quantities of corn and so reduced the prices the traders received.[26] As Reed shows, this implies that most of the traders were not covered by the law which obliged Athenian citizens and metics to carry grain to no port other than Athens.[27] It is an important point, and it indicates that throughout the fourth century the traders who came into Athens (and so probably into any other port) would expect to leave again within a short period. (D. Whitehead suggests that foreigners in Athens became liable to pay the metic tax after a month.)[28]

A text which may have a bearing on the predominance of persons foreign to the cities they called at in the shifting communities of traders around the Greek world is *P. Oxy.* 2538,[29] a fragment of an unidentified Attic orator, probably of the period of Lysias.[30] The speaker relates how his father, a merchant who made his living from the sea, came to Selymbria and made friends with one Antiphanes, whose daughter in due course he married. The speaker, the only one of the three sons of the marriage to survive, produces witnesses to show that his father introduced him to the members of his phratry in Athens and that after his mother's death he was sent to the same school as some others (perhaps children of a later or earlier marriage).[31] J. R. Rea shows that the text is part of a speech either aiming to vindicate the speaker's right to recognition as a citizen or claiming a share in an inheritance.[32] Perhaps the latter is the more likely, in view of the speaker's emphasis on what happened to him as a child, and in particular (since it survives) his account of how he was treated in his schooldays.[33] Rea argues that a defence of his citizenship would have required a plea that he was born in legitimate matrimony and was exercising citizen rights before 403/402, and that his treatment during his schooling as a member of his family would therefore have no legal bearing on whether he was a citizen.[34] After the re-enactment of Pericles' citizenship law in 403/402 an Athenian working as a trader would not have been able to offer a Selymbrian (or other non-Athenian) friend the prospect of citizen status at Athens for children of a daughter the trader might marry. This, while strengthening Athenian traders' connections with their own city by requiring them, if they cared about their children's status, to marry Athenian women, will have reduced the potential for firm personal connections between citizens of different cities who met as a result of one of them being a trader.

Therefore Athenian traders were obliged to behave as temporary and alien visitors while abroad, and to come home in order to act as respectable Greek people.[35] While they were on their summer tours (probably in their youth[36]) they had to have little to do with the cities they visited – to remain physically almost outside them, and ideologically entirely so.

If in these early years of the fourth century the trader's status and respectability abroad were compromised, first by his position as an alien and second by the strength of his own city's claims on him, he might still be regarded with some suspicion in his home city, or so the example of Andocides suggests. He complains that his legal adversaries indict him on the strength of his time as a ship's captain and as a trader.[37] The trader was insecure at home as well as abroad. His ties with the community – his own, let alone the communities he visited – were weakened. The next section will deal with the articulation and implications of these facts, and in particular with their relationship to what Greek writers had to say about trade and traders in the abstract.

The philosophical and theoretical writers

The embarrassing position Andocides' time as a ship's captain and trader put him in when he had to appear in court is easier to understand if consideration is given to a passage near the beginning of Plato's *Laws*. Plato defines what he means to treat as education (*paideia*, 'education aimed from childhood at excellence – producing a person whose aspirations and desires are towards being the perfect citizen') and specifically excludes as uneducated men trained 'for shopkeeping and ship-captaining and skill in other things of that sort'.[38] Expertise in trade is antithetical to the education needed for good citizenship. The point is not much developed in the treatise, but it is returned to in an *obiter dictum* in Book IV, at the beginning of the discussion of laws for a new Cretan city, where an inland site is preferred and the sea characterised as a 'salty and bitter neighbour' because of the harm done to a city's moral character by contacts made through trade.[39] A practical formula for avoiding the influence of traders without isolating the city from the benefits of trade[40] is given in Book XI: traders are to be received in markets, harbours and a public building outside the city.[41]

Similarly in the *Politics* Aristotle accepts the necessity of imports, of the things a city cannot supply itself, and of exporting surpluses;[42] but he postulates that a city should be a trading city for these two purposes only, observing that those who make themselves a market place for all and sundry do so for the sake of revenue. He adds that this is *pleonexia* ('aiming-to-get-more') and ought to be avoided.[43] The assumption is the same as Plato's, that traders will be liable to disturb the equilibrium of society. As A. E. Samuel comments:

> all Aristotle's reasoning is based on the fundamental assumption that stability in a society is a good, is achievable, and is the basic aim of all political and economic arrangements. Thus the designation of self-sufficiency as the chief good. It is so because self-sufficiency is the circumstance which will most certainly produce stability. So too, the attacks on certain kinds of exchange or commerce are based on the premise that they are undesirable insofar as they tend towards or promote instability.[44]

But whereas Plato theorises about the possibility of trade being respectable, or even praiseworthy, as a way of life (and sets out why the possibility is unlikely ever to become actuality),[45] Aristotle, asking the question whether the happiness of the state is the same as that of the individual,[46] and noting that the answer depends on which life it is better to choose – the life of being a citizen and sharing in a city or the life of a foreigner deprived of sharing in a city – elects not to express a preference between city and non-city life.[47] Having raised the question, it seems rather lame to avoid answering it on the ground that it is outside the scope of the political treatise.[48]

It is surprising how far the formula in *Laws* XI seems to reflect what was already being done in practice. It has been mentioned above that traders typically occupied the same quarter of a city as *hetaerae*;[49] as Vélissaropoulos comments, 'c'est toujours le souci d'empêcher que les contacts s'étendent au-delà des échanges matériels qui donne à l'emporion sa raison d'être'.[50] Aeneas Tacticus prescribes rules for the treatment of foreigners in a city under siege (it is envisaged that they will be in the city for trade),[51] restricting the places where they may go.[52] Later he describes how a city was captured as a result of weapons being brought through the gates 'in packing cases as if there was merchandise'. Customs men (*ellimenistai*) examined the boxes (but did not find the weapons), and Aeneas recommends inspection of incoming ships by harbour guards (*limenophulakes*) and inspectors (*apostoleis*).[53] The picture here is of wares being carried into the city from a separate place where vessels were unloaded. The fact that separation of this kind was usual explains Theopompus' tone when he comments on the people of Byzantium spending their time in the market place and the city's being a 'city by the emporium'.[54]

Rhetorical evidence

In the case of Byzantium it was only the closeness of the city's identification with its emporium which drew (hostile) comment. Political writers could accept the necessity of trade (and even look on it as a potentially noble calling),[55] but chose to prescribe protection of the city-state by endorsing in their treatises 'the marginality' (as Mossé has it) 'of the world of commerce'.[56] The orators, on the other hand, had less opportunity to choose which aspects of city life to write about, since they might be called on to compose speeches about whatever dispute had arisen. Demosthenes seems in some places to explain affairs at the emporium to the jurors as if they were likely to be innocent of any familiarity with the kind of things that went on there. He says in the Zenothemis speech, 'there is a gang of disreputable men that has gathered in the Peiraeus ...',[57] giving his story the quality of a shocking revelation about an unfamiliar aspect of life. Similarly, in the Lacritus speech he begins by characterising the Phaselites as 'the cleverest at borrowing money in the emporium',[58] insinuating into the hearer's mind on image of the emporium as full of tricky foreigners and the home of arcane techniques of doing business (on both counts unfamiliar and threatening).[59] On a more apologetic tack, the defendant in the Apaturius case says, 'I have given up seafaring, but I have a modest amount of money and I try to put it to work in maritime loans. Because I have been to the emporium often and spent time there, I know most of those who sail the sea ...',[60] so attempting to excuse himself for a much greater involvement in affairs at the emporium than it would be usual for a respectable Athenian to have.[61] But it would perhaps not be legitimate to generalise from these instances to the conclusion that the rhetorical treatment given by Demosthenes to the world of the emporium always relies on the assumption that jurors would have little knowledge about the place or the people who frequented it.

Mossé develops the argument about the marginality of the world of commerce[62] by suggesting that maritime loans at Athens in the fourth century were financed by two distinguishable groups of citizen lenders:

> the first group, composed of men of wealth, only concerned themselves indirectly with maritime loans and these loans represented no more than a fractional part of their total fortune ... the second group ... was composed of men of modest origins much more deeply involved in maritime commerce and it had far fewer connections with the life of the city.'[63]

But the case for the existence of the first group is compromised by the fact that Nausimachus and Xenopithes, identified by Mossé as having made a maritime loan, are mentioned in the passage he refers to[64] only as having had money owing to them in Bosporus. It is far from necessary to suppose that it was owed in the form of a maritime loan. In fact, in view of the stress laid by the defendant on the fact that Demaretus, his guardian, had never been to Bosporus and so could not have collected the money on behalf of the defendant (whose father had been Nausimachus' and Xenopithes' guardian),[65] it seems much more likely that it was not, since the debtor, in the case of a maritime loan, would normally have returned to the port in which the loan was made (in this hypothetical case presumably Athens) to repay it.[66] Mossé's first group is left with only two members, of whom Stephanus is regarded as only 'probably' coming into the category.[67]

Examining the members of the second group of Athenian citizens, Mossé finds that they were closely involved with, and very similar to, the metics and foreigners engaging in maritime business in the Athenian emporium.[68] This conclusion is supported by consideration of J. K. Davies's list of the 19 men known certainly to have been involved in financing sea voyages.[69] Though Attic oratory is the source for every entry in the list (all but two come from Demosthenes),[70] 12 or 13 of the 19 people were not Athenians. The fact that of the seven loans of 3,000 drachmas or more mentioned in the list three were subscribed to jointly by more than one lender suggests that quite often lenders would not have enough cash to finance a large venture alone. A financier of this kind found it difficult 'to secure large enough profit margins, or to operate on a large enough scale, to give him major financial status'.[71] If he was an Athenian, he 'in no sense belonged to the circles of leadership in the city'.[72]

The world of commerce, therefore, came to the attention of the city authorities most sharply when the Athenians began to be deprived of the benefits of trade during the Social war. In the mid-350s Isocrates expressed the hope that making peace would double the city's revenues,[73] and would cause it to be full again of 'merchants and foreigners and metics of whom the city is now empty';[74] but the burden of Xenophon's *Poroi* is to show that positive measures will be needed to restore prosperity.[75] His comments on ways of encouraging metics are not of primary relevance to the matter of traders, as his own strong change of subject at the beginning of chapter 3 shows,[76] and the proposals he makes, in sections 1–5 and 12–14 of chapter 3, all gain point from the assumption that the intended beneficiaries will be in Athens for a very short time. Being able to take good-quality silver instead of a return cargo would increase the ease and speed of the trader's visit;[77] the proposal for speedy settlement of legal disputes bears some similarity to what Athens did in the end for visiting traders;[78] the proposal to invite importers of outstanding goods to front seats in the theatre and civic meals is made with a view to securing more visits (rather than to inducing the traders to settle in Athens);[79] the suggestions about providing lodging houses and merchant ships for charter to the trading community show how Xenophon thought there was money to be made from offering facilities to Athens' temporary residents.[80] Action followed the literary encouragement of Isocrates and Xenophon,[81] and 'traders' suits' (*emporikai dikai*) were available to settle disputes for the second half of the fourth century and indeed beyond. There is no question that once the need to take measures encouraging merchants had become a point of discussion the Athenians gave the world of commerce the facilities it needed for Athens to become an attractive location.[82]

Athens and other locations

Even before the institution of 'traders' suits', and all the more afterwards, Athens was a uniquely well-frequented port. It had been committed to reliance on large-scale corn imports since the fifth century,[83] and though the dangers to the city's supply[84] were *ipso facto* dangers to its suppliers, Reed is certainly right to say that there was guaranteed work for the large number of men regularly engaged in the corn trade.[85] This suggests that Athens was a centre of the world outside the cities for traders in the same way as for certain other travelling workers.[86] But it was not the only such centre. Lycurgus makes much of the likely effect of Leocrates' spreading his comments on Athens to the traders at Rhodes and says that the traders sail all round the known world and proclaim what they have heard about the city from Leocrates.[87] He goes on to say, in particular, that Leocrates caused some traders and ships' captains not to come to Athens – and at a very awkward moment, after Chaeronea.[88] Unless Lycurgus is guilty of a very considerable exaggeration, Rhodes by this time was already becoming an important port of call. Its importance grew as the Greek world entered the Hellenistic Age, though the early medieval compilation extant under the name of Rhodian Sea Law echoes the city's significance as a centre of the commercial world in its title more than in its contents.[89]

Probably no other place attracted as much traffic as Athens or Rhodes. If Isocrates' hope of doubling trade-related revenue was at all realistic, in a year when Athens can be presumed to have received her full normal quantity of imported corn,[90] it is fair to infer that half or more of the imports arriving in a normal year were non-grain items carried by merchants to destinations chosen on the basis (presumably) of what port would be both easily reached and likely to offer a market in which the wares would fetch a good price. In normal circumstances Athens must often have come to mind when a merchant was weighing such considerations. Similarly with Rhodes, which was more easily reached from places in the East opened up by Alexander. Describing subdivisions of maritime occupations, Aristotle says that the 'trading form of business' is prevalent at Aegina and Chios,[91] but it is more plausible that, as Reed suggests, these locations were the home of many people who became merchants, rather than places which were filled with merchants in summer.[92]

There is a fragmentary passage of Hyperides which illustrates the difference between ports which expected an influx of summer visitors and cities which expected not to have much contact with traders. It shows how a city only a short distance from an international centre could be thoroughly remote from the network of emporia visited by travellers along the trade routes in summer. It is the story from the *Deliacus* of two Aeolians who came to Delos on a sightseeing tour of Greece.[93] They were not, apparently, engaged on a trading enterprise, as some travellers would have been, to finance their voyage: they had a large quantity of gold with them.[94] They were found dead on Rheneia.[95] The Delians accused the Rheneians of sacrilege. The Rheneians were annoyed, and made counter-accusations. At the arbitration,[96] they asked the Delians why they thought the two

Aeolians should have come to Rheneia: there were no harbours, no emporium nor any other attraction. Everyone, they said, went to Delos;[97] they themselves spent a good deal of time there. The Delians replied that the Aeolians had gone to Rheneia to buy sacrificial victims.[98] Why, in that case, asked the Rheneians, had they left their attendants in Delos instead of bringing them over to drive the victims back, and why, when they had walked around in the temple of Delos with shoes on, had they crossed to Rheneia without them when it was thirty stades along a rough road from the crossing point to the city of the Rheneians, where they would have had to go to make their purchase? The fragment ends at this point, but from the tone the reader is clearly intended to understand the overwhelming likelihood that the Aeolians were murdered in Delos and their bodies cast out on Rheneia: and the central feature of the Rheneians' argument is that, however many people frequent the harbours and emporium of Delos, hardly any visit Rheneia.

The fact that it cannot have been possible for Rheneia, any more than it was possible for any Greek city,[99] to be self-sufficient in all kinds of articles of consumption, might seem to constitute a difficulty here. But the difficulty is not serious. First, a small or backward city is likely to have needed a less wide range of imports than a larger one. Military and naval supplies, for instance, cannot have been proportionally as much in demand when a city was not large enough to have a foreign policy,[100] so that Isocrates' mention of the absence of harbour and emporium at Salamis in the days before Evagoras is a key element in the contrast between the city's former backwardness[101] and its present status as an impressively built and militarily powerful city.[102] Second, self-sufficiency in food was the norm in Greece, and large-scale importing was confined to a very few exceptional cities.[103] Third, there was little to attract a trader to a small place like Rheneia when there was virtually no commodity that would not be easier to sell in a much larger city like Delos. The likelihood is that the Rheneians brought what they needed from Delos in small craft.

It is worth noticing how in Scylax's *Periplus*[104] the phrase 'city and harbour' is used in some sections but not others.[105] This is because of the non-uniform composition of the work. Where the phrase occurs it is a cue to mariners that a city has harbour facilities, while places where it is not possible to put in are mentioned probably to aid navigation and recognition of localities. The implication is that the number of cities at which it is possible to call constitute only a fraction of all those on the coast.[106]

The inference is that the large slave-crewed cargo ships of the Aegean in the fourth century BC will have tended to travel between a fairly large but limited number of destinations. These destinations, cities with emporia which were in most cases districts separate, or at least distinct, from the rest of the built-up area[107] (often outside the walls),[108] were filled in summer with men who had at least temporarily gone to live outside the cities. Athens was the doyenne of these maritime cities, which formed between them a complex of locations whose connections with each other, through acquaintance between traders, were stronger than with the self-sufficient community life of the cities to which they were juxtaposed.[109]

Tourism and aristocratic traders

Hasebroek says of Solon:[110]

> his travels were inspired purely by the desire for knowledge, and he carried goods with him for sale abroad simply because at a time when any money that existed was current only within a narrowly restricted area and trade between one district and another had to be carried out on a barter basis, that was the only way in which he could support himself during his absence from home.

If Solon traded only to pay his expenses, than it would be fair to expect a decline in aristocratic trading as the money economy became established. This expectation would be strengthened by the mysterious case of the Aeolians at Delos, who were paying in gold.[111] But in the fourth century there were still Greeks from rich backgrounds who took cargoes of goods when they went abroad.

There was the plaintiff who commissioned Isocrates' *Trapeziticus*. He was the son of one Sopaeus, who held a position of trust and authority under Satyrus, king of Bosporus.[112] But when (in the speech he commissioned) he comments that 'the people who sail to Pontus' all know his father's position, it may perhaps show that his father had some official or business connections with the traders on their visits to Bosporus.[113] If that were the case, perhaps it could be expected that his father, who may have been used to loading ships with grain as part of his work in Satyrus' service, would load two ships with grain for his son, give him money and so send him to Greece.[114]

But it is perhaps less likely that Plato would have spent any part of his life selling olive oil in Egypt.[115] He was a man of good family who was interested in gaining knowledge, though: and even where a money economy operated it could easily be worth taking goods to sell on a trip abroad. Professional traders expected to make good profits, so clearly it was intelligent of a well-off traveller, instead of taking money with him, to spend it on a cargo and space in a ship, and sell the goods at destination for more than they cost him.[116] Comments in the dialogues should not be taken as indicative of Plato's own behaviour (where the views expressed are Plato's own, they represent his reflective outlook at the moment of writing). And there is a parallel for the combination of trade and study, besides Solon: the young man from Pontus who came to Athens to sell salt fish and learn philosophy.[117]

The chance survival of a proverbial phrase from the fourth century casts another small light on the relationship between philosophising and being a trader.[118] The phrase is tantalisingly referred to by Cicero, who writes to Atticus,[119] 'dic mihi, placetne tibi primum edere iniussu meo? hoc ne Hermodorus quidem faciebat, is qui Platonis libros solitus est divulgare, ex quo *logoisin Hermodoros*.' It is explained in the *Suda*:[120] 'Hermodorus, a disciple of Plato, used to take books written by Plato and sell them in Sicily.' Note the use of the imperfect: he used (regularly) to take loads of Platonic dialogues to Sicily and sell them.[121] Most likely it was an act of discipleship to become a long-range book exporter for Plato: but Hermodorus would hardly have done it unless it was possible to make money from it.[122] But as has been argued elsewhere in this book, philosophy, though it attracted students mostly from well-off backgrounds, was not in any exclusive sense an aristocratic pursuit in the fourth century.[123] This is where aristocratic, 'amateur' trade shades into ordinary trade, and it becomes clearer than ever that being a trader was more comparable with following another mobile skilled occupation than with other ways of life.[124]

Traders in New Comedy and Roman comedy

There are many references to traders in comedy: more in Latin than in Greek, because more Roman comedy is extant than Greek New Comedy. Discussion of the pertinence of comic material to consideration of what sort of people traders were is begun in a rudimentary way by Knorringa,[125] who surveys a list of references in Greek only. He says, 'we cannot find an opinion on traders in these authors',[126] and most of his short chapter is devoted to a list of objects of trade derived from his collection of references.[127] He gives no consideration to Latin sources.

Hasebroek says nothing of comedy. Reed, though he presents a useful collection of references, including many to Latin authors, deals with the subject of traders in comedy very briefly;[128] he argues that the authors' liking for making their characters merchants is a dramatic device for getting entrances and exits, and adds that there is no comment on the respectability of, or the necessity for, traders:[129]

indeed, he says there is no correspondence between traders in comedy and the figures in philosophy or oratory. Accordingly, he treats comic characters who are traders as 'amateur' traders.[130] 'Once they appear,' he sums up, 'we quickly forget their trading and concentrate on other features – usually on their family roles as father, son, uncle, family friend, etc.'[131]

The last point is an interesting one. The action of a comic play takes place in what is introduced to the audience as a city (at least in most cases). The 'return motif'[132] involves exploration of the difficulties and comic situations to which transfer from 'outside' to 'inside' gives rise in the case of characters who are returning home from abroad. Certainly in most cases the returning characters' family roles will be uppermost in the mind of the audience or reader through most of the play: the question is usually how the returning character is going to fit into his temporarily relinquished background.[133] It would be naive to suppose, because the playwrights' theme is family life,[134] that there is no serious treatment (in the measure in which New Comedy is a genre at least partly serious) of the issues raised by the ambiguous position of the returner-from-abroad;[135] in fact, the incidence of the 'return motif' in comic plays can be recognised as a symptom of awareness that relatives' absence from home as traders or soldiers, or indeed on state business, created tensions and awkward situations in a world where it was expected that people would normally live their whole lives within the social context of their own city.[136]

The statement that there is no correspondence between comic characters who are traders and the figures in philosophy and oratory may perhaps suggest that Reed has read Plato and Demosthenes with an insufficiently sceptical eye.[137] It is not surprising if Plato says that traders are rascals but comic writers do not.[138] Plato, writing at as high a level of theoretical abstraction as any writer, needs to distinguish, at that theoretical level, between the attainments of men educated as he himself was (for good citizenship) and men who had reached a high level of technical training in the complex business of being traders and ship captains.[139] He has no room to make a polite concession to the personal qualities of his counterparts in a different ideological tradition.[140] Writing in a period in which the city-state seemed to be losing the military imperative for its unchanged existence,[141] and was losing its able young men to the skilled mobile occupations,[142] and was dependent on traders for survival,[143] he was in a position where he had to use to the full his readers' predisposition in favour of the aristocratic/political style of education and life.[144] As for the characters in Demosthenes, they are the parties in lawsuits, and it is not surprising that they come out looking bad. G. M.

Calhoun makes a point which should not be neglected:[145] 'the trade could not, and would not, have been maintained on the basis of this type of contract [the maritime loan] had not the majority of adventurers been honest and upright men'.

And comedy has a number of pictures of traders and the trading life to present besides that of the reintegration of the returning trader into his family. An amusing fantasy appears in the mouth of the slave fisherman Gripus in Plautus' *Rudens*,[146] when he has caught a heavy chest which he imagines contains gold.[147] The first purchase after his freedom, he says, will be land, a house and slaves; then he will carry on trade in great ships; and he will become the very rival of the Successor kings.[148] It sums up the romance of trade, in the late fourth century, in six lines.[149] But there are more passages where trade is presented as dangerous to person and property: Pataecus in Menander's *Perikeiromene* describes how 'the wild sea of Aegean salt covered ... the ship'.[150] Davus in Terence's *Andria* rates as improbable the story he has been told of an Athenian's being shipwrecked on Andros.[151] What these and other pictures of the trader's life in comedy[152] yield is the information that being a trader was a way of acquiring and losing wealth with surprising speed and ease: and here, though the writers were naturally attracted to the extreme cases, comedy certainly was imitating life.[153]

So the idea that there is no correspondence between reality and the world of the trader of Greek and Roman comedy ought not to be entertained. Recognition of the plausibility of the comic character as trader is not damaging to the general Hasebroekian thesis that traders were persons of small account in society. It is not, after all, characteristic of Greek and Roman comedy to deal with characters whom Plato or Xenophon would have recognised as highly respectable – the abundance of *meretrices* and rascally slaves is an element in the temporary release from respectability which audiences welcomed. But the amount of information which comedy has to offer about typical trading activities is slight. Traffic in slaves appears in a number of places, but it is often connected with the personal histories of characters in the plays, and so cannot indicate the relative importance of slaves as an item of trade. Comedy's contribution to knowledge of what traders were like comes in its attestation of the at times uneasy relationship between individuals' lives inside the city (with their family) and outside it (doing business).

Notes

1 J. Hasebroek, *Trade and Politics in Ancient Greece* (New York, 1965), pp. 1–43. The book is a translation of *Staat und Handel in alten*

Griechenland (Tübingen, 1928).

2 C. M. Reed, 'Maritime traders in the Greek world of the Archaic and Classical periods' (Diss., Oxford, 1980), especially pp. xxiv–xxv. De Ste Croix, *Peloponnesian War*, p. 271 n. 6, says that Reed is going to produce a book on Greek maritime traders. It will presumably be substantially similar to the Oxford thesis referred to in this chapter.

3 Reed, 'Maritime traders', pp. 135–219.

4 Cf. Davies, *Wealth*, p. 2.

5 Reed, 'Maritime traders', *passim* and especially pp. xxiv–xxv; Hasebroek, *Trade and Politics*, pp. 44–96 (at pp. 44–5 there is a statement of the theory to which Hasebroek applies his critique). J. Vélissaropoulos, *Les Nauclères grecs* (Geneva and Paris, 1980), p. 6, argues for a theory exactly opposed to the theory of the rise of a commercial aristocracy, suggesting that the stability in the function and social role of the ship captain was such that the passing of a political regime (meaning changes such as that from Classical politics to Hellenistic monarchy, or from Hellenistic monarchy to Roman rule) brought no important change.

6 Reed, 'Maritime traders', pp. 1–99, deals with the people and conditions in fourth-century trade.

7 J. Vélissaropoulos, 'Le monde de l' emporion', *DHA* 3 (1977), pp. 61–85.

8 C. Mossé, 'The "World of the *Emporium*" in the private speeches of Demosthenes', in P. Garnsey, K. Hopkins and C. R. Whittaker (eds.), *Trade in the Ancient Economy* (London, 1983), at pp. 53–63.

9 Cf. above, pp. 152–4.

10 Vélissaropoulos, 'Le monde de l'emporion', p. 61 and n. 10; Pollux IX.34. Cf. Hasebroek, *Trade and Politics*, p. 160, who cites Strabo XVII.1.9 (=794) on Alexandria and Dicaearchus on Chalcis; the speech 'On the cities in Greece' ascribed to Dicaearchus was shown by F. Pfister to belong to Heraclides ('Die Reisebilder des Herakleides', *Sb. Ak. Wien* 227.2, 1951, a third-century author (pp. 44–5). Section 29 is the pertinent one (pp. 84–7).

11 Aeschines I(*Timarchus*).40. This is exactly the kind of accusation which may be a lie. There is no knowing. But (as modern writers who use Attic orators as sources often, and rightly, say) lies have to sound plausible to the jury. Aeschines' story must have fitted in with the kind of things Athenian citizens thought went on down near the docks.

12 Lucian, *Dialogi meretricii* 14.1–4. L. Casson, *Travel in the Ancient World* (London, 1974), p. 92, refers to this dialogue as 'an amusing skit in which a sailor from the Athenian navy storms at a courtesan because she threw him over for a toothless, balding fifty-year-old merchant'. This reveals a degree of misunderstanding: the sailor is not specified as being in Athenian service – Lucian probably did not intend to make his context exact, but it is apparently Hellenistic (the sailor has been (sections 2–3) to Sicyon, Syria, Samos, Cyprus, Caria, Patara, Gythium and, since the *saperdes* (cf. *LSJ* s.v.) was a fish associated with the Nile, to Egypt: this humorous list seems to envisage

routine peacetime naval activity in places which were under Persian control until the time of Alexander) so that it would make more sense to think of a Hellenistic king's navy. Nor does the sailor storm at the girl: he shows that he has given her all the presents he can afford, and she says (with a trace of sarcasm) that what he can afford will not persuade her to give up her (rich and generous) Bithynian merchant. Though Lucian is a late source this is an interesting dialogue, communicating a feel for the shifting population of seafarers who came in and out of a port (the list of destinations might perhaps suggest Rhodes as the scene of the action, but probably Lucian did not mean to be specific here either); but it must be said that none of the other *Dialogi Meretricii* refers to merchants in any way – 'merchant-and-*hetaera*' is only one of a very wide variety of available *topoi* in this area. On the other hand, the foreigners who did not come to Neaera in Megara ([Dem.] 59(*Neaera*).36) were quite likely merchants for the most part.

13 This point is amplified below, pp. 186–8.
14 De Ste Croix, *Class Struggle*, p. 266.
15 See below, n. 104.
16 *IG* II² 8548–825. Twenty-four of these texts (29 persons named) are identified in the corpus as belonging to the fourth century BC. One deceased person is identified as a steersman (8755), while another text commemorates a father, son and daughter who perished in the waves of the Aegean (8708). Most texts simply name the deceased, but many are located in the Peiraeus. The Heracleot community was certainly a community of traders.
17 Reed, 'Maritime traders', p. 98 and n. 175, treats Charinus as an 'amateur' merchant. This depends on a misunderstanding of the text: Charinus' father, Demipho, who had made his pile by selling up his farm and turning to maritime trade (Plautus, *Mercator* 73–9), is shown as sending his son to Rhodes to trade (11) in order to get him started on the serious business of following in his father's footsteps as a *mercator*. On Reed's opinions on traders in comedy cf. below, pp. 189–90.
18 Plautus, *Mercator* 87–97.
19 Plautus, *Mercator* 97–105.
20 Which was Philemon's *Emporos* (Plautus, *Mercator* 9).
21 He has a house to which to invite Charinus, and a slave girl to send to him at bedtime (Plautus, *Mercator* 97–105).
22 Plautus, *Mercator* 97–8.
23 Reed, 'Maritime traders', p. 56; G. E. M. de Ste Croix, 'Ancient Greek and Roman maritime loans', in H. Edey and B. S. Yamey (eds.), *Debits, Credits, Finance and Profits* (London, 1974), pp. 41–59, at p. 44, guesses that maritime loans began at this period: he mentions that the volume of the corn trade to Athens must have grown during the fifth century to become by the middle of the century 'the most important single item of Greek trade'.
    F. D. Harvey argues ('the maritime loan in Eupolis' "Marikas" (*P.*

Oxy. 2741)', *ZPE* 23 (1976), pp. 231–3) that the fragment *P. Oxy.* 2741 fr. 1B, col. ii, lines 16–18 (=C. Austin, *Comicorum Graecorum fragmenta in papyris reperta*, Berlin and New York, 1973, no. 95, lines 96–8) refers to maritime loans at 20 per cent. Since Eupolis' *Marikas* was produced in 421 (p. 233) this is the earliest reference to such a loan, and it seems that the maritime loan was already a familiar institution in 421.

24 This comment refers most sharply to treatment of Thucydides III.72–4. H. Knorringa, *Emporos* (Amsterdam, 1926), p. 59, for example, says, 'the *emporoi* who formed the aristocratic element in Corcyra, a town preeminently fitted for trade by its situation, live near the market and in the neighbourhood of the harbour'. A. W. Gomme in *HCT ad* III.72.3 says that 'those of the Corcyreans who were in charge of affairs' (III.72.2), were 'doubtless absentee landlords of wide agricultural domains, most of them; some of them merchants'. This is a more cautious comment, but neither Gomme nor Knorringa faces up to what III.74.2 (the place where merchants are mentioned) says: 'the few ... set on fire the houses round about the agora and the tenements, so that there would be no avenue of approach, and they spared neither their own property nor that of others, so that many wares belonging to merchants were burnt up ...'. This does not state or imply that any of 'the few' were merchants. M. I. Finkelstein, by contrast, makes sensible use of III.74.2 ('*Emporos, Naukleros* and *Kapelos*: a prolegomena to the study of Athenian trade', *CPhil* 30, 1935, pp. 320–36, at pp. 335–6 with n. 66) by pointing out that it shows how wares were stored near the agora. Trader and ship captain are grouped together in an Attic inscription (later than 434/433): *IG* I³ 133, e.g. at line 3.

25 Aristophanes, *Plutus* 904; cf. Reed, 'Maritime traders', p. 50.

26 Lysias 22(*Corn Dealers*).21 (on which cf. R. Seager, 'Lysias against the corn dealers', *Hist.* 15, 1966, pp. 172–84).

27 Reed, 'Maritime traders', p. 42.

28 Whitehead, *Ideology*, pp. 9–11.

29 J. R. Rea, *The Oxyrhynchus Papyri* XXXI (London, 1966), pp. 38–45.

30 Rea, *P. Oxy.* XXXI, pp. 39–40.

31 *P. Oxy.* 2538, col. ii.9–28, col. iii.1–8 and 14–20, col. iv.1–28.

32 Rea, *P. Oxy.* XXXI, pp. 38–9.

33 *P. Oxy.* 2538 col. iv.1–28.

34 Rea, *P. Oxy.* XXXI, p. 39. But the point is in a high degree unclear. *Birth* before 403/402 is presented as a defence at Demosthenes 57(*Eubulides*).30, but S. C. Humphreys, 'The Nothoi of Kynosarges', *JHS* 94 (1974), pp. 85–8, at pp. 92–3, suggests that Pericles' law of 451/450 disfranchised all sons of non-Athenian mothers not registered at the time of the law's passage, and C. Patterson, *Pericles' Citizenship Law of 451–50 B.C.* (New York, 1981), p. 145, argues that the re-enactment in 403/402 and non-examination of those coming of age before 403/402 (Schol. in Aeschines 1(*Timarchus*).39) were part of the general provisions for amnesty reflecting the turmoil of the preceding decade.

35 In Lysias 32(*Diogeiton*).4, for instance, it is related how Diodotus, who had made a lot of money in trading, was persuaded by Diogeiton to marry Diogeiton's daughter. This all happened in Athens, after Diodotus had made his money. By contrast *P. Eleph.* 1 (311/310) is a marriage contract between one Heraclides of Temnos and one Demetria of Cos – and, as the editor comments (O. Rubensohn, *Elephantine Papyri*, Berlin, 1907, p. 19), 'wir befinden uns hier offenbar im Kreis der Söldner der Garnison von Elephantine' ('here clearly we find ourselves in the circle of the mercenaries in the garrison of Elephantine'). But mercenary officers (the dowry is 1,000 drachmas: line 4) in this context would be planning for a career and settlement in Ptolemy I's Egypt.

36 It is only an impression that traders tended to start in young adulthood and retire (if their circumstances permitted) to less risky pursuits later. Some texts support it: Demosthenes 33(*Apaturius*).4 is the account given by a former trader, now a maritime moneylender, of his career; Plautus, *Mercator* (on which cf. above, n. 17) gives the same sort of picture, the father having returned after making a fortune and deciding to send his son out trading; and Diodotus (cf. above, n. 35) married after retiring with a fortune. Probably this course was open only to a small proportion of traders, the rest never growing rich enough.

37 Andocides 1(*Mysteries*).137. For substantiation of this, see Lysias 6(*Andocides*)30 and 48–9.

38 Plato, *Laws* I.643D–E. Cf. *Rep.* II.371A and *Politicus* 289D: traders characterised as '*diakonoi*', menials; it is *Rep.* II.271D which defines as *emporoi* tradespeople who wander from city to city. Cf. also Knorringa, *Emporos*, p. 112.

39 Plato, *Laws* IV.705A: '[the sea] fills [a city] with trading and moneymaking from shopkeeping – it breeds twisted and unreliable morals in souls and makes the city unreliable and no friend to itself – and just the same to other people'.

40 Plato, *Laws* XI.918B–C, is an unexpectedly frank and pleasant expression of the need for traders. Knorringa, *Emporos*, p. 69, is mistaken to say that Plato thinks trade has to be reduced to the smallest possible proportions: it comes nearer the mark to say, as at Knorringa, *Emporos*, pp. 110–11, that Plato may have asked himself 'in what way can I see to trade, which cannot be entirely abolished, exercising a minimum of demoralising influence on the citizens?'. Hasebroek, *Trade and Politics*, pp. 175–82, also seems to allow insuffient weight to this passage in the *Laws*.

Aristotle, *Pol.* I.1257a17–19, comes to the opposite conclusion to that of Plato, *Laws* XI.918B–C, and says that shopkeeping ('*kapelike*') is *not* by nature a part of money-making (*chrematistike*). This would point in the direction of a rejection of Plato's idea that people who are in trade are in a necessary and potentially noble occupation whose followers are corrupted by the exceptional degree of temptation to greed for gain to which they are subject.

41 Plato, *Laws* XI.952D–953A. Traders are mentioned as the first of four kinds of unavoidable foreign visitors: usually coming in summer (952D); 'trading for the sake of money-making, they fly from city to city for the length of the summer' (952E).

42 Aristotle, *Pol.* VII.1327a25–7.

43 Aristotle, *Pol.* VII.1327a–31.

44 A. E. Samuel, *From Athens to Alexandria: Hellenism and Social Goals in Ptolemaic Egypt* (Louvain, 1983), pp. 26–7. Samuel's book is as much concerned with reflective comment on Greek social thought in general as with Ptolemaic Egypt.

45 Cf. above, n. 40, and below, n. 55.

46 The phrase used by Aristotle at *Pol.* 1324a6, which is rendered here as 'the individual', is *heis hekastos tōn anthrōpōn*. This clear and elegant usage disproves G. E. M. de Ste Croix's contention (*Class Struggle*, p. 439) that 'this ... notion can hardly be expressed in Greek'. But the value of correcting a small point in such a highly tendentious passage is perhaps open to question.

47 Aristotle, *Pol.* VII.1324a13–17.

48 Aristotle, *Pol.* VII.1324a18–23: ending with 'but that is irrelevant: and the aim of this treatise is this ...' (lines 22–3). But it should be added that by 1334a15–16 he is saying that the purpose of men is the same 'both in common and individually' and 'that definition is necessary both for "the best man" and for "the best condition"'. This, considered in connection with the substance of n. 46 above, may suggest that the question Aristotle avoids is whether being a good man is a better thing to choose than a life outside the sphere in which virtue may be exercised and recognised.

49 Cf. the beginning of this chapter and nn. 8 and 10.

50 Vélissaropoulos, 'Le monde de l'emporion', p. 61: 'it is always concern to prevent contacts from extending beyond material exchanges which gives the emporium its reason for existing'.

51 Aeneas Tacticus 10.11 and 13.

52 Aeneas Tacticus 10.11–13.

53 Aeneas Tacticus 29.1–12. Herodotus VII.137.2 mentions a successful strategem of the kind a measure of this sort was intended to prevent.

54 Theopompus, *FGrHist* 115 F 62; cf. Vélissaropoulos, 'Le monde de l'emporion', p. 62 with n. 18, and p. 70, where it is pointed out that Theopompus' comments on the Byzantines are intended to account for their allegedly debauched character.

55 Plato, *Laws* XI.918B–C: Plato says that anyone who even out the uneven and unbalanced distribution of goods of any kind must be a benefactor, and adds that this is what coinage and traders are for. He goes on to look elsewhere for the reasons for the calling's disreputableness (918E–919C), ending with the observation that the problem with trade is the struggle against poverty and riches, whose moral dangers he sets forth (919B–C). At 919D–920C he provides that no citizen is to engage in shopkeeping or crafts, and that aliens who do so are to be under supervision. This is in contrast with the provision at *Rep.*

II.371A, where the traders are envisaged as a necessary element in the city population.

56 Mossé, 'The "World of the *Emporium*"', p. 53.

57 Demosthenes 32(*Zenothemis*).10.

58 Demosthenes 35(*Lacritus*).1.

59 Further on, Demosthenes develops the theme of arcane techniques, disclosing in 35(*Lacritus*).15 that Lacritus is Isocrates' pupil; and in sections 39–42, explaining Lacritus' alleged dishonesty as a result of his sophistic education, he warns that Lacritus is gathering paying pupils and has passed on to others (his brothers first) the evil and unjust 'education', namely the art of borrowing money as maritime loans in the emporium and not paying it back.

60 Demosthenes 33(*Apaturius*).4–5.

61 This apologetic tone is perhaps the factor which has given rise to the impression that the defendant in this case was an Athenian (cf. Mossé, 'The "World of the *Emporium*"', p. 54 (following L. Gernet) and Davies, *Democracy*, pp. 61–2): a metic might have felt able to describe his means of livelihood with less explanatory comment.

62 But note should be taken of the influence of traders and ship captains on getting decrees passed at Athens – see, for instance, *IG* II² 343, line 416, and the whole career of Moerocles (C. Ampolo, 'Tra finanza e politica: carriere e affari del signore Moirokles', *Riv. Fil.* 109 (1981), pp. 187–204). The marginality of the world of commerce from the point of view of public policy ought not to be over-stressed.

63 Mossé, 'The "World of the *Emporium*"', pp. 54–8; quotation from p. 56.

64 Demosthenes 38(*Nausimachus*).11; cf. Mossé, 'The "World of the *Emporium*"', p. 54.

65 Demosthenes 38(*Nausimachus*).11 and 14.

66 Cf. Knorringa, *Emporos*, pp. 93–4. Naturally the question arises what sort of loan *was* outstanding to Nausimachus and Xenopithes in Bosporus. The speech does not supply an answer. It seems odd that a rich Athenian (Nausimachus' and Xenopithes' father) should become so far separated from his money; but this should not be taken as showing that the money was lent to finance the voyage that took it away from its owner.

67 Mossé, 'The "World of the *Emporium*"', p. 54. Mossé does not mention the son of the strategos engaged in maritime loans attested at Demosthenes 34(*Against Phormio*).50. But this is hardly enough to save Mossé's model.

68 Mossé, 'The "World of the *Emporium*"', pp. 56–8.

69 Davies, *Democracy*, p. 68.

70 The others come from Lysias (No. 1: Diodotus) and from Hyperides plus Plutarch (No. 4: Demosthenes, the orator, himself).

71 Davies, *Democracy*, p. 68.

72 Mossé, 'The "World of the *Emporium*"', p. 58: which is in line with Davies' finding that it was not likely that anyone would be able to enter the liturgical class by financing maritime loans (*Democracy*, p.

68). But a counter-example against this generalisation is now available:
the Megaclides and Thrasyllus of Eleusis, who are attested as
borrowing 40 minas at Demosthenes 52(*Callippus*).20 (370s), arrived
in the liturgic class some 20 or so years later (*SEG* XXVII.19, which
combines J. Kirchner, *Prosopographia Attica*, Berlin, 1901 and 1903,
Nos. 9685 and 9686). Davies's arguments, though, are not such as to
be overthrown by one counter-example.

73 Isocrates 8(*Peace*).20–1.

74 Isocrates 8(*Peace*).21.

75 Xenophon, *Poroi, passim*.

76 Xenophon, *Poroi* 3.1: 'My next theme is the outstanding advantages
and profitability of our city as a trading centre ...'.

77 Xenophon, *Poroi* 3.2.

78 Xenophon, *Poroi* 3.3, suggests prizes for the administrators of the
emporium on just and quick settlement of disputes. 'Traders' suits' (on
which cf. below, n. 82), which were the solution actually adopted,
constituted perhaps a more radical answer; the implication of
Xenophon's suggestion is that in the first half of the fourth century,
and earlier, the administrators of the emporium had had at least an
informal part in the settlement of disputes (noted at Hasebroek, *Trade
and Politics*, pp. 171–2).

79 Xenophon, *Poroi* 3.4. Hasebroek, *Trade and Politics*, p. 26, misses out
of his summary of Xenophon's suggestions the important point that
only 'whoever seems to be benefiting the city with outstanding ships
and cargoes' is to get the prestigious invitations.

80 Xenophon, *Poroi* 3.12–14.

81 Which is not to say that legislation was influenced by the pamphlets:
more likely the pamphlets reflected a widespread consciousness that
something ought to be done.

82 Reed, 'Maritime traders', pp. 60–7, details what special measures were
taken to attract traders; and at p. 67 Reed says, 'Athens obviously *did*
act on behalf of maritime traders, due simply to the huge overlap of
their interests with those of the Athenian citizen body.' At p. 91 Reed
dates the introduction of 'traders' suits' between the composition of
Xenophon, *Poroi* (355), and that of Demosthenes 7(*Halonnesus*).12
(342), here following L. Gernet, 'Sur les actions commerciales en droit
athénien', *REG* 51 (1938), pp. 1–44, at pp. 1–2.

83 Cf. above, n. 23.

84 See, for example, de Ste Croix, *Class Struggle*, pp. 46–7, and Reed,
'Maritime traders', p. 18, referring to 'those willing to make the long
and dangerous voyages to the distant points, particularly Pontos, from
which Athens secured her grain'.

85 Reed, 'Maritime traders'.

86 Cf. above, pp. 151–4. On the central importance of the Peiraeus in the
Greek international world, cf. E. E. Cohen, *Ancient Athenian
Maritime Courts* (Princeton, 1973), pp. 6–8.

87 Lycurgus, *In Leocratem* 14–15.

88 Lycurgus, *In Leocratem* 18; cf. Hasebroek, *Trade and Politics*, p. 144.

89 Cf. W. Ashburner, *The Rhodian Sea Law* (Oxford, 1909), e.g. at p. lxvii: 'Part III, in the form in which we possess it, has nothing to do with the Rhodians' (Part III is the heart, and by far the largest part, of the extant text).

90 Cf. above, p. 185 and n. 73. In the year in the mid-350s referred to at Demosthenes 20(*Leptines*).31–2 the Athenians imported 800,000 medimni (this, as the only available figure for the annual Athenian corn import, has attracted comment in a number of places: de Ste Croix, *Class Struggle*, pp. 46–7, gives a brief explanation of it); the merchants whose ships brought this corn must have spent the usual length of time in Athens implied by a delivery there. Therefore the emporium of Athens must have seemed markedly emptier than usual, at any rate considering the whole summer period, when only the corn merchants were there.

91 Aristotle, *Pol.* IV.1291b17–24.

92 Reed, 'Maritime traders', p. 46, suggests Chios, Aegina and Massalia as the likely provenance of traders; Massalia because Nos. 19 and 20 in his catalogue (see above, n. 3) come from there, Chios and Aegina on the strength of the Aristotle passage (cf. above, n. 91). It should be added that Rhodes was also a provenance of traders: Polyaenus IV.6.16 says how in 305 Antigonus allowed safety to Rhodian traders (and sailors/fisherman – '*thalassurgoi*') provided that they did not sail to Rhodes.

93 Hyperides F.70, from Hyp. 13(*Deliacus*).

94 Hyperides F.70.1.

95 Ibid.

96 Hyperides F.70.2.

97 Ibid. This is an interesting testimony to the impression created in a small city by the busy influx of traders and travellers to a larger neighbour. It does perhaps represent a certain rhetorical overstatement.

98 Ibid. The Delian position has by now begun to look shaky: it cannot have been usual for visitors who wanted to make sacrifices to have to go far from a large temple to buy them.

99 Cf. above, pp. 181–2 for the theorists' acceptance of the necessity for all cities to participate in trade.

100 Ruschenbusch, *Untersuchungen*, p. 68, points out that a majority of Greek states were too small to have an independent foreign policy (=policy of war or peace: cf. p. 67). Since all cities maintained a hoplite force, all would require imports of metal, or of manufactured armaments; but as the large cities were centres of employment of mercenaries and of technical innovation, they must certainly have imported more *matériel* per citizen than the *Normalpoleis* (cf. Ruschenbusch, *Untersuchungen*, p. 9).

101 Isocrates 9(*Evagoras*).47; Isocrates points up the city's backwardness by observing that it was barbarised, that it did not welcome Greeks or know technical skills, that it did not use an emporium and that it did not have a harbour.

102 Ibid.
103 See de Ste Croix, *Class Struggle*, p. 46.
104 Text in A. Peretti, *Il Periplo di Scilace* (Pisa, 1979), at pp. 505–38.
   Noting the enormous amount of geographical material in the treatise,
   Peretti comments (p. 485) that it cannot all have been collected by a
   mid-fourth-century writer, and argues (p. 486) that the work, being
   independent of the famous literary works of the fifth century
   (Hecataeus, Herodotus), is representative of a tradition of know-how:
   'È il filone di un sapere empirico, fornito dalla secolare esperienza
   marinara dei Greci, rimasto nell'ombra come strumento della
   navigazione . . .' ('It is the product of practical knowledge drawn from
   centuries of Greek seafaring experience and collected together as a
   manual of navigation'; and cf. pp. 435–8, arguing that the extant text
   is the product of a redaction made in the Philippic age and including
   some earlier work). It is not contentious to speculate that this tradition
   of know-how was probably built up in the context of communities of
   professional seafarers and traders, just as the physicians build up their
   own traditions, the philosophers theirs and the cooks theirs (cf. above,
   chapter 6). This is another aspect of the traders' existence as a body
   of men with a cohesion between themselves, habitually living outside
   the city-state system.
      Reed, 'Maritime traders', pp. 93–7, argues that there was no
   cohesion among traders, except that there were religious ties, some of
   which were national in character (at pp. 94–5 Reed discusses Tod II
   189, the Athenians' response to a request from the Citians to be
   allowed to buy a plot of land and build a sanctuary to Aphrodite on
   it). The fact that he fails to find cohesion shows that his definition of
   cohesion has been inadequate for analysing the evidence: traders knew
   each other personally (cf. the beginning of this section, with n. 60) and
   their community had enough internal continuity over a long period for
   it to be possible for Scylax, *Periplus*, to come into existence.
105 See, for instance, Scylax, *Periplus* 67, and some of the sections in the
   80s.
106 It is typical of this text to refer to which cities are Greek cities when
   dealing with non-Greek areas. E.g. Scylax, *Periplus* 86, 'Choerades – a
   Greek city' – among the Mossynoeci.
107 Cf. above, the beginning of this chapter, with n. 10.
108 Cf. above, pp. 183 and nn. 51–3: Aeneas Tacticus assumes that wares
   brought ashore will subsequently need to be brought through a gate
   into the city.
109 Cf. above, n. 104. It need scarcely be added that revenue from
   harbours was important to governments, regardless of the self-
   sufficiency of community life in cities. See [Arist.] *Oeconomica*
   1340a16 on how Callistratus in Macedonia doubled the yield of the
   harbour tax.
110 Hasebroek, *Trade and Politics*, p. 13. Cf. Reed, 'Maritime traders', p.
   16.
111 Hyp. F.70.1; cf. above, p. 186 and n. 94.

112 Isocrates 17(*Trapeziticus*).4.
113 Ibid. Hasebroek, *Trade and Politics*, p. 13, is perhaps likely to be right in calling Sopaeus a 'rich landlord of Bosporus', but it should be noticed that the text gives no explicit support to the idea and that Sopaeus may have been a courtier rather than an indigenous nobleman. He was in charge (ibid.) of Satyrus' forces (probably mercenary forces, as Hasebroek, *Trade and Politics*, says), and so had possibly started his career as a travelling mercenary leader.
114 Isocrates 17(*Trapeziticus*).4.
115 Plutarch, *Solon* 2.4. Other sources (the earliest of which are Cicero, *Rep.* I.10.16 and *Fin.* V.29.87) stress only that he went to Egypt for study.
116 Commodities also probably had less attraction for thieves than precious metals; the Aeolians at Delos (cf. above, p. 186 and n. 94), after all, were probably murdered for their money.
117 D.L. VI.9.
118 On which cf. also above, n. 52.
119 Cicero, *ad Att.* XIII.21a: 'tell me – did you decide to publish right away without my permission? Not even Hermodorus did that – the Hermodorus who used to distribute Plato's books, whose name gives us the saying "Hermodorus travels in books"'.
120 *Suda* s.v. 'Logoisin Hermodoros emporeuetai'. Note also that the phrase is an iambic trimeter and so a comic fragment (Kock III, p. 456, Adesp. 269). The context cannot be guessed: Cicero clearly quotes it as a proverbial phrase.
121 A. Böckh, *Die Staatshaushaltung der Athener* I (third edition, Berlin, 1886), p. 62, suggests that trade in books over long distances was so unusual that Hermodorus became proverbial. This is not fully satisfactory in view of the facts (*a*) that the line began its career as part of a comic play; and (*b*) that at Xenophon, *Anab.* VII.5.14, books appear as part of a mixed cargo: Böckh thinks them likely to have been unwritten books (p. 61), but he is corrected by his editor, Fränkel (II, p. 14, n. 89). Fränkel's explanation is that Hermodorus was 'nach den Worten Ciceros ... nicht dadurch sprichwörtlich, dass er Buchhandel in die Ferne betreib, sondern durch die Art, wie er ihn betrieb', '(in Cicero's words) not proverbial because he engaged in long-distance trade in books, but because of the *way* in which he engaged in it' (II, p. 14, n. 89). This is right as far as it goes, but it should be made explicit that Cicero is referring to Hermodorus as an exceptionally devoted publicist of Plato's work: his message to Atticus could be paraphrased as 'you can be as devoted and effective a literary publicist as the greatest of them all, viz. Hermodorus, *without* publishing things without my permission'.
122 Cf. above, n. 121.
123 Cf. above, p. 159.
124 On 'amateur' traders, cf. below, pp. 189–91.
125 Knorringa, *Emporos*, pp. 74–6.
126 Knorringa, *Emporos*, p. 74.

127 Knorringa, *Emporos*, pp. 74–6.

128 Reed, 'Maritime traders', pp. 98–9.

129 It is perhaps not entirely surprising that there is not: but simply portraying traders (as Charinus in Plautus, *Mercator*, on whom see above, n. 17) as normal people, while it does not imply a value judgement on their occupation, disposes the audience or the reader to view traders as a part of Greek society which can be treated as familiar enough to be laughed at. Their existence is therefore affirmed as part of a generally genial *status quo*, rather than being (as, for example, in Plato) analysed as one of the less attractive implications of the need for distribution and exchange.

130 Reed, 'Maritime traders', p. 98 and n. 175. Here cf. above, n. 17; but Demeas and Niceratus in Menander, *Samia*, certainly seem, from their discussion at lines 96–111, to be amateur travellers (cf. 416–17).

131 Reed, 'Maritime traders', p. 98.

132 On which cf. S. M. Goldberg, *The Making of Menander's Comedy* (London, 1980), pp. 109–10, where attention is drawn to this motif in the context of 'the situations the tradition provides and the relationships they represent' (p. 109).

133 As, for instance, in the case of Clinia's return from military service in Asia with 'the king' in Terence, *Heautontimoroumenos* (see lines 110–17 for a military counterpart to Demipho's exhortation to his son to go trading in Plautus, *Mercator* (cf. above, n. 14)). Menander, *Aspis*, trades on the contrasts between the consequences of Cleostratus' return as corpse and as living man.

134 Cf., for instance, Goldberg, *Menander's Comedy*, pp. 109–21, on 'Menander and life'.

135 For example, the position of Theopropides in Plautus, *Mostellaria*, who expects to return to his position as head of his family, and to his property. But his son Philolaches has spent all the family fortune in his father's absence. Among the laughs there are moments of genuine poignancy, e.g. at lines 431–45 and 1153–65.

136 If people left their own city's territory it would most commonly be as part of a city military expedition. Plautus, *Truculentus*, makes sophisticated contrasts between Diniarchus, the townsman who has been abroad on state business (355–6), Strabax, the countryman come to town with a windfall of money in his pocket (647–55), and Stratophanes, the Babylonian soldier returning from campaigning (81–7). The differences, in success with the *meretrix* Phronesium, between the stay-at-home Strabax and Diniarchus and Stratophanes, make for many of the comic situations.

137 Note 129 above suggests a main reason for this apparent lack of correspondence.

138 Even in his most moderate moment (cf. above, n. 40) he speaks of riches destroying the souls of traders with luxury and poverty turning them to shamelessness (Plato, *Laws* XI.919B–C).

139 As at Plato, *Laws* II.643D–E.

140 Not that he is consistently rude about all who do not conform to his

gentlemanly ideal; cf. how he makes the contrast between doctors and doctors' assistants a type of the relationship between free people and slaves: Plato, *Laws* IV.720B–E. But he does not regard them as the equals of himself or people like himself, however necessary they are to his utopian plans (as in the case of the foreign schoolmasters required at Plato, *Laws* VII.804C–D).

141 The success of the Phocians, temporary as it was, showed what a tiny state could do with a large mercenary army.

142 Cf. above, pp. 157–60.

143 Cf. above, n. 40.

144 Certainly Plato was an enemy of democracy (de Ste Croix, *Class Struggle*, pp. 70–1), but he was as militantly in favour of being-a-good-citizen (cf. *Laws* I.643D–E). Aristocratic/political is a term intended to sum up this state of mind.

145 G. M. Calhoun, *The Business Life of Ancient Athens* (Chicago, 1926), p. 54. And Reed, 'Maritime traders', pp. 9–12, stresses the time necessary to build up a good reputation as a trader.

146 Plautus, *Rudens* 930–5.

147 Plautus, *Rudens* 925–6.

148 Plautus, *Rudens* 931, 'apud reges rex perhibebor'; and note what Gripus means to do (934–5): 'oppidum magnum communibo, ei ego urbi Gripo indam nomen, / monimentum meae famae et factis, ibi qui regnum magnum instituam'. M. N. Tod, 'Epigraphical notes on freedmen's professions', *Epigraphica* 12 (1950), pp. 3–26, at p. 6, notes six references to freedmen traders from the *catalogi paterarum argentearum: IG* II² 1157.59, 1558.91, 1559.39, 1566.2 and 1577.3(?). Cf. above, pp. 56–60.

149 On the romance of being a trader cf. Kock III, p. 443, Adesp. 181, which occurs in Aelian, *Ep.* 18 (from Demylus to Blepsias on the neighbour Laches who has taken to sailing and wishes he had not).

150 Menander, *Perikeiromene* 808–9.

151 Terence, *Andria* 223–4.

152 Cf. the lists of references in Reed, 'Maritime traders', pp. 98–9 nn. 173–81.

153 Cf. Aristophanes of Byzantium, Test. 32 K–T.

8

The kings' friends

Government under Alexander and the Successors

The Macedonian army under Alexander proved superior to all opposition. The achievements of conquest were consolidated from the beginning by foundations of Greek cities. But the effort of conquest was costly for Macedon: even by the end of Alexander's reign it was clear that his homeland could not be treated as an inexhaustible source of manpower.[1] Greek mercenaries were used in Alexander's campaigns of conquest and as settlers in his city foundations.[2] And from the beginning there were Greeks entrusted with administrative work. Eumenes of Cardia even managed, with a certain degree of ruthless opportunism, to use his position to carve out for himself a corner in the succession to Alexander.

Conditions during Alexander's reign were exceptional. Philip II had gained power in Greece through carefully planned intervention in politics, and established control through the League of Corinth. This organisation was an adaptation of forms familiar in fourth-century Greece. It made the states of southern Greece the allies of Philip, but at the outset there was no Macedonian government in southern Greece. The League of Corinth was not an administrative organisation, and until Alexander left for Asia the kingdom of Macedon was the sphere of operation of a government of a type which Alexander's and Philip's ancestors would not have found strange. Alexander himself lived with his army in foreign territory and his administration was always in a sense provisional. The initiative he took in government of the Greek world advanced its integration under Macedonian rule (the Exiles' Decree was a measure of particularly sweeping effect),[3] while the system which mediated royal commands from sovereign to distant subjects was the organising arm of the mobile military machine.

After Alexander's death the pace of change in Greek government hardly slowed. The effort to maintain the unity of Alexander's empire, while pursued with some persistence at the level of high politics, was not effective in preventing the almost instant establishment of governments capable of resisting the centre. Ptolemy's first move on reaching Egypt in 323 was to begin securing his position by recruiting Greeks. Diodorus notes that he was gathering mercenaries and forming an army, and continues by saying that a large number of 'friends' (*philoi*) gathered round him 'on account of his fairness'.[4] By 321, after Perdiccas' failed attempt to dislodge him, Ptolemy had forced recognition of his effective autonomy: he was confirmed as satrap of Egypt because there was no alternative.[5]

Evidence for the mechanics of government in the period of the Successors is apt to be problematic. Diodorus does not go beyond campaigns and diplomacy; inscriptions, while substantially useful, have to be interpreted with care. Greek papyri of second-century and later dates have been found in Egypt in very large numbers, but there are extremely few Greek papyri from the first generation of Greek government there. During this brief period, though there was movement towards the developed type of Hellenistic government, there were areas where older forms of record-making and bureaucracy persisted for a long time. At Babylon the temple scribes carried on their chronicles well into the third century, retaining a position in the imperial establishment into the second generation of Greek rule.[6]

Recruitment and officialdom

Service in government in the period of the Successors was personal service to a particular king. Ptolemy's recruitment of 'friends' in 323 delineates the model for this, even if his reputation for fairness was written into the tradition rather than acting as a beacon for potential administrators as soon as he got to Egypt. And Theophrastus in the *Characters* gives a detailed (though allusive and deprecating) picture of the sort of person involved.[7] He tells someone he meets in the street how he campaigned with Evander (Alexander): he brags that he has had three letters from Antipater begging him to come to Macedonia and offering a tax concession – duty-free exports of timber. He claims that his reason for refusing was to safeguard himself against being the victim of sycophancy in Athens. Theophrastus' aim is to construct a stereotypical Boastful Man, so there is another side to his picture. The speaker has really never been out of the country; and his boasts include good deeds done to Athens. The effect of extreme hyperbole is achieved by capping cosmopolitanism and the courtier's life by making the subject a (pretended) patriot – and of the most generous, aristocratic kind. The ideology of city-state life is finally presented as definitive: the highest expectation, or proudest boast.

But perks were available for those prepared to move outside their cities and work for the kings. Real city aristocrats, with an income from land, would seldom be attracted to leaving home to enter other men's service. It would in any case seem slavish to people whose idea of freedom made paid labour analogous (in part) to slavery.[8] A Hellenistic king was not generally, in the Greek context, referred to as king of a particular place or people,[9] and his servants or officials were members of a personal retinue. The similarity in function and prestige between the kings' 'friends' and the 'companions' of earlier Macedonian sovereigns – as also the *amici principis* of the imperial period at Rome – are clear to the modern student,[10] even though many city-state Greeks would not have valued the opportunity to join the improvised *Gefolgschaft* of an ambitious Macedonian.

The formal titles of court functionaries are attested with more complexity and refinement at later stages in the Hellenistic period,[11] but there is a particular reason for the virtual absence of such titles in fourth-century inscriptions and literary sources referring to the period of the Successors. G. Herman notes how anecdotes about the Successors recall flatterers, parasites and slaves surrounding the kings – but not officials. He argues that ambiguity in referring to royal officials in city decrees (even though as bringers of rescripts and as general channels of communication between kings and cities they were powerful, and capable sometimes of achieving benefits for the cities they were in contact with) reflects the ambiguous position of the 'friends' in Greek city society.[12]

To illustrate the point Herman catalogues 57 inscriptions of the period between 330 and 200 from Athens, Samos, Delos and Ephesus. They all imply that the honorand is being rewarded for benefactions carried out by virtue of his connections with a ruler.[13] Herman's analysis shows formulae of two types used in the inscriptions to refer to the relationship between honorands and rulers. Formulae of his Type I run along the lines of '*staying with* the king' and do not carry the idea of paid service or give precise information about the person's place at court. Type II formulae are more explicit, giving a technical title and offices.[14] Herman's finding is that Type I formulae do not usually recur in a city's inscriptions after the first use of a Type II formula; Type II formulae come in as early as 302 in Ephesus, but not until 270/260 in Samos, and not until 260/250 in Athens.[15] The inference is that court titles were omitted from inscriptions because of their pejorative connotations in the Greek cities,[16] and that the progressive appearance of Type II formulae attests a process of legitimation in the third century BC for the role of royal officials in the Greek world.[17]

Autigonus' letter to Scepsis in 311, and the decree which goes with it, give a clear example of the contact a royal official could have with a city on official business. Acius went to Scepsis with Antigonus' letter which announced the treaty between Antigonus and Cassander.[18] The letter refers to Acius by name at line 70 – and, as C. B. Welles comments, the decree must have been sent out widely.[19] Even with each official making a tour and visiting several cities, a number of Aciuses must have been needed to publicise Antigonus' arrangement with Cassander and his professed aim of securing the freedom of the Greeks. But the use of manpower in this instance was probably very cost-effective. The companion document, a decree passed by the city of Scepsis, grants honours to Antigonus: a precinct, an altar, a statue, sacrifice, games, a festival – and, more prosaically, a 100-stater gold crown for Antigonus himself and a 50-stater gold crown for each of his sons, Demetrius and Philip.[20] As well as publicity, Acius' journey had a fund-raising function.

The Scepsis letter and decree illustrate a system of administration which was beginning to achieve some success in communication between the court and the cities. But there were definite limits on what Hellenistic governments could do. Regular taxation tended to be insufficient when from time to time high expenditure was called for; irregular taxes and crowns were collected from the cities at such times.[21] The civil servants were deployed to administer this crisis-response financing, which had to sustain not only the utilitarian requirements of government but also the magnificence of court life.[22]

There is no direct way of telling what numbers of Greeks were taken into service as 'friends' of Macedonian rulers. It is, though, possible to say that non-Macedonian Greeks – most of them from the city-states – must have formed a majority,[23] and that non-Greeks did not play a part in the government of Hellenistic states at the level of courts or capital cities.[24] L. Mooren gives a prosopography of Ptolemaic officials, and though the period before about 275 is more thinly represented than subsequent years, some inferences can be suggested from the half-dozen names available.[25] Cilles and Callicrates are attested as Macedonians: they were both army officers.[26] Nicanor and Argaeus have no attested provenance, but are both referred to in Diodorus as 'friends' of Ptolemy: they were put in charge of military operations.[27] When Tyre fell to Ptolemy in 312 the garrison commander, Andronicus of Olynthus, who had been working for Antigonus and Demetrius, was accepted as one of Ptolemy's 'friends' and, Diodorus says, given advancement.[28] These were all military men (the source being Diodorus, the focus of the narrative is military) but there was also a need on Ptolemy's staff for technical experts; Sostratus of Cnidos was an architect and engineer,[29] who collected honours from several Greek cities in the course of his work.[30] The ruler's likely strategy (as the acceptance of Andronicus of Cnidus illustrates) was to accept as a 'friend' anyone who seemed likely to be useful.

Scopas of Aetolia, for instance (at a slightly later period than the first generation of Hellenistic government), arrived at Alexandria destitute and three years later was running the whole army.[31] His story is obviously not typical, but it is illustrative, because Scopas' rise would not have been possible if the king and his followers did not form a little face-to-face society of a quite intimate type. Meteoric advancement, where it happened, was a matter of the ruler's personal assessment of a 'friend'. In this sense the kings and their 'friends' did form, as C. Habicht has it,[32] a 'dominant society'. The 'friends' spend the day with the king whatever he does, and advise him on all points.[33] Where cities make sacrifices, they make them for the health of the king, his 'friends' and the army.[34]

The holders of civil offices, military commands or sacred positions were all members of this face-to-face society. Two views are possible on the degree of specialisation and differentiation of functions among the 'friends'. The more widespread supposes that in the Successors' courts anyone might be turned to any necessary work. Habicht and F. W. Walbank both quote the examples of Persaeus, the Stoic philosopher who lost the Acrocorinthus for Antigonus Gonatas, Apollophanes, the physician who carried his view in Antiochus III's war council in 219, and Hegesianax, poet and historian, who was Antiochus' ambassador to Rome.[35] But Herman outlines a case for significant qualification of this: there were from the beginning people with the titles of strategos, nauarchos, somatophylax, phrourarchos, satrap.[36] Literary sources allow H. Bengtson to identify 45 generals from 330 to 280, when only five out of 50 benefactors in inscriptions are designated by titles.[37] Court titles may have been quite extensively granted, on this argument, at a stage when the nature of surviving sources, and the social stigma attached to being a courtier of one of the Hellenistic rulers, prevented their being attested.

Habicht comments that the kings could get the best and brightest people to enter their service.[38] There is perhaps some danger of exaggeration here: the rulers had a choice, presumably, but there is a lack of information about how it was exercised. It did not come to involve formal measurement of intellectual and cultural competence, on the lines of examination for entry to the Chinese mandarinate, and personal recommendation by people already influential with a ruler is likely to have been important; but initial entry to the body of 'friends' may not have been a particularly difficult hurdle.[39] Taking the analogy of the clients of an eminent Roman, it may be that provision for less influential 'friends' was not very costly.

It is quite attractive to suppose that exiles provided a particularly important source of recruits to the staffs of the Hellenistic courts. Habicht argues that it was exile – a permanent consequence of party strife in the cities – which meant that members of the intelligentsia were available.[40] In favour of this view is the fact that a fair proportion of exiles must have been oligarchs and, until they were banished, rich; many of them must have had access to education. But the assumption that displaced owners of land were the most likely recruits is disputable. The expanding tradition of travelling to find opportunities for professional success – the informal career style of doctors and philosophers, *hetaerae* and the rest[41] – is quite likely to have served as a model for men whose training and outlook inclined them to seek their fortune as 'friends'. Athens was the cultural centre and had most to offer an ambitious philosopher or *hetaera*, as has been argued above,[42] and the position of Athens in the literary world (and so in the extant texts) gives it more prominence now than the courts which were the locus of the life and influence of the 'friends'.

Kings and courtiers in the Hellenistic world

The Successors' courts, in their early years at least, demonstrated a sort of dialectic between Alexander's style of government from the mobile camp and a more static model. In the generation after his death the cities of Antigoneia, Cassandreia, Lysimacheia, Thessalonice and Demetrias were set up as new capitals.[43] Ptolemy, who had made Memphis his base when he first came to Egypt, came to use Alexandria as the heart of Greek administration – and also to found a city named after himself.[44] It was not a seat of government, and fitted uneasily into the pattern of Greek settlement and organisation in Egypt, but eventually all the serious rivals named cities for themselves.[45] These places housed the courts when there was no campaign in hand, and they illustrate the innovative nature of the government the kings and courts exercised. The ancient capitals of the eastern states which Alexander had conquered were progressively made marginal to administration.[46] (It appears, in contrast, that Alexander himself had planned to use Babylon as the capital of his empire.[47]) The men who governed in and from these cities were a ruling class, obviously – but the rich people of the capitals, as such, did not become the 'friends' of the kings.

Some of the things Hellenistic rulers could give – titles, personal attention – were held in contempt by city-state Greeks of the conventional type. But other things led to recognition. Money and particularly land were flexible and effective forms of reward for service. So in 275 Antiochus I granted 2,000 plethra of land in the Troad to Aristodicides of Assos:[48] a complicated transaction, partly because (as appears from the correspondence) the government's information about what land it held in the Troad was rather hazy.[49] Detailed arrangements had to be made at the local level.[50] But when Aristodicides had decided which city he wanted his land joined to (he had chosen between Scepsis and Ilium) a letter was sent from Meleager, the secretary, to the council and people of Ilium, stressing what an honour it was to be chosen by Aristodicides, and recommending them to grant him whatever privileges he might suggest.[51] From being an outsider, Aristodicides had been imposed on the people of Ilium as a leading local personage. The older and newer power structures coexisted, but the most successful of the kings' men could retire to – or simply keep estates in – Greek cities: the new ruling class could *do* more.

They came from a wide variety of places. No statistical measurement is possible, but in Herman's sample of honorific decrees (57 from Athens, Samos, Delos and Ephesus, with seven others) there is a great range of provenance.[52] With six lost and 16 not specified, there are eight Macedonians,[53] four Athenians and four Lampsacenes, two Perinthians, two Coans, two Rhodians and two Spartans; and one each from Cyzicus, Aeniania, Larisa, Bargylia, Otrynia, Thriasia, Iasos, Cardia, Cyrene, Arcadia, Elis, Lycia, Chalcis, Thessalonica, Plataea, Acarnania, Theangela, Miletus and Caunus. The list represents many areas of the Greek world. Macedonians account for just under a fifth of the persons whose origins are given. Other than Macedonia, no place is dominant.

So there was a two-way process in the Hellenistic courts' becoming what they were. The rulers – kings, as they began to call themselves – had the military might which was the basic requirement in their imposition of authority ('spear-won' territory formed an element in the ideology which was developed to legitimise their rule[54]); but the presence and the advice of self-confident and ambitious Greeks was a substantial element in the organisation of captured land into units accustomed and reconciled to responding to rulers' requirements. In 302, when Antigonus and Demetrius decided to reuse the device of a League of Greek states based on Corinth, it was the work of Adeimantus of Lampsacus as Demetrius' chief agent which communicated the kings' wishes to the states in their sphere of influence.[55]

As well as helping to shape the administrative and political nature of the Hellenistic kingdoms, the wider circle of courtiers defined the style of the royal households. The kings had a liking for the culture and entertainment of Greece. Philosophers may sometimes have suspected that the invitation to join a court circle was likely to work more to the ruler's advantage than their own: to his worldly, rather than moral or intellectual, advantage, as a result of imputed respectability.[56] As for *hetaerae*, they and the kings afforded each other some of their best opportunities for stylish gestures and clever comments:[57] anecdotes preserved for the reading public the edited highlights of smart-set life.[58]

The smart set of the anecdotes, where anecdotes concerned the royal courts, was the cosmopolitan world of courtiers; but, as Herman notes, the conventional city-state ideology has led to an unflattering portrayal of the people who surrounded the kings. They appear as slaves, parasites, flatterers, not as administrators or statesmen.[59] 'Flattery,' Theophrastus comments in the *Characters*,[60] 'might be understood as a sort of converse that is dishonourable but at the same time profitable to him that flatters.' This puts a 'friend', whose relationship to the king is necessarily one of dependence, in a position which could be rationalised as that of a 'flatterer'. Herman instances two anecdotes which illustrate a tension between the perceptions of kings' followers by their own circles and by city-state Greeks.[61] One, from Alexis, shows a parasite talking to his master and distinguishing between two types of parasite: the distinction allows him to speak of parasite generals and parasite satraps.[62] This makes the differential in value judgements almost explicit. The second is the elephantarch anecdote:[63] Demetrius' people speak of him as king, Seleucus as elephantarch, Ptolemy as navarch, Lysimachus as treasurer, Agathocles as nesiarch of Sicily. The flattering point is that Demetrius is treated as the real king and the others as government functionaries. The bureaucracy is taken for granted: the people who joked about Demetrius' rivals were themselves the officials who spent the days with the king and formed the governmental machine.

Discussing the philosophers, professional men and royal officials who formed their prosperous element in the world of outsiders, J. K. Davies characterises them as a 'tiny but influential minority in a world which was still largely a long way behind them'.[64] This analysis, while it puts into perspective the extent to which the Hellenistic world became a cosmopolitan world, is perhaps unnecessarily belittling. The Greek world was in an important sense not *behind* them: they formed part of a dominant structure which, though it progressively changed the world, did not seek to assimilate the world to itself. To some extent the fifth-century Athenian democrats had tried to make others like themselves by promoting democracy. But the courts were the product of the kings' successful exploitation of the resources available for consolidating their rule. Their all-Greek character, in one sense a reactionary feature by comparison with Alexander's use of local ruling classes in non-Greek areas, represented (at least outside Greece) an innovative way of governing: not local, not in the Greek tradition, not more than vestigially similar to earlier Macedonian kingship. In the courts and governments of the age of the Successors, people who had become outsiders from the Greek cities were instrumental in bringing in an era of central authority in the Greek world, and Greek-speaking authority across the Near East.

Notes

1 See A. B. Bosworth, 'Alexander the Great and the decline of Macedon', *JHS* 106 (1986), pp. 1–12. Bosworth argues that the Macedonian population was seriously depleted and states paradoxically that 'Alexander's conquests ... were ultimately fateful for the military and political destiny of Macedon' (p. 10). Militarily it is a little unclear what more the Macedonians could have achieved; but the substantially non-Macedonian nature of royal administrations set up after Alexander's death could perhaps support the idea that Macedon's 'political destiny' (whatever Bosworth thinks that was) went unfulfilled.

2 See Griffith, *Mercenaries*, pp. 12–25.

3 *Syll.*³ 306: see A. J. Heisserer, *Alexander the Great and the Greeks* (Norman, 1980), pp. 203–29. At pp. 227–9 Heisserer notes how Alexander had progressively eliminated the League of Corinth from the process of government.

4 D.S. XVIII.14.1: *philoi* here are not people for whom Ptolemy had a personal affection but able, educated people who could help him manage his interests. The comment about his fairness is the clue that *philoi* here is the standard Hellenistic term dealt with below.

5 D.S. XVIII.39.5.

6 S. Smith, *Babylonian Historical Texts* (London, 1924), pp. 124–49.

7 Theophrastus, *Characters* 23 (Boastfulness).

8 Aristotle, *Rh.* 1367a32: 'the condition of the free man is that he does not live for the benefit of another'.

9 F. W. Walbank notes this at *CAH* VII.1² (Cambridge, 1984), pp. 65–6.

10 Cf. L. Mooren, *The Aulic Titulature in Ptolemaic Egypt* (Brussels, 1975), pp. 1–3. Mooren observes that whenever there is a *Gefolgschaft* it is designated by a name from everyday life, hence simply 'friends'.

11 F. W. Walbank at *CAH* VII.1² (Cambridge, 1984), pp. 70–1, reviews the hierarchical structure of the second-century Seleucid court: 'friends', 'first friends', 'first and specially honoured friends', 'kinsmen'.

12 G. Herman, 'The "friends" of early Hellenistic rulers: servants or officials?', *Talanta* 12–13 (1980–1), pp. 103–149, at p. 103.

13 Herman, '"Friends"', p. 104.

14 Herman, '"Friends"', pp. 106–7.

15 Herman, "'Friends'", p. 107.
16 Herman notes (p. 107 n. 13) that cities not dealt with in his analysis conform to the same pattern; on the negative evaluation of court service see pp. 108–9, 115, 121 and 126–7.
17 Herman, "'Friends'", pp. 103 and 127.
18 *OGIS* 5, which is No. 1 in C. B. Welles, *Royal Correspondence in the Hellenistic Period* (New Haven, Conn., 1934). Acius comes in at line 70.
19 Welles, *Royal Correspondence*, p. 11.
20 *OGIS* 6 (Welles, *Royal Correspondence*, No. 2).
21 Rostovtseff, *History*, p. 138.
22 On the lavish nature of life at the courts see, e.g., Plutarch, *Mor.* 182 (*Apophthegmata regum*); not, *Cleomenes* 13; the story at *Demetrius* 27.1 of Demetrius' handing the 250 talents collected from Athens to Lamia and the *hetaerae* for soap shows the king using extraordinary taxation together with whimsical largesse as a deliberate insult.
23 See below, p. 214, nn. 52 and 53.
24 F. W. Walbank at *CAH* VII.I² (Cambridge, 1984), p. 69 n. 1, and C. Habicht, 'Die herrschende Gesellschaft in den hellenistischen Monarchien', *Vierteljahrschrift für Sozial- und Wirtschaftsgeschichte* 45 (1958), pp. 1–16, at p. 5, both note this point. Hannibal in Macedon at the turn of the third and second centuries was an anomaly. E. Will at *CAH* VII.I² (Cambridge, 1984), p. 28, notes how Alexander had put Persians in administrative posts and in his own entourage, but that that practice ended when he died – leaving the way open for Greeks to find work in Macedonian governments.
25 Mooren, *Aulic Titulature*, pp. 52–7: there are eight entries for 320 to 275, but one of them is Seleucus and another is Demetrius of Phalerum. Neither of them really fits the category of a court official.
26 Mooren, *Aulic Titulature*, Nos. 4 and 6; Cilles: D.S. XIX.93.1–2; Callicrates: D.S. XX.21.1. Callicrates appears as a flatterer at Athenaeus VI.251d (=Euphantus, *FGrHist* 74 F 1); cf. also *IG* XI.2 2038, lines 77–8, and *IG* XI.2 161B, lines 54–5 and 89–90.
27 Mooren, *Aulic Titulature*, Nos. 1 and 5; Nicanor: D.S. XVIII.43.2; Argaeus: D.S. XX.21.1–2.
28 Mooren, *Aulic Titulature*, No. 3; D.S. XIX.86.1–2.
29 Mooren, *Aulic Titulature*, No. 8; a 'friend' of the kings: Strabo XVII.1.6; and cf. Fraser, *Ptolemaic Alexandria* I, pp. 18–20.
30 Sostratus' honours included *OGIS* 67 (League of Islanders); *IG* XI.4 563 (Delos); *OGIS* 68 (Caunus) and *OGIS* 66 (Delphi).
31 See Habicht, 'Die herrschende Gesellschaft', p. 9, and R. Flacelière, *Les Aitoliens à Delphes* (Paris, 1937), pp. 288–310.
32 The connection between kings and 'friends' always had a personal character, as Habicht notes (p. 10): between them they formed the 'herrschende Gesellschaft' he refers to in his title.
33 Habicht, 'Die herrschende Gesellschaft', pp. 2–3.
34 Habicht, 'Die herrschende Gesellschaft', p. 4.
35 Habicht, 'Die herrschende Gesellschaft', p. 7 and Walbank, *CAH* VII.I² (Cambridge 1984), pp. 69–70.

36 Herman, '"Friends"', p. 110.
37 H. Bengtson, 'Die Strategie in der hellenistischen Zeit' III, *Münchener Beiträge* 36 (1967²), pp. 403–21, and Herman, '"Friends"', p. 110.
38 Habicht, 'Die Herrschende Gesellschaft', p. 8 – and Walbank, *CAH* VII.I² (Cambridge, 1984), p. 69 n. 1, speaks of a nobility chosen by the kings solely on the basis of ability.
39 The argument for this conjecture is as follows. It would be a mistake to think that becoming a 'friend' of a king was precisely analogous to being appointed to a vacancy in a modern bureaucracy. It is unlikely to have involved choosing an available person from outside the group of 'friends' for a particular function. More probably if a person appeared at a court with an introduction from an established friend, or a convincing style and self-presentation, he would be able to begin following the king around in an informal way – receiving something towards maintenance rather as the urban client of a great Roman aristocrat might have done at a later date. When the king had to assign someone to a particular task he would probably choose someone who had been around the court for a while. There would not be any substantial reward unless one got assigned to something – so 'friends' who did not attract work at court would probably, after a certain period, be deterred from staying there.
40 Habicht, 'Die herrschende Gesellschaft', p. 8.
41 Cf. above, chapter 6.
42 Cf. above, pp. 150–4.
43 Cf. Rostovtzeff, *History*, p. 137. Antigoneia did not last long, and the Seleucid foundations in Syria, Seleuceia-in-Pieria, Laodicea-on-the-sea, Apamea and principally Antioch, formed the eventual backbone of Greek government in that area.
44 See above, p. 58 and n. 265 for the date.
45 Founding and naming these cities was an element in the move towards establishment of new kingdoms: Cassandreia came ten years before the Successors became kings, and the other cities followed over about a generation.
46 On this see Rostovtzeff, *History*, pp. 132–5 and 423–36.
47 For instance, at D.S. XVII.112.1–116.4 he seems to be setting up a peacetime administration there in 324/323.
48 Welles, *Royal Correspondence*: Nos. 10–12 deal with Aristodicides' grant.
49 Welles, *Royal Correspondence*, p. 66.
50 Welles, *Royal Correspondence*, notes that at a later period when Antiochus II sold land, not far away from the same area, to Laodice, he knew it was his to sell and could describe its boundaries (*Royal Correspondence*, No. 18). Not here. But it would be unwise to draw any general conclusion from comparing the two individual cases.
51 Welles, *Royal Correspondence*, No. 13.
52 Herman, '"Friends"', pp. 128–49.
53 Counting an Aegaean (a person from Aegae, the ancient capital of Macedonia) as a Macedonian.

54 Walbank, *CAH* VII.I² (Cambridge, 1984), p. 64.
55 L. Robert, 'Adeimantos de Lampsaque et la ligue de Corinthe sur une inscription de Delphes', *Hellenica* II (1946), pp. 15–36.
56 A point Stilpo may have had in mind: cf. above, chapter 6 n. 215.
57 See, e.g., Athenaeus XIII.577d–f and 579a (both from Machon) – girls' comments. A king's comment – Plutarch, *Mor.* 180F (*Apophth. reg.*).
58 So literary figures, *hetaerae*, philosophers and kings attracted anecdotes: they held the commanding height, by the last quarter of the fourth century, in terms of public visibility in Greece.
59 Herman, '"Friends"', p. 118.
60 Theophrastus, *Characters* 2(*Flattery*).1.
61 Herman, '"Friends"', pp. 119–20.
62 Athenaeus VI.237B–D.
63 Plutarch, *Dem.* 25.3–5 (cf. *Mor.* 823c–d).
64 J. K. Davies at *CAH* VII.I² (Cambridge, 1984), p. 310.

Bibliography

Accame, S., *La lega ateniese del sec. IV. A.C.* (Rome, 1941).
Altieri, N., *Museo archeologico nazionale di Ferrara* I (Bologna, 1979).
Ampolo, C., 'Tra finanza e politica: carriere e affari del signore Moirokles', *Riv. Fil.* 109 (1981), pp. 187–204.
Anderson, J. K., *Ancient Greek Horsemanship* (Berkeley and Los Angeles, 1961).
Anon. rev. of Ormerod, *Piracy in the Ancient World, JHS* 45 (1925), p. 149.
Ashburner, W., *The Rhodian Sea Law* (Oxford, 1909).
Asheri, D., *Distribuzioni di terre nell'antica Grecia* (Turin, 1966).
— 'I coloni elei ad Agrigento', *Kokalos* 16 (1970), pp. 79–88.
Austin, C., *Comicorum Graecorum Fragmenta in Papyris Reperta* (Berlin and New York, 1973).
Austin, M. M., *The Hellenistic World* (Cambridge, 1981).
Baden, H., 'Untersuchungen zur Einheit der Hellenika Xenophons' (Diss., Hamburg, 1966).
Badian, E., 'Harpalus', *JHS* 81 (1961), pp. 16–43.
— 'A king's notebooks', *HSCP* 72 (1967), pp. 183–204.
Barker, E., 'Greek political thought and theory', *C.A.H.* VI (Cambridge, 1927), pp. 505–35.
Barnes, J. W. B., Parsons, P., Rea, J. and Turner, E. G., *The Oxyrhynchus Papyri* XXXI (London, 1966).
Baynes, N. H., *Byzantine Studies and Other Essays* (London, 1960).
Bean, G. E. and Cook, J. M. 'The Carian coast III', *BSA* 52 (1957), pp. 58–146.
Beloch, K. J., *Die Bevölkerung der griechisch-römischen Welt* (Leipzig, 1986).
— *Griechische Geschichte* IV (1) (second edition, Berlin and Leipzig, 1925).
Bengtson, M., 'Die Strategie in der hellenistischen Zeit' III, *Münchener Beiträge* 36 (1967²), pp. 403–21.
Bensel, J. F., 'Hippocratis qui fertur De Medico libellus ed codicum fidem recensitus', *Philologus* 78 (1923), pp. 88–130.
Berve, H., *Das Alexanderreich auf prosopographischer Grundlage* I (Munich, 1926).
— *Die Tyrannis bei den Griechen* (Munich, 1967).

Bevan, E., *A History of Egypt under the Ptolemaic Dynasty* (London, 1927).

Bickermann, E., and Sykutris, J., 'Speusipps Brief an König Philipp', *Berichte über die Verhandlungen der Sächsischen Akademie der Wissenschaften zu Leipzig* 80 (1928, No. 3), pp. 1-86.

Blinkenberg, C., 'Triemiolia: étude sur un type de navire rhodien', *Archaeologisk-Kunsthistoriske Meddelelser* II, 3 (1938), pp. 1-59.

Blümner, H., 'Fahrendes Volk im Alterthum', *SBA* (1918), Abh. 6, pp. 1-53.

Boardman, J., rev. of G. Navarra, *Città sicane, sicule e greche nella zona di Gela*, *CR*, n.s. 16 (1966), pp. 213-15.

Böckh, A., *Corpus Inscriptionum Graecarum* I (Berlin, 1828).

— *Die Staatshaushaltung der Athener* I, ed. M. Fränkel (third edition, Berlin, 1886).

Bon, A., 'Les ruines antiques dans l'île de Thasos et en particulier les tours helléniques', *BCH* 54 (1930), pp. 174-94.

Bosworth, A. B., 'The Congress Decree: another hypothesis', *Hist.* 20 (1971), pp. 600-16.

— *A Historical Commentary on Arrian's History of Alexander* (Oxford, 1980).

— 'Alexander the Great and the decline of Macedon', *JHS* 106 (1986), pp. 1-12.

Braun, K., 'Der Dipylon-Brunnen Bl: Die Funde', *Ath. Mitt.* 85 (1970), pp. 114-269.

Bravo, B., 'Sulân. Représailles et justice privée contre des étrangers dans les cités grecques', *ASNP*, Ser. III, 10 (1980), pp. 675-987.

Briant, P., 'Colonisation hellénistique et populations indigènes. La phase d'installation', *Klio* 60 (1978), pp. 57-92.

— 'Colonisation hellénistique et populations indigènes II. Renfort grecs dans les cités hellénistiques d'Orient', *Klio* 64 (1982), pp. 83-98.

Brown, P., *Augustine of Hippo* (Berkeley and Los Angeles, 1967).

— *The Cult of the Saints* (London, 1981).

Brown, T. S., 'Suggestions for a *vita* of Ctesias of Cnidus', *Hist.* 27 (1978), pp. 1-19.

Brunt, P. A., *Italian Manpower 225 B.C. - A.D. 14* (Oxford, 1971).

Burford, A., 'The economics of Greek temple building', *PCPhS*, n.s. 11 (1965), pp. 21-34.

— *The Greek Temple Builders at Epidaurus* (Liverpool, 1969).

— *Craftsmen in Greek and Roman Society* (London, 1972).

Burn, A. R., *The Warring States of Greece* (London, 1968).

Calhoun, G. M., *The Business Life of Ancient Athens* (Chicago, 1926).

Cargill, J., *The Second Athenian League* (Berkeley and Los Angeles, 1981).

Cartledge, P., 'Hoplites and heroes', *JHS* 97 (1977), pp. 11-27.

Casson, L., *Travel in the Ancient World* (London, 1974).

Cataldi, S., 'La *boetheia* dei geloi e degli herbitaioi ai Campani di Entella', *ASNP*, Ser. III, 12.3 (1982), pp. 887-904.

Cavaignac, E., 'Les dekarchies de Lysandre', *REH* 90 (1924), pp. 285-316.

Cawkwell, G. L., *Philip of Macedon* (London, 1978).

217

Bibliography

Ciaceri, E., *Storia della Magna Grecia* II (Milan, Rome and Naples, 1927).

Cohen, E. E., *Ancient Athenian Maritime Courts* (Princeton, 1973).

Cohen, G. M., *The Seleucid Colonies, Hist.* Einzelschrift 30 (Wiesbaden, 1978).

Cohn-Haft, L., *The Public Physicians of Ancient Greece* (Northampton, Mass., 1956).

Cook, J. M., 'Old Smyrna, 1948–1951', *BSA* 53 (1958), pp. 1–34.

— *The Troad* (Oxford, 1973).

— *The Persian Empire* (London, 1983).

Cornford, F. M., *Thucydides Mythistoricus* (London, 1907).

Corsaro, M., 'La presenza Romana a Entella: una nota su Tiberio Claudio di Anzio', *ASNP*, Ser. III, 12.3 (1982), pp. 993–1032.

Crapanzano, V., *The Hamadsha: A Study in Moroccan Ethnopsychiatry* (Berkeley and Los Angeles, 1973).

Davies, J. K., *Athenian Propertied Families* (Oxford, 1971).

— *Democracy and Classical Greece* (Glasgow, 1978).

— *Wealth and the Power of Wealth in Classical Athens* (New York, 1981).

Diller, H., *Wanderarzt und Aitiologe* (Leipzig, *Philologus*, Supplementband 26, Heft 3, 1934).

Donlan, W., *The Aristocratic Ideal in Ancient Greece* (Lawrence, 1980).

Dover, K. J., *Lysias and the Corpus Lysiacum* (Berkeley and Los Angeles, 1968).

— *Greek Popular Morality in the Time of Plato and Aristotle* (Oxford, 1974).

Dunbabin, T. J., *The Western Greeks* (Oxford, 1948).

Edelstein, L., *Plato's Seventh Letter* (Leiden, 1966).

— *Ancient Medicine* (Baltimore, 1967).

— *Peri aeron und die Sammlung der hippokratischen Schriften* (Berlin, 1931).

Ellis, J. R., 'Population transplants under Philip II', *Makedonika* 9 (1969), pp. 9–17.

Englemann, H., Knibbe, D., and Merkelbach, R., *Die Inschriften von Ephesos* IV (Bonn, 1980).

Errington, R. M., 'From Babylon to Triparadeisos, 323–320 BC', *JHS* 90 (1970), pp. 49–77.

— 'Alexander in the Hellenistic world', *Entretiens Fondation Hardt* 22 (1975), pp. 137–79.

Evans, A. J., 'The "Horsemen" of Tarentum', *NC*, Ser. III, vol. 9 (1889), pp. 1–228.

Ferguson, W. S., *Hellenistic Athens* (London, 1911).

Finkelstein, M. I. (M. I. Finley), ʽἜμπορος, Ναύκληρος and Κάπηλος: a prolegomena to the study of Athenian trade', *CPhil* 30 (1925), pp. 320–36.

Finley, M. I., 'The Black Sea and Danubian regions and the slave trade in antiquity', *Klio* 40 (1962), pp. 51–60.

— *The Ancient Economy* (London, 1973).

— *Problèmes de la terre en Grèce Ancienne* (Paris, 1973).

— *The Use and Abuse of History* (London, 1975).

Flacelière, R., *Les Aitoliens à Delphes* (Paris, Bibliothèque des Ecoles françaises d'Athènes et de Rome, 143, 1937).

Fraser, P. M., 'Inscriptions from Ptolemaic Egypt', *Berytus* 13 (1960), pp. 123–61.

— *Ptolemaic Alexandria* (Oxford, 1972).

Freeman, E. A., *The History of Sicily from the Earliest Times* III (Oxford, 1982).

Fuks, A., 'Isocrates and the social-economic situation in Greece', *Ancient Society* 3 (1972), pp. 17–44.

Galbraith, J. K., *The Affluent Society* (second edition, Harmondsworth, 1970).

Gardner, E. A., Loring, W., Richards, G. C. and Woodhouse, W. J., *Excavations at Megalopolis 1890–1891*, Society for the Promotion of Hellenic Studies, Supp. Paper No. 1 (London, 1982).

Garlan, Y., *Recherches de Poliorcétique grecque* (Bibliothèque des écoles françaises d'Athènes et de Rome, fasc. 123, 1974).

— 'Signification historique de la piraterie grecque', *DHA* 4 (1978), pp. 1–16.

Garnsey, P. D. A., and Whittaker, C. R., *Imperialism in the Ancient World* (Cambridge, 1978).

— Hopkins, K. and Whittaker, C. R. (eds.), *Trade in the Ancient Economy* (London, 1983).

Genière, J. de la, 'C'è un "modello" Amendolara?' *ASNP*, Ser. III 8.2 (1978), pp. 335–54.

Gernet, L., 'Sur les actions commerciales en droit athénien', *REG* 51 (1938), pp. 1–44.

Ghiron-Bistagne, P., *Recherches sur les acteurs dans la Grèce antique* (Paris, 1976).

Gitti, A., 'La colonia ateniese in Adriatico del 325/4 a.c.', *PP* 9 (1954), pp. 16–24.

Glover, T. R., *Greek Byways* (Cambridge, 1932).

Goldberg, S. M., *The Making of Menander's Comedy* (London, 1980).

Goldsberry, M., 'Sicily and its cities in Hellenistic and Roman times' (Diss., University of North Carolina, Chapel Hill, 1973).

Gomperz, T., *Greek Thinkers* I (London, 1901).

Gow, A. S. F., *Theocritus* II (Cambridge, 1950).

Green, P., rev. of de Ste Croix, *The Class Struggle in the Ancient Greek World*, *TLS* 4167 (11 February 1983), pp. 125–6.

Griffith, G. T., *The Mercenaries of the Hellenistic World* (Cambridge, 1935).

— 'The union of Corinth and Argos', *Hist.* 1 (1950), pp. 236–56.

Grote, G., *History of Greece* XII (London, 1856).

Gude, M., *A History of Olynthus* (Baltimore, 1933).

Guthrie, W. K. C., *A History of Greek philosophy* IV (Cambridge, 1975).

Habicht, C., 'Samische Volksbeschlussen der hellenistischen Zeit', *Ath. Mitt.* 72 (1957), pp. 152–237.

— 'Die herrschende Gesellschaft in den hellenistischen Monarchien', *Vierteljahrschrift für Sozial- und Wirtschaftsgeschichte* 45 (1958), pp. 1–16.

Bibliography

— 'Hellenistische Inschriften aus dem Heraion von Samos', *Ath. Mitt.* 87 (1972), pp. 191–228.

Hamilton, J. R., *Plutarch: Alexander, a Commentary* (Oxford, 1969).

Hammond, N. G. L., 'The sources of Diodorus Siculus XVI. I. The Macedonian, Greek and Persian narrative', *CQ* 31 (1937), pp. 79–91.

— *Epirus* (Oxford, 1967).

— and Griffith, G. T., *A History of Macedonia* II (Oxford, 1979).

Harvey, F. D., 'The maritime loan in Eupolis' "Marikas" (*P. Oxy.* 2741)', *ZPE* 23 (1976), pp. 231–3.

Hasebroek, J., *Trade and Politics in Ancient Greece* (New York, 1965).

Head, B. V., *Historia Numorum* (second edition, Oxford, 1911).

Heinen, H., *Untersuchungen zur hellenistischen Geschichte des 3. Jahrhunderts v. Chr.*, *Hist.* Einzelschrift 20 (Wiesbaden, 1972).

Heisserer, A. J., *Alexander the Great and the Greeks* (Norman, 1980).

Herman, G., 'The "friends" of early Hellenistic rulers: servants or officials?', *Talanta* 12–13 (1980–1), pp. 103–49.

Hornblower, J., *Hieronymus of Cardia* (Oxford, 1982).

Hornblower, S., *Mausolus* (Oxford, 1982).

— *The Greek World 479–323 B.C.* (London and New York, 1983).

Humphreys, S. C., 'The Nothoi of Kynosarges', *JHS* 94 (1974), pp. 88–95.

Jaeger, W., *Diokles von Karystos* (Berlin, 1938).

Jones, A. H. M., *The Greek City from Alexander to Justinian* (Oxford, 1940).

— *Athenian Democracy* (Oxford, 1957).

Kahrstedt, U., *Beiträge zur Geschichte der thrakischen Chersones* (Baden-Baden, 1954).

Kant, I., *Critique of Pure Reason*, trans. N. Kemp Smith (second edition, London, 1929).

Kerferd, G. B., *The Sophistic Movement* (Cambridge, 1981).

Kett, 'Prosopographie der griechischen historischen Manteis bis auf die Zeit Alexanders des Grossen' (Diss., Erlangen-Nürnberg, 1966).

Kindstrand, J. F., *Bion of Borysthenes*, Acta Universitatis Uppsalensis, *Studia Graeca Uppsalensia* II (Uppsala, 1976).

Kirchner, J., *Prosopographia Attica* (Berlin, 1901 and 1903).

Knorringa, H., *Emporos* (Amsterdam, 1926).

Köhler, L., 'Die Briefe des Sokrates und der Sokratiker', *Philologus* Suppl. 20, Heft 2 (1928).

Kraay, C. M., *Archaic and Classical Greek Coins* (London, 1976).

Kroll, J. H., 'An archive of the Athenian cavalry', *Hesp.* 46(1977), pp. 83–140.

Lacroix, M., 'Les Etrangers à Délos pendant la période de l'indépendence', *Mélanges Gustave Glotz* II (Paris, 1932).

Lane Fox, R. J., *Alexander the Great* (London, 1973).

Larsen, J. A. O., *Greek Federal States* (Oxford, 1968).

Lawrence, A. W., *Greek Aims in Fortifications* (Oxford, 1979).

Leaf, W., 'On a commercial history of Greece', *JHS* 35 (1915), pp. 161–72.

— 'Strabo and Demetrius of Skepsis', *BSA* 22 (1916–18), pp. 23–47.

Lejeune, M., 'Noms grecs et noms indigènes dans l'épigraphie hellénistique

d'Entella', *ASNP*, Ser. III, 12.3 (1982), pp. 787–99.
Lévêque, P., 'De Timoléon à Pyrrhos', *Kokalos* 14–15 (1968–9), pp. 135–51 and debate at pp. 151–6.
Lewis, D. M., 'Notes on Attic inscriptions', *BSA* 49 (1954), pp. 17–50.
— 'Dedications of Phialai at Athens', *Hesp.* 37 (1968), pp. 368–80.
— *Sparta and Persia* (Leiden, 1977).
Lintott, A., *Violence, Civil Strife and Revolution in the Classical City* (London and Canberra, 1982).
Lombardo, M., 'Il Sinecismo di Entella', *ASNP*, Ser. III, 12.3 (1982), pp. 849–86.
Lord, L. E., 'Watchtowers and fortresses in Argolis', *AJA* 43 (1939), pp. 78–84.
Lotze, D., 'Die chronologische Interpolationen in Xenophons Hellenika', *Philologus* 106 (1962), pp. 1–13.
— *Lysander und der peloponnesische Krieg*, Abhandlungen der Sachsischen Akademie der Wissenschaften zu Leipzig, philologisch-historische Klasse, 57.1 (Berlin, 1964).
– 'War Xenophon selbst der Interpolator seiner Hellenika I–II?', *Philologus* 118 (1974), pp. 215–17.
Lynch, J. P., *Aristotle's School* (Berkeley and Los Angeles, 1972).
MacDonald, B. R., 'The emigration of potters from Athens in the late fifth century B.C. and its effect on the Attic pottery industry', *AJA* 85 (1981), pp. 159–68.
– 'The authenticity of the Congress Decree', *Hist.* 31 (1982), pp. 120–3.
– 'ΛΗΙΣΤΕΙΑ and ΛΗΙΖΟΜΑΙ in Thucydides and in *IG* I³ 41, 67 and 75', *AJP* 105 (1984), pp. 77–84.
MacKay, R. A., 'Klephtika: the tradition of the tales of banditry in Apuleius', *G&R*, 2nd Ser. 10 (1963), pp. 147–52.
MacMullen, R., *Enemies of the Roman Order* (Cambridge, Mass., 1967).
Meister, K., 'Die Sizilische Geschichte bei Diodor von den Anfängen bis zum Tod des Agathokles' (Diss., Munich, 1967).
Meritt, B. D., 'Greek inscriptions', *Hesp.* 9 (1940), pp. 53–96.
Millar, F., 'The world of the Golden Ass', *JRS* 71 (1981), pp. 63–75.
Miller, S. G., 'Excavations at Nemea, 1978', *Hesp.* 48 (1979), pp. 73–103.
Moggi, M., *I Sinecismi interstatali greci* (Pisa, 1976).
Momigliano, A., *Essays in Ancient and Modern Historiography* (Oxford, 1977).
Mooren, L., *The Aulic Titulature in Ptolemaic Egypt* (Brussels, 1975).
Moretti, L., *Olympionikai, i vincitori negli antichi agoni olimpici* (Rome, 1957).
— *Iscrizioni storiche ellenistiche* (Florence, 1967).
Mossé, C., *Athens in Decline, 404–86 B.C.* (London and Boston, Mass., 1973).
– 'The "World of the *Emporium*" in the private speeches of Demosthenes', in P. Garnsey, K. Hopkins and C. R. Whittaker (eds.), *Trade in the Ancient Economy*, pp. 53–63.
Navarra, G., *Città sicane, sicule e greche nella zona di Gela* (Palermo, 1964).

Bibliography

— 'E Gela e Katagela', *Röm. Mitt.* 82 (1975), pp. 21–82.

Nenci, G., 'Considerazioni sui decreti da Entella', *ASNP* Ser. III 12.3 (1982), pp. 1069–83.

Orlandini, P., 'Storia e topografia di Gela dal 405 al 282 a.c. alla luce delle nuove scoperte archeologiche', *Kokalos* 2 (1956), pp. 158–76.

Ormerod, H. A., *Piracy in the Ancient World* (Liverpool, 1924).

Parke, H. W., *Greek Mercenary Soldiers from the Earliest Times to the Battle of Ipsus* (Oxford, 1933).

Patterson, C., *Pericles' Citizenship Law of 451–50 B.C.* (New York, 1981).

Pečirka, J., 'Homestead farms in Classical and Hellenistic Hellas', in M. I. Finley (ed.), *Problèmes de la terre en Grèce ancienne* (Paris, 1973), pp. 113–47.

Peretti, A., *II Periplo di Scilace* (Pisa, 1979).

Petrakos, B. Ch., 'Νέαι πηγαὶ περὶ τοῦ Χρεμωνιδείου πολέμου', *Arch. Delt.* 22 (1967), pp. 38–52.

Pfister, F., 'Die Reisebilder des Herakleides', *Sb. Ak. Wien* 227.2 (1951), pp. 1–252.

Phillips, E. D., *Greek Medicine* (London, 1973).

Pickard-Cambridge, A. W., *Demosthenes and the Last Days of Greek Freedom* (New York and London, 1914).

– *The Dramatic Festivals of Athens* (second edition, Oxford, 1968).

Pippidi, D. M., *Inscripţiile din Scythia Minor greceşti şi latine* I (Bucharest, 1983).

Plaumann, E., *Ptolemais in Oberägypten* (Leipzig, 1910).

Pomeroy, S. B., *Goddesses, Whores, Wives and Slaves* (London, 1976).

Pouilloux, J., 'ὁ ἐπικέφαλος ὀβολος', *BCH* 73 (1949), pp. 177–200.

— *L'histoire et les cultes de Thasos* I, Etudes Thasiennes III, Paris, 1954.

Powell, J. E., *A Lexicon to Herodotus* (Oxford, 1938).

Pritchett, W. K., 'The Attic stelai I', *Hesp.* 22 (1953), pp. 225–99.

— 'The Attic stelai II', *Hesp.* 25 (1956), pp. 178–317.

— *The Greek State at War* I (Berkeley and Los Angeles, 1974).

— *The Greek State at War* III (Berkeley and Los Angeles, 1974).

— *The Greek State at War* II (Berkeley and Los Angeles, 1979).

Pugliese Carratelli, G., 'Sanniti, Lucani, Brettii e italioti dal secolo IV a.c.', *Convegno di Studi Sulla Magna Grecia* 11 (1971), pp. 37–55.

Randall, R. H., 'The Erechtheum workmen', *AJA* 57 (1953), pp. 199–210.

Rankin, E. M., *The Role of the Mageiroi in the Life of the Ancient Greeks* (Chicago, 1907).

Reed, C. M., 'Maritime traders in the Greek world of the Archaic and Classical periods' (Diss., Oxford, 1980).

Rhodes, P. J., *The Athenian Boule* (Oxford, 1972).

— *A Commentary on the Aristotelian Athenaion Politeia* (Oxford, 1981).

Richter, G. M. A., *Sculptors and Sculpture of the Greeks* (fourth edition, New Haven and London, 1970).

Robert, L., 'Adeimantos de Lampsaque et la ligue de Corinthe sur une inscription de Delphes', *Hellenica* II (1946), pp. 15–36.

Robert, L. and J., 'Une inscription grecque de Téos en Ionie: l'union de Téos et Kyrbissos', *JS* (1976), pp. 153–235.

Robinson, D. M., *Excavations at Olynthus* II (Baltimore, 1930).
— *Excavations at Olynthus* XII (Baltimore, 1946).
Roebuck, C., 'The settlements of Philip II in 338 BC', *CPhil.* 43 (1948), pp. 73–92.
Roesch, P., 'Une loi fédérale béotienne sur la préparation militaire', *Acta of the Fifth International Congress of Greek and Latin Epigraphy, Cambridge, 1967* (Oxford, 1971), pp. 81–8.
Rostovtzeff, M. I., *Social and Economic History of the Hellenistic World* (Oxford, 1941).
Roy, J., 'The mercenaries of Cyrus', *Hist.* 16 (1967), pp. 287–323.
Rubensohn, O., *Elephantine Papyri* (Berlin, 1907).
Ruschenbusch, E., *Untersuchungen zu Staat und Politik in Griechenland vom 7.–4. Jh. v. Chr.* (Bamberg, 1978).
— 'Zur Wirtschaft- und Sozialstruktur der Normalpolis', *ASNP*, Ser. III, 13.1 (1983), pp. 171–94.
— 'Die Zahl der griechischen Staaten und Arealgrösse und Bürgerzahl der "Normalpolis"', *ZPE* 59 (1985), pp. 253–63.
Ryder, T. T. B., *Koine Eirene* (Oxford, 1965).
Ste Croix, G. E. M. de, *The Origins of the Peloponnesian War* (London, 1972).
— *The Class Struggle in the Ancient Greek World* (London, 1981).
— 'A worm's eye view of the Greeks and Romans and how they spoke: martyr-acts, parables, fables, and other texts', *Latin Teaching* 37.4 (1984), pp. 16–30.
— Edey, H. and Yamey, B. S. (eds.), *Debits, Credits, Finance and Profits* (London, 1974), pp. 41–59.
Salmon, J. B., *Wealthy Corinth* (Oxford, 1984).
Samuel, A. E., *From Athens to Alexandria: Hellenism and Social Goals in Ptolemaic Egypt*, Studia Hellenistica 26 (Louvain, 1983).
Schachermeyr, F., 'Die Letzten Pläne Alexanders des Grossen', *JÖAI* 41 (1954), pp. 118–40.
Schaps, D., 'The woman least mentioned: etiquette and women's names', *CQ*, n.s. 27 (1977), pp. 323–30.
Schede, M., 'Aus dem Heraion von Samos', *Ath. Mitt.* 44 (1919), pp. 1–46.
Seager, R., 'Lysias against the corn dealers', *Hist.* 15 (1966), pp. 172–84.
Segre, M., 'Due novi testi storici', *Riv. Fil.* 60 (1933), pp. 446–61.
Seibert, J., *Die politischen Flüchtlinge und Verbannten in der griechischen Geschichte* (Darmstadt, 1979).
Sherwin-White, S. M., *Ancient Cos* (Göttingen, 1978).
Smith, S., *Babylonian Historical Texts* (London, 1924).
Snodgrass, A. M., 'The hoplite reform and history', *JHS* 85 (1965), pp. 110–22.
— *Arms and Armour of the Greeks* (London, 1967).
Sokolowski, F., *Lois sacrées des cités grecques* (Paris, 1969).
Stern, S. M., *Aristotle and the World-State* (Oxford, 1968).
Stroud, R. S., 'Greek inscriptions, Theozotides and the Athenian orphans', *Hesp.* 40 (1971), pp. 280–301.
Talbert, R. J. A., *Timoleon and the Revival of Greek Sicily, 344–317 B.C.*

Bibliography

(Cambridge, 1974).

Tarn, W. W., *Antigonos Gonatas* (Oxford, 1913).

— *Alexander the Great* II (Cambridge, 1948).

— *The Greeks in Bactria and India* (second edition, Cambridge, 1951).

Thompson, W. E., 'Arcadian factionalism in the 360's', *Hist.* 32 (1983), pp. 149–60.

Tscherikower, V., *Die hellenistischen Städtegründungen von Alexander dem grossen bis auf die Römerzeit, Philologus*, Supplementband 19, Heft 1 (Leipzig, 1927).

Tod, M. N., 'Epigraphical notes on freedmen's professions', *Epigraphica* 12 (1950). pp. 3–26.

Tuplin, C. J., 'Xenophon's *Hellenica*: introductory essay and commentary on VI.3–VI.5' (Diss., Oxford, 1981).

Vallet, G., 'Athènes et l'Adriatique', *Mélanges de L'Ecole Française de Rome* 62 (1950), pp. 33–52.

Vélissaropoulos, J., 'Le monde de l'emporion', *DHA* 3 (1977), pp. 61–85.

— *Les Nauclères grecs* (Geneva and Paris, 1980).

Waele, J. A. de, 'La popolazione di Akragas antica', *Philias charin. Miscellanea di studi classici in onore di Eugenio Manni* III (Rome, 1979), pp. 747–60.

Wehrli, F., *Die Schule des Aristoteles* I–X (Basel, 1944–59).

Welles, C. B., *Royal Correspondence in the Hellenistic Period* (New Haven, Conn., 1934).

Wendland, P., *Anaximenes von Lampsakos* (Berlin, 1905).

Westlake, H. D., 'Phalaecus and Timoleon', *CQ* 34 (1940), pp. 44–6.

Whitehead, D., *The Ideology of the Athenian Metic* (Cambridge, *PCPhS*, Supp. vol. 4, 1977).

Witt, N. W. de, *Epicurus and his Philosophy* (Minneapolis, 1954).

Woodhead, A. G., rev. of G. Navarra, *Città sicane, sicule e greche nella zona di Gela, JHS* 87 (1967), pp. 188–9.

— 'The "Adriatic empire" of Dionysius of Syracuse', *Klio* 52 (1970), pp. 503–12.

Woodhouse, W. J., *Aetolia* (London, 1897).

Woodward, A. M., rev. of Tod II, *JHS* 68 (1948), p. 161.

Young, J. H., 'Studies in south Attica: country estates at Sounion', *Hesp.* 25 (1956), pp. 122–46.

Young, R. S., 'An industrial district of ancient Athens', *Hesp.* 20 (1951), pp. 135–288.

Zahrnt, M., *Olynth und die Chalkidier* (Munich, 1971).

Ziebarth, E., *Beiträge zur Geschichte des Seeraubs und Seehandels im alten Griechenland* (Hamburg, 1929).

Index

Index